Bureaucracy and Society
in Modern Egypt

PRINCETON ORIENTAL STUDIES

SOCIAL SCIENCE, NO. 1

Bureaucracy and Society in Modern Egypt · A STUDY

OF THE HIGHER CIVIL SERVICE

by Morroe Berger

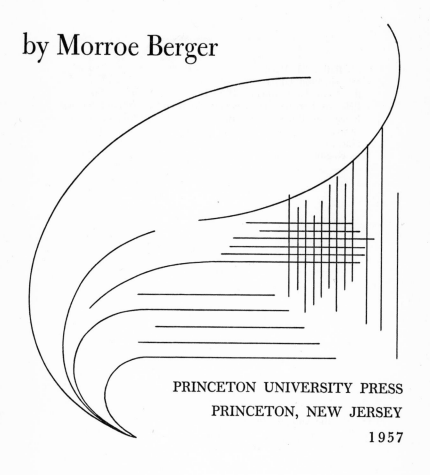

PRINCETON UNIVERSITY PRESS
PRINCETON, NEW JERSEY
1957

MORROE BERGER, who is assistant professor of sociology
at Princeton University, spent a year of study and travel in
the Near East, during 1953-1954, in preparing this book.
Prior to that, he served as consultant on the National Security
Resources Board, executive office of the President. He is a
contributor to various social science journals, general magazines, and newspapers, author of *Equality by Statute*, as well
as co-editor of *Freedom and Control in Modern Society*.

Printed in the United States of America
by Princeton University Press, Princeton, New Jersey

In Memory of My Mother

Foreword

Perhaps the most significant development in education and scholarship in the 20th century has been the coming of age of the social sciences. Certainly one of the most interesting developments in American higher education during the postwar decade at the center of the century has been the recent interest in area studies. In the enthusiastic embrace of this new interest, and especially in the application of the social sciences to area studies, there has been a flood of articles, and even books, of a broad and general character attempting to illuminate areas of culture in the modern world, with the implication that here at last is the light from on high for want of which we have been groping in the darkness. Without denying that such studies may serve a useful purpose, especially for newcomers still unoriented to an area's cultural patterns and for old residents still complacent in their self-made ruts, some of us may be forgiven perhaps for continuing to believe that contemporary area studies would be enriched by perception of the depth of their rootage in history, and invigorated by the acquisition of a wide variety of detailed analyses made by individual disciplines. In such contributions of the social sciences to area studies can the new frontiers of knowledge discovered by such studies be mapped and conquered.

It is for the publication of the results of such pioneer research that Princeton is extending its Oriental Series to include a sub-section on Studies in the Social Sciences. The series will consist of contributions from the various social science disciplines to the explication of segments of the culture of the Orient, primarily that of the Near and Middle East.

To begin this sub-series, it is a pleasure to commend this specific sociological study of the higher civil service of Egypt by Professor Morroe Berger, since 1952 the representative of sociology on the staff of Princeton's Special Program in Near Eastern Studies.

T. CUYLER YOUNG, *Chairman*
Department of Oriental Studies
Princeton University

Acknowledgments

This study has been made possible by the help many persons and organizations have given, for which the author is very grateful. The first who ought to be mentioned are the 249 higher civil servants of Egypt who consented to be interviewed and whose responses are presented and analyzed here. They must be nameless, of course. Their cooperation was freely extended, for, although the procedure of this study was unfamiliar, its goal of scientific analysis was fully understood and appreciated.

Government officials at all levels were equally cooperative. Permission to interview civil servants in their respective ministries was kindly granted by Dr. Abdel Razaq Sidqy, Minister of Agriculture; Dr. William Selim Hanna, then Minister of Municipal and Rural Affairs; Dr. Ali A. I. El Gritly, then Vice Minister of Finance and Economy; and Dr. Shafiq Ghorbal, Under-Secretary in the Ministry of Education and by Dr. Ahmad Shafiq Zaher, who succeeded him upon his retirement. All of these gentlemen were helpful, also, in some of the substantive details of the study. I am especially indebted to Dr. El Gritly for his constant encouragement and his considerable support at several crucial moments. Significant aid came, also, from Dr. Abbas Ammar, then Minister of Social Affairs and later of Education; Dr. Ismail Sarwat, Director of the Civil Service Commission (Diwan al Muwazzafin); and Dr. Abdel Moneim El Shafei, then Under-Secretary in the Ministry of Finance and Economy. To Dr. Sarwat's technical assistant, Mr. Yehia Riad Sallam, I owe a special debt; he provided much information about the civil service, its history and organization, and arranged many meetings indispensable to the progress of the work.

Many Egyptians kindly gave assistance at various stages of the interviewing procedure. For help in revising the original questionnaire and in the crucial process of translating it into Arabic, I am indebted to Mr. Nessim Habib, of the American University at Cairo; Mr. Saad el Din el Shishiny, of the Ministry of Finance and Economy, who was helpful in many other ways; Dr. Ali R. Ansary, of the Ministry of Education; Mr. Yehia Riad Sallam, of the Civil Service Commission, men-

tioned earlier; Mr. Hamid El Kabbani, of the Ministry of
Finance and Economy; and Dr. Mahmoud Amin Anis, then in
the same ministry.

For help in obtaining interviewers I am indebted chiefly to
Dr. Badrawy Muhammad Fahmy Badrawy, of the Cairo School
of Social Work and President of the Egyptian Association of
Social Workers. His general support and counsel, indeed, were
selflessly given. The interviewers themselves, of course, were
indispensable; already advanced in their profession, they did
their work expertly and with genuine interest in the project.
They are: Abdel Rahman Khalid Nadim, Abdel Wahab Abul
Khair, Abdel Wahab Mansour, Abdullah Mustafa, Abdullah
Mustafa Salem, Abdel Hamid Yusuf Kamal, Ahmad Abu Raya,
Ahmad Khairi Abdel Rahman, Ahmad Kamal Hassan Zaki, Aziz
Nashid, El Sayid Hussein Ashour, Gamal Farahat, Habib Bot-
ros, Hassan Ibrahim Karawia, Ibrahim Abdel Meguid, Kamal
Nagi, Mahmoud Ibrahim Mahmoud, Mahmoud Munir al Gindi,
Mahrous Sawiris, Muhammad Abdel Latif Hussein, Muhammad
Hashim Dawood, Muhammad Kamel el Batrik, Muhammad
Khairi Muhammad Ali, Muhammad Mahmoud Omar, Muham-
mad Morsi Hussein, Muhammad Nabih Fouda, Sabri Sami.

Several of the interviewers also coded the questionnaire returns. On the coding and tabulating a great deal of help was
provided by Mr. Michel Fahim, of the British Tabulating Machine Corporation. The interviews were recorded in Arabic and
the coding was done from these Arabic returns; translation of
the returns into English was by Mr. Izzat Fahim Yusif.

On methodology, interpretation, and presentation I have been
fortunate enough to be able to call on my colleagues in several
departments: Gabriel A. Almond, Marver Bernstein, Ibrahim
Abdelkader Ibrahim, Sheldon L. Messinger, Wilbert E. Moore,
Frederick F. Stephan, Gresham M. Sykes, Lewis V. Thomas,
Melvin M. Tumin, and Farhat J. Ziadeh. My most important
debt on this score is to a former colleague, William M. Evan, on
whose considerable knowledge of survey analysis, the Near East
and bureaucratic development I was allowed to draw at will. I
have also had the benefit of comments from other scholars:
Reinhard Bendix (University of California at Berkeley), Walter
R. Sharp (Yale University), Albert Hourani (Oxford University), and F. R. C. Bagley (McGill University).

x

I am indebted to the late Dr. Zdenek K. Ullrich for making available several studies made under his excellent direction by students in the Institute of Sociology and Social Science of Alexandria University.

For valuable assistance in checking data and running down some elusive facts I am indebted to Mr. Richard P. Mitchell (who also helped on some Arabic sources) and to Mr. Charles C. Moskos.

Thanks are due the following journals for permission to use material which first appeared in their pages: *The Public Opinion Quarterly*, Vol. xx, No. 1, Spring, 1956; *Administrative Science Quarterly*, Vol. i, No. 4, March 1957.

Financial assistance for this research was provided by the Princeton University Program in Near Eastern Studies, under whose auspices I spent a year of study and travel in that area. I owe a great debt to Professor Philip K. Hitti, then Chairman of the Program and now retired, for his wise counsel and support not only in this connection but also in other matters over many years. The Princeton University Research Fund was also generous in its grants. The Social Science Research Council, finally, provided a grant-in-aid to enable me to prepare the manuscript.

This long list of debts would be far from complete without mention of the genuine hospitality Egyptians everywhere extended the author and his family. They made our stay one of our most enjoyable and exciting experiences. The Egyptian government was likewise hospitable and encouraging in facilitating the study. At no time was there any question but that I would be free to proceed as the study-plan required.

Finally, I must mention several persons whose friendship and assistance can hardly be separated; they helped in more ways than can be simply stated here. They are: Mr. Mahmoud Hassan, then a director of several business enterprises but formerly, and for many years, Egyptian ambassador to the United States; Major General Muhammad Khalifa, of the Egyptian Air Force, retired; and Mr. Z. Misketian, a businessman whose hospitality and help date back to our friendship in Cairo during World War II.

M. B.

Contents

Bureaucracy and Society
in Modern Egypt

Chapter 1. Introduction: The Social Setting of the Egyptian Civil Service

In the spring of 1954 the world was thrilled by the discovery of a solar ship, said to be 5,000 years old, near the great pyramid of Cheops a few miles from Cairo. Insensitive to romance and mystery, this writer was less interested in the description of the ship or in the drama of its discovery than in the administrative byplay that followed. For, according to newspaper reports, the find precipitated a serious dispute between the young discoverer and his superiors. The prime minister himself stepped into the affair, it was reported, and, supporting the younger man against his chiefs, warned that officials who were unfair to their subordinates would be taught a lesson. A year later the discoverer was world-famous. He had lectured to large audiences in America. He was widely quoted by reporters for Western newspapers. Despite this acclaim and the public announcement of support by the prime minister, however, he found himself shorn of one responsibility after another by his chiefs until he was even denied access to the solar ship itself.

This administrative subplot to the main drama, appropriately played on the site of man's oldest recorded bureaucracy, carries several implications for the study of the public bureaucracy of Egypt today. The prime minister's support of the younger man exemplifies the effort to build a new relationship between the rulers of Egypt and the civil servants upon whom they must rely to realize the reforms they have promised the nation. As a result of the regime's intention to eradicate the spirit and the deeds of its royal predecessor, hundreds of high officials have been removed or have resigned or retired early, and younger subordinates have found easier access to responsible posts through ability and diligence. But the administrative eclipse of the discoverer of the solar ship, despite the prominence of his support, reveals the old bureaucracy's firm control over some aspects of day-to-day government business. It is significant, too, that the bureaucracy's resistance to the power-holders' intervention was confined to a question of relations between superior and subordinate in the hierarchy and did not touch matters of policy. For, as we shall see, the Egyptian civil service is more cohesive in the area of self-protection than in that of policy-making. It will challenge the political rulers less on public policy than on its own private interests.

This aspect of the Egyptian civil service—its place as a social group in the larger society—will concern us in this study, rather than its administrative functions. From the standpoints of both public administration and sociology the public bureaucracy of any country is an interesting subject of study. Especially in view of the myriad technical assistance programs, the prescriptions for industrializing the technologically retarded or the poor countries, and the innumerable plans adopted by these countries themselves, it is unnecessary to dwell at length upon the importance of the administrative task in such areas or upon that of the social groups who execute it.

Many countries that are primarily agricultural, including Egypt, are seeking to industrialize and thereby, they hope, to raise their living standards and to increase their national power in the international community. At the same time they want to avoid the social evils that accompanied industrialization in the West and which the West overcame only long after its economic growth. Such a combination of aims is laudably humane but to realize it a nation will require a high degree of expertise in public administration as well as in other arts and sciences. In Egypt and other countries where the state is likely to have to undertake a substantial part of the task of industrialization, the public bureaucracy, heretofore largely administrative, will have to add many more technicians in the sciences; this necessity is already felt in the Egyptian civil service and is soon bound to have its repercussions on the system of higher education. The role of public administration in easing the transition from rural-agricultural to urban-industrial society is given great importance by a prominent student of English industrialization, who says: "If the industrial revolution was not able to bring its rewards in full measure to the ordinary man and woman it is to the defects of administrative, and not of economic processes, that the failure must be ascribed."[1]

[1] T. S. Ashton, *Industrial Revolution 1760-1830*, Home University Li-

Even if this judgment is accepted only in part, the importance of the civil service would be considerable in societies seeking to industrialize. The civil servants themselves, thus, constitute a significant social group. In countries like Egypt they are a large proportion of the educated population and may comprise the main section of such a middle class as may be found in them. From what elements in the population do they come? What are their goals? How cohesive a group do they form? What administrative and technical capacities do they have? Such questions are of both sociological interest for the scholar and of practical consequence for the nation trying to industrialize.

Moreover, because it is one of the few outlets for the educated elite, the civil service has been a focus of much local political struggle and of nationalist agitation against the colonial powers. It is in this sense that the civil service of Egypt, for example, has been intimately involved in politics. It has been a weapon of partisanship among the Egyptian political parties and an articulate ally of all these parties in their struggle against British power. Yet in matters of public policy—as distinct from partisan politics—the Egyptian civil service has been a relatively pliant tool in the hands of any executive power rather than a rival seeking to exercise control over broad policy issues of government not directly affecting the exercise of political power itself. One reason for this pliability has been the fact that the group in power could bend the civil service to its will because of the absence of a strong system of job-tenure. Another is that the political parties themselves, except for some extremist groups, have not seriously divided on questions of public policy which were not connected with the issue of the British occupation or with the exercise of political power itself. The humdrum administration of day-to-day affairs is at least as important as larger political goals in the creation of public attitudes toward a regime and a system of government. In countries where new social classes are emerging and the distribution of power and prestige is shifting, the level of public administration affects the degree of confidence in orderly processes of government; a low level can destroy the promise and hope that people feel when

---

brary of Modern Knowledge, No. 204, Oxford University Press, London, 1948, pp. 139-141.

5

they have gained political independence and embark upon programs of economic development.

The kind of public administration available to governments in technologically underdeveloped areas assumes added importance because of the intertwining of certain political and economic goals. The most dramatic recent example of this mingling is Egypt's nationalization of the Suez Canal company in July 1956, which embodied the political goal of obtaining greater Egyptian control over the waterway and the economic goal of bringing more revenue to Egypt. The political-economic ideology of many Near Eastern, Asiatic, and Latin American countries moves them in the direction of nationalization of foreign-owned, highly developed enterprises.

Egypt's nationalization of the Canal company brought it, for the first time as an independent state, into high international politics. It also posed the problem whether Egypt could operate the Canal. Both issues placed new responsibilities upon the higher civil service and put it to severe tests. Those who made the extraordinary decisions in July and August of 1956 must have needed expert technical advice of several kinds: political—the probable reaction of the Western powers and the Soviet Union; military—the strategic position of British and French forces and the capacity of Egypt to meet a threat from them; economic—the effect of a possible diversion of Western shipping from the Canal; technological—the ability of Egypt to operate the Canal as a national enterprise, and for how long.

Irrespective of the merits of the nationalization of the Canal from the standpoint of international law, Egyptian military and civil staff work seems to have been of a high order—higher, indeed, than had been expected in the West, considering Egypt's socio-economic and technological foundation. The capacities of the public bureaucracy in countries like Egypt are thus among the factors that are most likely to determine the success or failure of governmental plans not only to develop industry and agriculture but also to control and operate industrial enterprises of various kinds. We may, indeed, look upon the nature and capacities of the public bureaucracy as a mirror of a society in which are reflected, with varying degrees of clarity, its technological base, educational level, the kind of economic opportunities it affords, the fluidity of its class structure, the extent of its national unity, and the nature of the loyalties evoked in it.

The following chapters do not deal with all these subjects but they do examine some of them: the legacy of past Egyptian society and public administration to the present; the social origins of the higher civil servants today; the reasons for the attraction this career has for so many of the educated elite; the changing socio-economic status of the higher civil servants; their loyalties and the extent of their professionalization; and their attitudes toward such norms of bureaucratic behavior as impartiality, impersonality, subordination to one's superior, and the exercise of a permitted degree of personal initiative.

To throw light on these subjects, this book reports and analyzes data gathered in two ways: historical research, and the replies that 249 higher civil servants of Egypt gave in 1954 to a long questionnaire about their backgrounds, attitudes, and opinions. (The questionnaire appears in Appendix 1.) Most of the historical data are discussed in Chapter 2. In the remaining chapters the responses to the questionnaire are analyzed at length, and historical and documentary data are used to set forth the problems dealt with and to illuminate the replies given by the civil servants who were interviewed. We do not rely exclusively, then, upon one kind of research but try to combine the historical and the questionnaire-survey approaches in order to give our discussion depth in time as well as relevance to the present. The two approaches are complementary; each is used where it is best suited to the problem posed. If we are interested in the influences that have brought the higher civil service of Egypt to its present position, we must consider the Ottoman and British legacies. If we want to know the social origin of the present senior officials in Egypt, we can find out only by asking them the appropriate questions, for such information is nowhere available. There are, of course, limitations to the questionnaire method. We have tried to overcome as many of them as we could by judicious wording and spacing of questions, by the inclusion of items that can be checked against one another, and by setting up the most favorable interview-situation possible in the circumstances. Properly applied and interpreted, the questionnaire can be useful for some purposes. The newness of the method in Egypt was taken into account in planning the questions, and great effort was expended in developing several ways of increasing the probability that either the answers given were the respondents' true answers or that skillful interpretation of all the answers could reveal which were true and which were not true—and what significance should be placed upon the answers deemed to be conscious or unconscious evasions.

In analyzing the survey data, we shall have two tasks. First, we shall try to see the differences in the public bureaucracy of Egypt and that of most Western states. Second, we shall compare one group of Egyptian civil servants with another—the older with the younger, the administrative with the technical workers, those more exposed to Western influences with those less exposed, and so on. The first of these two kinds of comparisons will be the more difficult one, for there are few studies of the higher civil servants of Western states with whom we can compare the Egyptian officials we interviewed. Studies of the socio-economic background of senior officials in the United States, England, and France have been published in recent years, and these permit a few comparisons of social origin, age, and position. But there are no studies that would permit a comparison of the opinions and attitudes of Egyptian and Western higher civil servants. Such comparisons of this order as are found in the following pages, therefore, are based, on the Egyptian side, on the specific data collected in the questionnaire, and on the Western side only on what the author takes to be the generally accepted notions in the literature on its public bureaucracies.

One of the main themes we shall develop will be the degree to which the Egyptian higher civil service approaches Western norms of professionalization and bureaucratic behavior. This focus is not an ethnocentric weakness but, on the contrary, is dictated by Egypt's own goals and intentions as expressed in recent efforts to industrialize, in the long-term trend toward secularism in government, and in reforms in the civil service itself. Moreover, the goals announced by the leaders of regimes both before and since the end of the monarchy in 1952-1953 imply movement in the direction of a typically Western economy and polity (irrespective of the leadership's attitude toward the West at any given moment), although they see this process as one of "modernization," rather than of "Westernization." In the light of these Egyptian social changes and policies (and not as

8

a reflection of Western bias) we are interested in learning how far the civil service, a social group essential to realization of these goals, has moved in a direction consistent with the kind of society the Egyptians want to create in their land.

Egypt is not the only country seeking to move in this direction. To what extent are our findings about Egypt applicable to other countries in the Near East, Asia, or even Latin America? The author prefers, in the absence of comparable studies, to leave the answer to readers familiar with the public bureaucracies of these areas. One could easily lump together all the "underdeveloped" lands and assume their civil service corps are like the Egyptian in many ways. But Egypt is far from being the "typical" "underdeveloped" area. Its civil service has a long tradition. Its population, unlike that of many non-industrial areas, is dense rather than sparse in settlement. Its efficient agriculture may indeed be said to be overdeveloped in some respects. It has, for a basically rural-agricultural economy, highly developed commercial and banking institutions. Its educational system is probably more advanced than that of most countries at the same level of economic development. Even within the Near East, Egypt can hardly be said to be typical; regarding our own focus of interest in this study, the Arab countries alone (not to mention Israel, Turkey, and Iran) have public bureaucracies ranging from those that are no more than personal advisers to the reigning family to the relatively modern civil service of the Egyptian republic.

Yet there are similarities among the "underdeveloped" countries, as a United Nations study group has pointed out: "The problems of underdeveloped countries that may be related to public administration are primarily problems of transition: transition from semi-feudal and traditional to more responsible and rational forms of administration; from an agricultural and extractive economy to an economy of industry and trade; from a colonial regime conducted by foreigners to a national government."[2] Indeed, studies of other aspects of some Near Eastern countries, touching on public administration, mention characteristics similar to those we find in Egypt: the civil service as a

[2] United Nations, Technical Assistance Administration, Report by the Special Committee on Public Administration Problems, *Standards and Techniques of Public Administration*, N.Y., 1951, par. 12, p. 5.

9

social class, its peculiar status and prestige, and its special loyalties. These studies (dealing only incidentally and briefly with what is our central concern here) cover Syria, Iraq, Turkey, Iran, and Afghanistan.[3] Other studies cover Mexico, Cuba, Guatemala, Nicaragua, Burma, Siam, and Malaya.[4] Although such studies have been made, caution must be exercised in pointing to similarities, for we cannot know their significance until we know, through more detailed investigation than has thus far been made available, the full range of differences as well.

The Bureaucratic Atmosphere

To the reader interested in the "feel" or the "climate" of the Egyptian public bureaucracy all the statistics in the world are probably beside the point. Even if the studies of other bureaucracies now lacking were to become available overnight and all the precise statistical comparisons made, such a reader would be hardly satisfied. The bureaucratic "atmosphere" is a subject for the artist, a Daumier or a Balzac, not for the social scientist. Moreover, the artist's evocation is likely to be so general in scope that it encompasses all bureaucratic systems and would hardly permit us to distinguish one national expression of this

[3] The International Bank for Reconstruction and Development has published reports on Syria, Iraq, and Turkey: *The Economic Development of Syria*, The Johns Hopkins Press, Baltimore, 1955, pp. 193-199; *The Economic Development of Iraq*, The Johns Hopkins Press, Baltimore, 1952, pp. 77-80; *The Economy of Turkey*, I.B.R.D., Wash., D.C., 1951, pp. 198-200. On Iran, see Arthur C. Millspaugh, *Americans in Persia*, The Brookings Institution, Wash., D.C., 1946, pp. 83-91. On Afghanistan, see Peter G. Franck, "Economic Planners," in Sydney N. Fisher, ed., *Social Forces in the Middle East*, Cornell University Press, Ithaca, 1955, pp. 149-153.

[4] On Mexico, see Nathan L. Whetten, *Rural Mexico*, University of Chicago Press, 1948, pp. 545-554; and Luccio Mendieta y Nuñez, *La Administración Publica en Mexico*, Imprenta Universitaria, Mexico, 1942, pp. 293-303. On Cuba, Guatemala, and Nicaragua, see the volumes by the International Bank for Reconstruction and Development: *Report on Cuba*, I.B.R.D., Wash., D.C., 1951, pp. 453-455; *The Economic Development of Guatemala*, I.B.R.D., Wash., D.C., 1951, pp. 262-264; *The Economic Development of Nicaragua*, The Johns Hopkins Press, Baltimore, 1953, pp. 85-87. On Burma, Siam, and Malaya, see the series published by the Royal Institute of International Affairs: F. S. V. Donnison, *Public Administration in Burma*, London, 1953, pp. 81-86; W. D. Reeve, *Public Administration in Siam*, N.Y., 1951, pp. 31-39, 60-67, 80-82; S. W. Jones, *Public Administration in Malaya*, London, 1953, pp. 116, 124-125.

spirit from another. Consider the following two descriptions by novelists:

"As government offices are at present constituted, four hours out of the nine which the clerks are supposed to give to the State are wasted, as will presently be seen, over talks, anecdotes, and squabbles, and, more than all, over office intrigues. You do not know, unless you frequent government offices, how much the clerks' little world resembles the world of school; the similarity strikes you wherever men live together; and in the army or the law-courts you find the school again on a rather larger scale. The body of clerks, thus pent up for eight hours at a stretch, looked upon the offices as classrooms in which a certain amount of lessons must be done."

———

"I scribbled at the bottom of the page: 'To be filed with Report,' and clasped my head in my hands, wondering what was to be done next in this case, and whom we could interrogate so as to bring our Report up to a minimum of twenty pages. For I have never forgotten what a Public Prosecutor said to me one day when he received a ten-page Report.

" 'What's all this? A contravention or a misdemeanor?'

"When I replied that it was a murder-case, he shouted at me in astonishment:

" 'A Murder case investigated in ten pages! An assassination! The murder of a human being! All in ten pages?'

"When I replied that with those ten pages we had managed to get the murderer, he paid no attention whatever, and went on weighing the Report in his hand with careful accuracy.

" 'Who would ever have believed that this Report could be of a murder case?'

"I replied instantly: 'Next time, God willing, we shall be more careful about the weight!' "

However much we may admire the skill of these writers, we should have to admit that they are depicting much the same kind of behavior, although the first quotation is from Balzac's novel of early nineteenth-century France and the second from Towfiq el Hakim's[5] novel of contemporary Egypt.[6] The social scientist does not aim to communicate an "atmosphere" in this sense; the artist does not have the social scientist's aim of developing precise statements of relations that fit into larger systems and can be compared with statements about similar phenomena in other times and places.

Yet, below the level of things all bureaucracies have in common, there are differences even in the intangible impressions they leave. These may be only stereotypes, but they can nevertheless embody a core of truth. The "typical" British civil servant, with bowler and tightly-rolled umbrella, is reserved, aloof, and very correct. The "typical" French *fonctionnaire* sits among his papers, inaccessible, and never permits the public business to prevent him, every day at the same time, from reaching into the bottom drawer of his desk for his lunch wrapped in brown paper. The "typical" Egyptian clerical *muwazzaf*, for the author, is a man sitting at a desk in his overcoat, his *tarbush* (or fez) hanging on a nail on the wall behind him, his newspaper spread out, one hand holding his demitasse of Turkish coffee and the other reaching for his buzzer to call in a messenger.

Such stereotypes, of course, are akin to the public image of any bureaucracy and are equally unflattering. Through the stereotypic lens all bureaucracies appear alike and unattractive. To the Western visitor, nevertheless, the surface aspects of the Egyptian government office are considerably different from anything he has seen. The first thing he notices is the presence of men, rather than women, in the reception rooms. Women are employed in only a few ministries. The outer office presided over by a female secretary or two, so familiar in the West, is never seen in Egypt. Nor can one usually see the large office with scores of desks at which typists, clerks, and machine operators are working. Instead, there is a combination reception room and outer office manned by one or two male secretaries who do no typing or stenography but who handle appointments, pass and

[5] Transliteration of Arabic names and words in this book follows common usage rather than any linguistically consistent system.

[6] The first quotation is from Balzac's *The Government Clerks* (*Les Employés*, 1836), tr. by James Waring, vol. 24 in *The Works of Honoré de Balzac*, The University Society, N.Y., n.d., pp. 260-261. The second is from Towfiq el Hakim, *Maze of Justice* (*Mudhakkirāt Nā'ib fi al-Aryāf*, 1937), tr. by A. S. Eban, The Harvill Press, London, 1947, pp. 11-12.

receive papers, and exercise much more influence than do their closest counterparts in the West. Leading off this room is a much larger one occupied by a superior official. Here the furnishings are more elegant. Serving both offices and others along the corridor are a large number of servant-messengers, in uniforms of varying degrees of completeness, who usher in visitors, transmit papers, run errands, and bring Turkish coffee. Coffee-drinking (and, to an increasing extent, Coca-Cola drinking) is usually the first order of business when the official arrives and practically each time someone comes to see him. As a visitor enters, indeed, he usually finds many others there before him, most of them whispering to each other quietly, yet not in a conspiratorial air; this is simply the way things are done, for in Egyptian government offices the really private audience is almost unknown. The official simultaneously handles three or four items of business and converses with three or four visitors or colleagues who stand or sit around his desk. The number of such persons milling around an office gets to be considerable. Several years ago it reached a point where the Minister of Communications tried to forbid all "private" visits to officials in his ministry. At the same time he sought to end delays in work by requiring that every matter be studied for no more than twenty-four hours, after which, finished or not, it must yield its place to another item.[7] Perhaps the most striking thing to a Western visitor will occur at noon, when he may hear the Muslim call to prayer resound through the building. In a few minutes the faithful will form their ranks in the courtyard and corridors for the noon prayer. Those who join these ranks, however, are the messengers, porters, janitorial and kitchen workers—the clerks and senior officials remain at their desks.

Change is slow in the public bureaucracy of any country. Writing over a hundred years ago, in 1839, an Englishman described the conduct of business in Egyptian government offices in a way that anyone can still recognize despite the changes that have taken place. "The public business in Egypt," wrote John Bowring, "as generally in the East, is dispatched in a divan, presided over by a principal functionary. The correspondence is opened and read, and answers dictated to the surrounding scribes,

[7] *The Egyptian Gazette* (Cairo), October 29, 1953, p. 5.

13

who are almost invariably Copts. Sometimes there is a discussion, and the opinions of the different members of the divan are consulted; but a predominant weight is invariably given to that of the president. A sort of publicity pervades all these proceedings. There is a perpetual succession of auditors and spectators, many of whom have no interest in the matters under discussion."[8]

Egypt is, of course, not unique in the conservatism of its bureaucracy. Like that of France, for example, according to a recent interpretation by Herbert Lüthy, the government apparatus has supplied a continuity that the politicians have not been able to achieve, and has managed to keep all administrative authority centralized in its own hands. Lüthy says of France that the bureaucracy functions so automatically "that the only sphere of activity it concedes to politics is that of pure and irrelevant ideology."[9] The same cannot be said about the Egyptian government bureaucracy for, concerned as it has been with self-protection rather than public policy, the only major sphere of activity it has conceded to politics has been that of power. In other respects, however, the Egyptian public bureaucracy resembles the French even more than it does the British, despite the latter's greater political power in the area since the late nineteenth century. Other government institutions, as well as some features of all levels of the educational system, likewise owe much to French inspiration.[10]

⟋ The Public Bureaucracy in Egyptian Society

A public bureaucracy functions within a particular form of government and a particular kind of society. Differences between bureaucracies can be traced to the differences in the broader political, social, and economic spheres they serve. What are these broad differences between Egypt and the Western world? The following observations are not based on our questionnaire

---

[8] John Bowring, *Report on Egypt and Candia*, Sessional Papers 1840, Vol. xxxv, H.M.S.O., London, p. 48.

[9] Herbert Lüthy, "Democracy and Its Discontents. II. France," *Encounter* (London), Vol. II, No. 5, May, 1954, pp. 23-24, and *France against Herself*, Praeger, N.Y., 1955, p. 18.

[10] On the civil service, see especially Walter R. Sharp, *The French Civil Service*, Macmillan, N.Y., 1931, chapters I, II, XIV.

survey, but the results of the survey, reviewed in the remaining chapters, illustrate and in part substantiate them.

In Egypt, as in most of the Arab-Muslim world, the connection between economic and political power has been closer than in the West. Egypt is thus at a stage of development comparable to a much earlier era in the West, when these two types of power were less distinct in their exercise and in the groups of individuals who enjoyed their possession. The power of the upper economic classes in Egypt has not been private economic power as we know it in the West but, whether based on land or trade or industry, has been derived from their close relationship to the holders of political power. Government in the Near East is the major source of any organized social power, and no class wields much power outside it. Consequently government is respected and feared, for few persons have the economic independence to risk incurring its hostility. Owing to this close connection between economic and political power, and to the depressed state of the vast majority of the population, government posts have been largely a preserve of the upper and (more recently) the middle classes. Although the middle groups stand between the classes above and below them, they are much nearer the upper class in education, economic interest, goals and aspirations, and general attitude and taste. The prestige of the civil servant in the Near East is higher than in the West, for two reasons: first, because government and those who speak for it are more respected and feared; second, because the civil servant himself is likely to come from a higher socio-economic group. (A third but different sort of reason is that government in Egypt has been associated for thousands of years with foreign conquerors.)

When an Egyptian goes to the post office or police station or even to a railroad ticket office, he is almost certain to meet government officials who earn more than he does and who are better educated. In the West the situation is more likely to be just the opposite. Such contacts serve constantly to reinforce the prestige of the civil servant in the Near East. The mere fact that he can read and write places even the lowliest clerk above the vast mass of the illiterate population.

Egypt has been a society in which (irrespective of changing regimes) the relations between the people and their government

15

are not so precisely articulated as they have become in the West. The state has for generations performed functions that lead to considerable contact between the people and the government; yet the rights and duties of both parties have not been so clearly defined as to permit much of this contact to become routine. Rather, there is still ignorance and uncertainty among the citizens, while among government officials there has always been a tendency to take advantage of such latitude as the law and public apathy allow. There are several reasons for this relatively vague structuring of relations between people and government. One is precisely the fact that Egypt has been ruled by a strong executive (at first foreign and then native, even during the constitutional regimes from 1923 to 1952), and has never known rulers responsible to a strong legislature representing an educated electorate. Second, the proliferation of government services and functions (often under Western influence) has been beyond the capacity of the public and the civil service to absorb quickly enough and probably even beyond the capacity of the largely rural nation to understand. It would be difficult to demonstrate fully, but it appears that the result of this lack of clarity is a disproportionately large number personal contacts between citizen and government representative—disproportionate to the size and urbanization of the population and to the functions and services the state performs. One reason for this situation may be that the Near East has not yet developed the network of voluntary associations and interest-groups, known in the West, which can meet some individual needs directly or can represent individuals before the government. Moreover, where rights and responsibilities are vague (despite—perhaps because of—the presence of myriad laws and rulings) it is probably worth a trip to a government office to try to get a decision one wants even if it appears offhand that prospects are not good. Much more than in the West, people in the Near East seem to feel there is always a way to get around a regulation or to find one that helps instead of hurts your case. Such a situation, of course, adds to the power and prestige of the civil servant—and increases the temptation to act arbitrarily or upon the basis of irrelevant loyalties.

This vague structuring of relations between citizen and government exemplifies the fact that Egypt has not yet become a rational, secular state of the Western type, in spite of its efforts to do so. Much of what we may call a pre-bureaucratic character remains—that is, remnants of an older society in which the state was not clearly differentiated and government was personal instead of the impersonal, rational, uniform administration that is the goal (if not the performance) of modern bureaucracy. Egypt does not lack a long bureaucratic history. This history has been, most of the time, one of what Max Weber has called an administrative system based upon "traditional authority" rather than upon "legal authority." Both types of authority employ administrative staffs but Weber reserves for the staff of a "legal authority" the name of bureaucracy, with its now-familiar traits of impersonal obligation, hierarchical organization, legal jurisdiction, selection through technical qualification, remuneration and tenure governed by fixed principles, and so on. The administrative staff of a "traditional authority" lacks these features; instead, in it powers and duties shift with the decision of the chief, the staff is attached to the chief's household, functions are not permanently defined and assigned to certain posts, selection and promotion occur by grace of the chief, and so on.[11] It is immediately clear that Egypt's public bureaucracy has been moving from the model of "traditional authority" to that of "legal authority" and that vestiges of the older model persist to this day.

Another Egyptian (and perhaps Near Eastern) legacy is the tension between the local community and the central government. The village has fiercely resisted the advent of national or imperial authorities even where economic necessity has dictated it. Paralleling this tension has been a pervading difference in the pattern of social control between the periphery and the center. The village, especially in Egypt, is loosely structured, practically barren of formal controls, and those it has have been administered informally by the *umda*, the notable or mayor. The central government, in contrast, has been highly organized and has claimed control (on either secular or religious grounds) over the most minute and private aspects of life, although usually in effect it has scarcely touched the local community. Thus, in the village

[11] Max Weber, *The Theory of Social and Economic Organization*, ed. by Talcott Parsons, Oxford University Press, N.Y., 1947, pp. 333-336, 342-345.

authority has been wielded by the heads of the patriarchal families and by the notables. The absence of formal, political controls, however, has had a curious concomitant: a tendency to "politicize" interpersonal relations. Individuals tend to judge and assess one another in terms of social position and social power. The result is a pattern of ingratiation and manipulation which is political in motivation and effect but which proceeds on a level of interpersonal relations which virtually excludes concern with politics as a struggle for, and the exercise of, formal governmental controls.[12]

Any government of Egypt seeking to revamp its civil service has to contend with this broader and older legacy of society and government as well as with the more specific problems engendered by the system of public administration that it has inherited.

[12] See Hamed Ammar, *Growing Up in an Egyptian Village*, Routledge and Kegan Paul, London, 1954, especially chapters IV-VI; and El-Demerdash Abdel-Meguid Sarhan, *Interests and Culture. A Comparative Study of Interests, Concerns, Wishes, Likes, Dislikes, and Happiest Days of Egyptian and American Children*, Teachers College, Columbia University, Contributions to Education, No. 959, N.Y., 1950, especially chapter IX.

Chapter 2. The Public Bureaucracy in Modern Egypt

The inclusion of Egypt among the "underdeveloped" countries conceals the fact that in some ways, for example, in agricultural land use, it is rather highly developed. In public administration, too, Egypt has a long history of highly developed bureaucracy. Its centralized civil service may be traced back thousands of years, not in the regimes it has served but in the social sources from which it has been recruited and in many of the functions it has performed. Egypt is a unified state with a population dependent upon the fullest use of the waters of the Nile. As a river civilization, Ancient Egypt had a highly centralized state and a well-developed professional bureaucracy. Indeed, although it functioned in a subsistence rather than a money economy, the civil service of the New Kingdom 1,500 years before the Christian era was, according to Max Weber, "the historical model of all later bureaucracies."[1] The prestige of this bureaucracy was as high then as it has been in the recent past. One historian's observations have a contemporary ring. "In Ancient Egypt," says A. M. Hocart, "to administer and to make a record are synonymous: the official is a scribe. Then, as now, government employment enjoyed the greatest prestige and appeared to offer the most desirable career, because it seemed an easy life compared with other occupations and ensured a steady livelihood from the government, or, as the ancients expressed it, 'from the king's house.' "[2]

Arab-Islamic Conquest

Similarities between the present bureaucracy and that of Ancient Egypt do not, of course, establish a direct link between the two. Many economic, political, and cultural influences have intervened. The most significant influence for contemporary

[1] Max Weber, "Bureaucracy," in *From Max Weber*, H. H. Gerth and C. Wright Mills, translators and editors, Oxford University Press, N.Y., 1946, p. 204.
[2] A. M. Hocart, "The Legacy to Modern Egypt," in *The Legacy of Egypt*, ed. by S. R. K. Glanville, Oxford University Press, London, 1942, p. 375.

Egypt was the Arab-Islamic conquest in the seventh century A.D., which imposed a form of political absolutism based upon religious doctrine that discouraged popular initiative in political life.[3] At the same time that the new rulers retained much of the Byzantine administrative system they found in Egypt, they re-introduced a degree of the old centralization that one historian has called "almost excessive."[4] It is probably at this point that Egypt felt the power of influences whose traces may still be seen in the present government service as described in the following chapters. From then on the country was ruled by Islamic regimes with varying degrees of non-Egyptian loyalty until, several hundred years later, much of the administration was in the hands of a special class recruited from abroad by the Mameluke sultans. The Ottoman conquest of Egypt in the early sixteenth century perpetuated foreign administration of a servile character.[5] Yet many Egyptians all through these centuries had managed to enter the government service and to maintain their positions by transmitting their skills from generation to generation. Government posts were thus inherited, but in a functional sense, through education, rather than in the usual feudal manner of succession in office and title.[6]

The tone of administration during these centuries was set by the tone of Ottoman political control. There was little connection, according to Gibb and Bowen,[7] between rulers and ruled except the exercise of force. Cynicism in the former was given free reign by apathy in the latter. Between these two classes stood the public bureaucracy, which provided some degree of stability because it changed more slowly than did the regimes it served. The population grew to expect that authority meant

[3] H. A. R. Gibb and Harold Bowen, *Islamic Society and the West*, Volume One, Part I, Oxford University Press, London, 1950, pp. 26-30.

[4] H. I. Bell, "The Administration of Egypt under the Ummayad Khalifs," *Byzantinische Zeitschrift*, 1928, Vol. 28, Nos. 3-4, p. 279.

[5] Gibb and Bowen, *op.cit.*, note 3 above, pp. 42-43, 208, 215-216, 224-225; and Albert H. Lybyer, *The Government of the Ottoman Empire in the Time of Suleiman the Magnificent*, Harvard University Press, Cambridge, 1913, pp. 36, 55, 196.

[6] See Gibb and Bowen, *op.cit.*, note 3 above, p. 210, and J. Heyworth-Dunne, *An Introduction to the History of Education in Modern Egypt*, Luzac and Co., London, n.d. (preface dated September, 1938), pp. 87, 92, 146.

[7] *Ibid.*, pp. 205, 207, 209-210.

not only legitimate power but also a display of harshness and violence; it accepted authority as a form of special privilege, not merely as a form of defined power. This attitude persisted into the middle of the nineteenth century, according to a contemporary observer. The British economist Nassau Senior reported that the British consul general in Cairo told him in 1856 that the Egyptian ruler (the Viceroy of the Turkish Sultan) had only two motives to call upon in ruling the Egyptians. "They are indeed only hope and fear; and as he can hold out hope only to a few, but fear to all, fear is his principal instrument."[8]

This observation emphasizes the survival of Ottoman characteristics through the Napoleonic invasion of Egypt and the brief French occupation (1798-1801). But the shock of this Western penetration was nevertheless considerable. Napoleon raised the banner of nationalism in Egypt as he did in Europe. Upon his arrival he announced: "All Egyptians shall be called upon to manage all posts; the wisest, the most learned, the most virtuous shall govern, and the people shall be happy."[9] He thus challenged the traditional Mameluke and Turkish power and administration in what we recognize as modern accents. This injection of European nationalist influence had an immediate effect, for only four years after the French were forced to evacuate, Egypt was ruled by Muhammad Ali, who, although he nominally represented the Turkish Sultan, pursued an independent policy that set the stage for the emergence of modern Egyptian nationalism.

From Muhammad Ali to the British Occupation

Muhammad Ali sought to transform rural, agricultural Egypt, steeped in tradition and with no knowledge of the scientific and technological revolution that was gripping the West, into an industrial society with a modern military apparatus. He mobilized as much as he could of the nation's human and material resources into his own hands, creating a state-controlled economy in the Near East with Egypt as its center. To manage his varied enter-

[8] Nassau William Senior, *Conversations and Journals in Egypt and Malta*, ed. by his daughter, M. C. M. Simpson, 2 volumes, Sampson Low, Marston, Searle, and Rivington, London, 1882, vol. 2, p. 35.

[9] *Correspondance de Napoleon Ier*, Plon and Dumaine, Paris, 1860, No. 2723, 2 July 1798, vol. IV, p. 191.

prises he wanted an efficient but subservient civil service. According to Deny, who classified the Turkish archives in Cairo, two principles governed Muhammad Ali's administrative organization: first, all matters had to be studied by a council and decided by majority vote; second, Muhammad Ali retained absolute control over every detail.[10] While he wanted expert advice, he also wanted to share none of his administrative and policy control. In an effort to draw upon the Egyptian population for his technical and administrative staffs, he set up schools in Egypt and sent several hundred young men to European institutions. In 1829, for example, following a change to European methods of accountancy, he established a school to train civil servants in the new system.[11] From 1813 to 1848 he sent abroad 339 students for technical and humanistic training. All but twelve were enrolled in technical studies in medicine, industry and engineering, and agriculture, mainly in France and England.[12] It was this policy of instituting secular, technical education only for the specific purpose of training government employees and advisers that was instrumental in encouraging generations of Egyptians to think of non-religious education only as a means to a civil service appointment. From this attitude it was only a step to the expectation that such an education, however meager, entitled one to a government post.

Although Muhammad Ali trained Egyptians at home and abroad, he continued to rely upon foreigners, Copts, and Turks to fill the higher administrative and technical posts. A contemporary British observer, John Bowring, writing in 1839, reported that, "with the exception of the situations filled by Christians, the Turks have nearly a monopoly of all high official functions in Egypt." He reported, nevertheless, that Egyptians were finding their way into important government posts for the first time. "Till of late years," he commented, "the Arab and Egyptian Mussulman races never reached any post of influence or power . . . [but] a change has been gradually introduced in favor of the Egyptian people. Egyptian functionaries, formerly

[10] Jean Deny, *Sommaire des Archives Turques du Caire*, Société Royale de Geographie d'Egypte, Cairo, 1930, pp. 33-34.

[11] Heyworth-Dunne, *op.cit.*, see note 6 above, p. 148.

[12] M. M. Mosharrafa, *Cultural Survey of Modern Egypt*, 2 Parts, Longmans, Green, London, 1947, Part 2, p. 54.

wholly excluded, are now found in the establishments both civil and military. Both Copts and Arabs are sometimes invested with official power."[13] Less than a decade later, as a result of a systematic policy of negating the work of Muhammad Ali, Khedive Abbas I had removed all of these foreign and Egyptian advisers.[14] A former official under Muhammad Ali told Nassau Senior in 1856 that no Egyptians were in high offices any more: ". . . of the many Egyptians whom Mehemet Ali educated, at home, in France, and in England, not one distinguished himself in after life. They have all sunk into obscurity. To a certain extent this may be attributed to the compact phalanx of Turks who defend all public employments against all intruders; but I attribute it in part to the languor and apathy produced by twenty centuries of oppression."[15]

Following Muhammad Ali, Egypt's rulers seem to have begun the familiar process of getting rid of the upper ranks of the civil service left by their predecessors. Thus the successor to Abbas I, Said, according to Senior's reports of his conversations in Cairo, replaced the higher functionaries left to him and substituted his own appointees.[16] Moreover, he tried to direct affairs himself, from matters of high policy down to questions of detail.[17] It was under Said that Europeans began their penetration of Egypt in earnest, by financial manipulation and exploitation of the local rulers' extravagances and ambitions.[18] His successor, Ismail, did little to alter the administrative habits of Egypt, for he soon became embroiled in international finance to a degree that brought the European powers closer and closer to political control over the country. That point was not reached, however, until 1882, when the British, ostensibly seeking to restore the authority of Turkey during the revolt led by Ahmad Arabi, an Egyptian colonel of peasant origin, occupied the land and led it into the widening imperialist orbit of the West.

[13] John Bowring, *Report on Egypt and Candia*, Sessional Papers 1840, Vol. xxxv, H.M.S.O., London, pp. 6-7.

[14] George Young, *Egypt*, Scribner, N.Y., 1927, p. 64.

[15] Senior, *op.cit.*, see note 8 above, vol. 1, pp. 251-252.

[16] *Ibid.*, vol. 1, p. 48.

[17] *Ibid.*, vol. 2, p. 140.

[18] See David Landes, "Bankers and Pashas," in William Miller, ed., *Men in Business. Essays in the History of Entrepreneurship*, Harvard University Press, Cambridge, 1952, especially pp. 32ff.

The British Occupation

The occupation of Egypt is perhaps a classic example of what is meant when Britain is charitably said to have acquired an empire in a fit of absentmindedness. Even as Cromer was on his way to Cairo in 1883 Gladsone's foreign minister told him of the cabinet's desire to see an immediate withdrawal of British troops from Cairo.[19] This reticence was of course more related to European than to local politics, for the British intervention in Egypt followed repeated assurances to France that Britain would not act unilaterally. "These latter assurances," writes Harold Nicolson, "were, at the moment, passionately sincere. British statesmen are usually blind to their own tendencies, but vividly aware of their own disinclinations. . . . This gap between our conscious realization of what we do *not* want to do, and our unconscious realization that in the end we shall have to do it, is inevitably interpreted by foreign observers as indicating hypocrisy or even worse. The mistake our critics make is to state in terms of ethics a problem which is essentially psychological."[20] Whatever the British awareness of their intervention, or their motivation and intention, they soon found good reasons for staying on. Lord Dufferin, the ambassador in Constantinople, was sent to Egypt on a special mission in 1882. Arriving in November, he asked the local British representatives to ascertain the "views and feelings of various sections of the Egyptian community." The report he got from the consul a month later was filled with irresistible reasons to continue the occupation and embark on a reform program. In this early public opinion study the consul stated: "I have come into contact with representatives of the Ulema, the gentry, the mercantile classes, and tradespeople. To have descended lower in the social scale would have been neither profitable nor advisable." Most of the persons questioned, he reported, strongly disapproved of the rebellion the British had put down and expressed "gratitude to England for having saved the country from anarchy and the exactions of the chiefs of the insurrection." He found, in addition, some dissatis-

[19] The Marquess of Zetland (L. J. L. Dundas), *Lord Cromer*, Hodder and Stoughton, London, 1932, pp. 87-88.
[20] Harold Nicolson, *Portrait of a Diplomatist*, Harcourt, Brace, N.Y., 1930, p. 27.

faction at the "rare employment of native Egyptians in the higher grades of the public service. . . ." The Egyptians, he reported, nevertheless expressed a "unanimous and earnest wish . . . that Englishmen should be associated with Egyptian Governors, Judges, and functionaries of every description, to keep them in the paths of rectitude and duty, and to give confidence to the people that henceforward right and justice would take the place of venality, arbitrariness, and the law of the strongest." How could Egyptians complain of foreign officials and ask for English tutelage in almost the same breath? The consul transmitted to Dufferin the following comforting viewpoint of the Egyptians: "To the objection that the employment of foreigners was precisely one of the cries of the rebels, the answer was that their numbers were unnecessarily large, and their salaries excessive; moreover, they should be exclusively English, and not a mixture of all nationalities."[21]

The justification for intervention and occupation established, the rationale for a policy of indefinite control was easily developed. A few months after his retirement from Egypt in 1907, Cromer stated with special clarity, from the vantage point of his long experience there, the philosophy of his regime. Urging caution in the attempt to develop "free institutions" uncongenial to the "Oriental mind," he pointed out that "our primary duty is, not to introduce a system which, under the specious cloak of free institutions, will enable a small minority of natives to misgovern their countrymen, but to establish one which will enable the mass of the population to be good according to the code of Christian morality."[22] In 1885, less than two years after his arrival in Egypt, he was able to report substantial progress in the elimination of corruption;[23] obviously, the occupation was fulfilling its mission so well that it ought to continue.

The Egyptians, nine tenths of them Muslims, were to be guided in the "code of Christian morality" by Englishmen in the

[21] Great Britain, Egypt, No. 2 (1883). *Correspondence Respecting Reorganization in Egypt* (Cd. 3462), p. 26.

[22] Lord Cromer, "The Government of the Subject Races" (January, 1908), in *Political and Literary Essays 1908-1913*, Macmillan, London, 1913, p. 28.

[23] Sir E. Baring to Earl Granville, from Cairo, Feb. 10, 1885, in Great Britain, Egypt, No. 15 (1885). *Reports on the State of Egypt, and the Progress of Administrative Reforms* (Cd. 4421), pp. 2-3.

various government departments. They ruled from the top. Cromer in 1891 commented that British control was exercised by exactly 39 officials, who formed the "backbone of the Egyptian Civil Administration."[24] Many observers, British as well as Egyptian, agree that little was done to develop the capacity for self-government.[25] Cromer himself in 1913, in listing what he took to be the achievements of his administration from 1883 to 1907, asked what things were not done. He answered, ". . . little, if any, progress was made in the direction of conferring autonomy on Egypt," and he offered as reasons the preoccupation with finances, the Anglo-French tension, and the Capitulations.[26] Englishmen who had served in Egypt confirmed Cromer's self-evaluation but without his self-justification. Elgood argued that by 1900 Britain could have withdrawn entirely from Egypt, having done what it had set out to do. But Cromer, believing the Egyptians incapable of self-government, tightened British control by adding a more numerous British staff to the few British advisers.[27] Willcocks, more bitter, commented: "Throughout his long tenure of office Lord Cromer had sedulously depressed and kept down every independent Egyptian and had filled all the high posts with cyphers, with the result that the natural leaders of the people had no opportunity of leading the people."[28] The historian-diplomat, Young, confirms these judgments.[29]

An interesting question arises here: Why did the British not do in Egypt what they did in India? Among British, Indian, and foreign observers there is some agreement that the Indians were well trained in the civil service under British tutelage. No one says the same for the British in Egypt. There are several clues that point to an answer to this question. One is simply that the British were in India much longer than in Egypt. Moreover, they

[24] Great Britain, Egypt, No. 3 (1891). *Report on the Administration and Condition of Egypt and the Progress of Reforms* (Cd. 6321), p. 28.

[25] This review of course omits Cromer's and his successor's achievements in Egypt; our concern here is with problems of the civil service rather that of financial policy, administration of justice, etc.

[26] Lord Cromer, "The Capitulations in Egypt" (July, 1913), *Political and Literary Essays 1908-1913*, pp. 159-162.

[27] P. G. Elgood, *Egypt and the Army*, Oxford University Press, London, 1924, pp. 9-10.

[28] William Willcocks, *Sixty Years in the East*, William Blackwood and Sons, London, 1935, p. 269.

[29] Young, *op.cit.*, see note 14 above, pp. 166-167.

were much more secure in India than in Egypt, for they had moved into India early in the age of imperialism whereas they occupied Egypt when imperialism was already on the wane and the new anti-colonial ideology on the rise. Consequently, even at the start the British in Egypt confronted, in addition to rivals among the European powers and hostility on the part of the Egyptians, a considerable amount of criticism at home. British interest in India was always more direct than its interest in Egypt, whose importance was primarily to guard communications in the Empire. In these circumstances British influence did not penetrate Egyptian society so deeply and widely as it did Indian society. In India British administrators reached the provinces and villages more regularly and intimately than they did in Egypt, where they were largely confined to posts in the central government. The Egyptian people, therefore, having little or no experience with Western administration, developed no expectation of a kind of rule different from what they had been forced to endure for centuries. In the central administration, meanwhile, British policy was set by Cromer, whose personality and philosophy brooked no sharing of power, especially with the "subject races." At one point, indeed, the British wanted to take on local administrative and judicial functions, but the Egyptians objected that such action would have meant superseding rather than supplementing the authority of Egyptian governors. Nubar Pasha, Egyptian prime minister in 1884, vigorously opposed the plan and his success marked the end of the possibility that the British would rule in any way except through control at the center.[30] A final factor of importance was that the British occupied Egypt after nearly a century of French influence in public administration, education, and economic relations, which made British influence all the more difficult to make itself felt.

Yet the British have been able, as Cromer did so often, to rationalize their failure to develop autonomy in Egypt. Cromer's main rationale was, as we have seen, that transferring power and administration to Egyptians would simply have meant misgovernment. Sir Auckland Colvin, who held several high offices in Egypt just before Cromer's arrival on the scene in 1883,

[30] See Cromer, *Modern Egypt*, 2 vols., Macmillan, London, 1908, vol. 2, pp. 482-490, and Young, *op.cit.*, see note 14 above, pp. 168-169.

worked out a subtler rationale. He warned against giving a dependent people too good a government. "We must be careful," he wrote, "not to confound the public interests with the interests of State administrators. There is a point at which the community may reasonably rest satisfied, while the public servant is still impatient to achieve results." He warned against too much administrative progress in areas under foreign control, for the greater the progress the less the native population would be governing itself. "The gulf between the foreigner and the native is thus widened," he concluded, "and there grows up gradually a detached, if highly efficient official class, which, from its almost exclusive control over the wheels of State progress, seems rather to retard than assist the efforts of popular endeavor."[31] This attitude suggests that the choice is no better than one between native administration and good administration. Colvin seems to be saying that stable, efficient government is too good for dependent peoples. One is reminded of the comment by Sir Ronald Storrs concerning England's creation of a government in Iraq: "It seems such a very doubtful benefit—government—to give a people who have long done without."[32]

With so pessimistic an approach to the task of governing Egypt it is not surprising that everyone has been dissatisfied with the job. Each observer has his own special complaint and explanation. For our purpose, to show something of the recent history of the public bureaucracy in Egypt as it affects the higher civil service today, we need to discuss two points in particular: the emphasis upon the school certificate as an entitlement to a government post, and the reserving of the higher posts for Englishmen.

As early as 1885 Cromer reported that "a commencement has been made of the formation of something like a regular Civil Service." He was referring to the promotion of lower officials to the post of provincial governor.[33] Seven years later, early in 1892, the provincial civil service was further systematized. In the same year the service in the central government was likewise

[31] Sir Auckland Colvin, *The Making of Modern Egypt*, 2d ed., Dutton, N.Y., 1906, p. 324.
[32] Ronald Storrs, *Orientations*, Nicholson and Watson, London, 1943, p. 204 note.
[33] See note 23 above, p. 28.

reformed. The major innovation was the creation of an upper division, appointment to which required a secondary school certificate, and a lower division, which called for a primary school certificate. This policy merely formalized and solidified a practice and an attitude that went back many years. As we have seen earlier in this chapter, under Muhammad Ali secular education was identified exclusively with entrance into government employment. Now the certificate became more than ever the badge of education that opened the door to a civil service post. Cromer was quite aware that this reform would have such an effect, and he may even have intended it to produce the result it did. In reporting the innovation, he observed: "Besides improving the material from which the public service is recruited, the system I have described above will give a very great impetus to the spread of education in this country. With an assured prospect of employment in the Administration before them, a very considerable increase must take place in the number of those who apply for the secondary and primary certificates of education. Parents will more willingly spend money in having their children taught when they feel that they are thereby providing them with a certain future."[34] The certificate thus became a guarantee of public employment. Surveying the effects of British educational policy thirty years later, the Milner mission remarked that it might have been justified in the beginning as a means of educating Egyptians to "undertake clerical duties in State departments which had hitherto been largely performed by non-Egyptians" but that there was little attempt to revise the system as time passed.[35]

Most of the Egyptian holders of the primary and secondary school certificates could not aspire to rise very high in civil service, for only a few years after the institution of these reforms in 1892 the recruitment of Englishmen for the higher posts was likewise systematized.[36] This question of the distribution of posts

[34] Lord Cromer to the Earl of Rosebery, from Cairo, March 9, 1893, in Great Britain, Egypt, No. 3 (1893). *Report on the Finances, Administration, and Condition of Egypt, and the Progress of Reforms* (Cd. 6957), pp. 25-26.

[35] Great Britain, Egypt, No. 1 (1921). *Report of the Special Mission to Egypt* (Cd. 1131), pp. 9-10.

[36] See Elgood, *op.cit.*, note 27 above, pp. 10, 16-17; also Humphrey Bowman, *Middle-East Window*, Longmans, Green, London, 1942, p.

at various levels between Egyptians and foreigners (especially Englishmen after 1882) was a constant irritant and a focus of nationalist attack upon the occupying power.

Lord Cromer, we saw earlier, once claimed that British control over Egyptian administration was accomplished by only thirty-nine Englishmen. But there were many more than that number in the employ of the Egyptian government and they were accompanied by hundreds of other non-Egyptians as well. When the British occupied the country, they reduced the number of all appointments to government posts. From 1883 to sometime in 1886 only about 200 appointments were made annually, whereas in the period 1880-1882 the rate was well over 600 annually and more than 300 annually during 1863-1879.[37] Attendant upon this contraction, however, was an increase in the number of foreigners remaining in the service; this increase occurred mainly in the three services charged with the maintenance of public order: the police, the army, and the coast guard. Excluding these three services, however, the increase in the number of foreigners was negligible; in 1882 there were 1,199 and in 1886 only eight more. Foreigners of all nationalities except the English declined in number; the English, understandably, increased from 264 to 299.[38] Cromer summed up their functions as follows: "The army, the Financial Department, and the Public Works Department are mainly in European hands. In these Departments a considerable number of French, Italian, Austrian, German, and Greek subordinates are employed. The principal places are, however, held by Englishmen, and the administrative systems of these Departments distinctly bear the mark of English influence. On the other hand, the Home Department, which includes that of Public Instruction, as well as the Department of Justice, are in Egyptian hands. . . ." The departments in which Englishmen were predominant, he pointed

37, and Coles Pasha, *Recollections and Reflections*, St. Catherine Press, London, no date (preface dated October 1, 1918), p. 168.

[37] Great Britain, Egypt, No. 11 (1887). *Further Correspondence Respecting the Finances of Egypt* (Cd. 4942), pp. 6-7.

[38] The English in the Egyptian civil service included English-born subjects of the Crown, Maltese, and English-protected persons. (See note 40, this chapter, p. 15 of the report cited.)

out, were the essential ones, the ones in need of reform, and those related to foreigners.[39]

What proportion of the civil service in 1882 were foreigners? The answer depends upon which categories of government workers are considered. A British estimate put the total figures at 52,974 Egyptians, drawing salaries aggregating £.E. 1,648,-503, and 1,067 Europeans receiving £.E. 305,096. Europeans thus constituted two per cent of the service and drew 16 per cent of the total salaries.[40] Excluding the armed forces, another British estimate placed the total number of civil servants at about 20,000, of whom five per cent were Europeans. Finally, omitting customs, railways, and similar services, the total was said to be 10,000, of whom eight per cent were Europeans.[41]

In accordance with the policy of reducing the influence of other nations in Egypt, the number of non-English Europeans in the civil service continued to decline. By 1898 the number of Englishmen was 455, compared to only 299 in 1886. In addition, of course, they occupied the highest positions. Of 10,600 Egyptians in 1898 only 45 received a monthly salary of £.E. 70 or more, whereas 47 of 455 Englishmen did so.[42]

Much has been made of the over-staffing of the Egyptian civil service and of the difficulty of reducing its swollen ranks. The British, seeking to get rid of Europeans early in the occupation, found this particular task not an easy one. Lord Dufferin in 1883 suggested the need to reduce the number of Europeans in the service, "especially where it has been duplicated for political reasons."[43] Drummond Wolff, on a mission a few years later, reported that the foreign civil servants' consular representatives

[39] Great Britain, Egypt, No. 6 (1887). *Despatches from Sir E. Baring Respecting the Employment of Europeans in the Egyptian Public Service* (Cd. 4997), pp. 3-6.

[40] Sir E. Malet to Earl Granville, from Alexandria, September 11, 1882, in Great Britain, Egypt, No. 3 (1883). *Papers Respecting Europeans in the Service of the Egyptian Government* (Cd. 3463), p. 2.

[41] The Earl of Dufferin to Earl Granville, from Cairo, April 3, 1883, in Great Britain, Egypt, No. 14 (1883). *Further Correspondence Respecting the Reorganization of Egypt* (Cd. 3696), pp. 18-19.

[42] Lord Cromer to Marquis of Salisbury, from Cairo, February 26, 1899, in Great Britain, Egypt, No. 3 (1899). *Report by Her Majesty's Agent and Consul-General on the Finances, Administration, and Condition of Egypt and the Sudan in 1898* (Cd. 9231), pp. 47-48.

[43] Great Britain, Egypt, No. 6 (1883). *Further Correspondence Respecting Reorganization in Egypt* (Cd. 3529), pp. 66-68.

would seek to retain them in their posts. "By this means official misdemeanors are often condoned," he remarked, "and a foreign employe is retained in a post for which he is manifestly unfit from incapacity or misconduct, or his fall is lightened by an undue addition to the Pension List." He concluded that: "In measures of retrenchment the rights of native officials have too often, in former times, been sacrificed to the foreigners. . . ."[44] This special form of corruption was thus prevalent long before the Egyptians began to control their own government employment.

The number of British officials in Egyptian civil administration was steadily increasing. By World War I it had grown enormously. In 1920 the Milner mission found Egyptians in less than one quarter of the higher posts. Reviewing the changes since 1905, it found that the proportion of Egyptians in *all* posts had increased from 45 to 51 per cent. In the *higher* posts, however, they had declined from 28 to 23 per cent, while the proportion of the British in such posts had increased from 42 to 59 per cent.[45]

During the period of the protectorate (1914-1922) and since the achievement of a growing degree of independence, the patterns set in the years we have just reviewed continued to prevail. The growing nationalist movement and the accompanying grants of autonomy meant the steady elimination of foreigners from the civil service and its "Egyptianization." This process was accelerated by the British declaration of Egypt's independence in 1922. The British left to the Sultan and the Egyptian people the matter of the "creation of a Parliament with a right to control the policy and administration of a constitutionally responsible Government. . . ."[46] The Egyptians did not wait long to adopt a systematic policy of removing and retiring British and European officials in the civil service over which they assumed complete control. According to Lord Lloyd, British High Commissioner in Egypt from 1925 to 1929, the number of Europeans in the Egyptian civil service dwindled to a handful in the first

[44] Sir H. Drummond Wolff to the Earl of Rosebery, from Cairo, March 3, 1886, in Great Britain, Egypt, No. 5 (1887). *Reports by Sir H. Drummond Wolff on the Administration of Egypt* (Cd. 4996), p. 15.

[45] Milner Mission, see note 35 above, p. 30 note.

[46] Arnold J. Toynbee, *Survey of International Affairs 1925. Vol.* I, *The Islamic World Since the Peace Settlement,* Royal Institute of International Affairs, Oxford University Press, London, 1927, pp. 194-195.

five years of the country's independence.[47] More and more, meanwhile, the service became an object of domestic politics. The educational system continued to be geared to the expectation of a government post, still held in high esteem. During these latter years Egypt had full control over most of public employment but did little to combat the weaknesses it had pointed to previously. Several starts in the direction of reform soon faded. Government posts became a recognized spoil of political victory. The palace likewise exerted a corrupting influence. By 1949, however, a culmination of reform efforts produced a draft law revamping the civil service. The following year the Egyptian government invited a British expert to examine its civil service system and to suggest means to improve it. One of his recommendations was the establishment of an independent civil service department "reporting to the Council of Ministers through, and under the authority of, the Prime Minister."[48] Two years later, in 1952, after the extraordinary changes the army introduced following its seizure of power and the abdication of the king, Egypt had a Civil Service Commission and the beginnings of a new civil service establishment.[49]

The Commission's functions are to recruit and place government workers, designate the numbers and grades of civil servants, and in general carry out the provisions of civil service regulations. An indication of the state of government employment in 1952 may be gleaned from the Commission's detailed review, in its first annual report, of the needs of the public service. These needs, defining the tasks of the Commission itself, may be summarized as: (1) elimination of unnecessary posts and bureaus; (2) classification of posts with job descriptions and appropriate grades and salaries; (3) assignment of personnel to posts for which they are qualified; (4) proper dis-

[47] Lord Lloyd, *Egypt since Cromer*, 2 vols., Macmillan, London, 1934, vol. 2, pp. 105, 198, and chapters 5, 6.

[48] A. P. Sinker, *Report on the Personnel Questions of the Egyptian Civil Service* (Nov. 27, 1950), Ministry of Finance of Egypt, Government Press, Cairo, 1951, par. 31.

[49] The Civil Service Commission (Diwan al Muwazzafin) was created by Law No. 190 of 1951 (October 22). This law was superseded by Law No. 78 of 1952 (June 7), which was in turn replaced by Law No. 158 of 1952 (August 18), which is still the statute that defines the functions of the Commission. Law No. 210 of 1951, as modified, regulates the civil service itself.

tribution of work among the agencies of the government; (5) establishment of a training program for the service; (6) strengthening of the Commission's position in the government and enlargement of its jurisdiction.[50]

The regulations governing the civil service of Egypt today are much like those of Western countries, with certain exceptions. Appointments to most posts are to be made according to the applicant's scores in written and oral examinations. Civil servants are to be paid the salary fixed for the posts which they occupy even if they may be qualified for higher posts; and salary scales are published together with the schedule of increments. Promotion is by merit or seniority, and the proportion of each is fixed for the various grades. Disciplinary action is defined in nine steps from warning to dismissal. An unusual feature is that several of these steps provide for temporary or permanent reductions in salary without changes in grade.

As to the general conduct of the civil servant, the Egyptian law, in common with Western law, forbids him to engage in politics or in business connected in any way with his government employment. In addition, however, the Egyptian law includes some restrictions derived from the country's own experience and illustrative of the problem of conflicting loyalties which we shall discuss later; and these are features far from common in Western codes governing the conduct of civil servants. The Egyptian law requires the government official to give an annual statement of his financial position. The civil servant's place of residence is regulated to the extent that he must live in the area in which he works (although this is not defined in the law) except for urgent reasons approved by his ministry. He is also forbidden to hold other employment after working hours except by special permission. He is forbidden to gamble in clubs and public places and to speculate in the stock market. Finally, one article forbids an official to ask another person to intervene on his behalf in any matter relating to his post, and he is himself forbidden to intervene on behalf of another official. These provisions were designed to meet the special problems of the government in its relations with the civil servants; their vagueness makes them susceptible to differing interpretations, as is the case whenever personal

[50] Civil Service Commission, *Annual Report, 1952* (in Arabic), Government Press, Cairo, 1953, pp. 31-34.

taste and motivation are made the subjects of legal regulation.

Basic salaries in the civil service are given in detail in Law 210 of 1951. The annual salaries of cabinet ministers and the highest officials down to heads of departments were set at £.E. 2,500 to 1,200 (about $7,000 to $3,400). Salaries for the high technical and administrative workers (the group of which our 249 respondents constitute very nearly the highest grades) were fixed at £.E. 1,140 to £.E. 180 (about $3,200 to $500). Salaries in the medium technical and clerical class range from £.E. 540 to £.E. 72 (about $1,500 to $100). To these basic salaries a cost of living bonus of 15.5 per cent to 150 per cent was added in 1950;[51] the size of the bonus was reduced in 1953.[52] Further, normal salary increments were suspended in 1953-1954 and restored only on July 1, 1955.[53]

Progress toward the six goals the Commission set for itself in 1952 has been definite but slow. The important point is that the policies the Commission aims to carry out imply a different set of values from that apparently still surviving vigorously even in the upper ranks of the civil service. Resistance to the Commission, according to its own reports, has added to the original difficulties facing it when it was first constituted.[54] Its activity in conducting examinations and in filling openings has nevertheless increased. The Commission has reported that it conducted 57 written examinations in 1954, compared with 31 in 1953, and that in 1954 about 13,000 candidates sat for these examinations as against only 5,600 the year before. In addition, it received an increasing number of requests from the ministries to supply personnel; in 1954 it received about 6,300 such requests, a sharp increase over the 1,700 in 1953.[55]

[51] Ministry of Finance, General Administration of Government Employees, *Circular Letter*, February 26, 1950 (in Arabic), based upon a decision of the Council of Ministers on February 19, 1950.

[52] Decision of the Council of Ministers, June 30, 1953, carried out in Circular Letter No. 41/1953 of the Civil Service Commission, in *Collection of Circular Letters Issued by the Commission since Its Establishment in 1952* (in Arabic), Government Press, Cairo, 1954, p. 60.

[53] Text of law in *Al Ahram* (Cairo), June 30, 1955, p. 9, col. 4.

[54] Civil Service Commission, *Annual Report, 1952*, see note 50 above, pp. 1-2; and *Report of the Commission on Budgetary Proposals for the Fiscal Year 1953-1954* (in Arabic), Government Press, Cairo, 1953, pp. 1, 2, 15.

[55] Republic of Egypt, Civil Service Commission, *Annual Report of the*

Some of the problems we shall discuss in succeeding chapters are aggravated by the absence of formal regulations such as the Commission now seeks to introduce. The lack of job-descriptions and codes, for example, discourages the government official from using his initiative even if he is able to overcome other powerful deterrents. Since he is not certain where his authority and functions begin and end, the civil servant has one more reason to play everything safely by assuming that the responsibility lies elsewhere than upon himself. In a recent report the Commission has listed its tasks as: (1) reclassification of posts to relate grade to function, in order to correct the legacy of planless or corrupt appointments; (2) development of a proper recruitment and placement policy; (3) introduction of administrative reforms to eliminate improvisation, increase efficiency and output, and reduce violations of laws and regulations.[56] When the formal structure of the Egyptian civil service has attained this character it will have come a long way in its evolution from its role as a personal adjunct to the ruling power.

Commission on Budgetary Proposals for the Fiscal Year 1955-1956 (in Arabic), Government Press, Cairo, 1955, pp. 31-32.

[56] Republic of Egypt, Civil Service Commission, *Annual Report of the Commission on Budgetary Proposals for the Fiscal Year 1954-1955* (in Arabic), Government Press, Cairo, 1954, pp. 6-11.

Chapter 3. The Background of the Higher Civil Servants Today

Despite changes in political leadership, the abolition of the monarchy, the departure of the British, and the considerable reform effort since 1952, the Egyptian civil service today is the direct lineal descendant of the corps whose history we have just reviewed. Our main evidence for the contemporary higher civil service comes from the questionnaire[1] answered by 249 government officials and from reports and rulings by the Civil Service Commission. Both types of evidence point to certain characteristics and problems of the service that are easily traced to the influences described in previous chapters. The past lives on in the very changes it has wrought in the corps of Egyptian higher civil servants.

Before examining in detail the results of the questionnaire survey and their relationship to other kinds of information, we ought briefly to describe the way in which the survey was carried out, the selection and interviewing of the sample of higher civil servants, and their backgrounds. Then we can see, broadly, certain characteristics and problems of the respondents to the questionnaire and the aspects of their socio-economic background that help explain them. This summary review of the survey findings will set the stage for more detailed reporting and analysis later.

Selection and Interviewing of Respondents

To learn certain things about the higher civil service of Egypt today it was necessary to go directly to the officials themselves, since there were no published or unpublished data on their socio-economic background, their conceptions of the role of the civil servant, and their attitudes toward the performance of the tasks involved in government. It was immediately decided to omit the "sensitive" ministries such as those of Foreign Affairs, Interior, and War. These and other considerations led to the selection of the following four ministries: Agriculture, Education (excluding classroom teachers), Finance and Economy, and

[1] The entire questionnaire, in the original Arabic and in an English translation, appears in Appendix 1.

Municipal and Rural Affairs. The focus of our interest was the higher civil service in Cairo, where the overwhelming majority of the central civil service is stationed. Respondents were sought among grades 2, 3, and 4. Grade 1, the highest, was omitted because it would have provided too many of the very highest supervisory officials, including some in the rank of director-general or department head. The number of officials in each of these three grades in each of the four ministries was obtained from the personnel officers. As Table 1 shows, the total number of civil servants we wanted to learn about was 1,556, of whom 129 were in the Ministry of Agriculture, 687 in Education, 602 in Finance and Economy, and 138 in Municipal and Rural Affairs.

TABLE 1

Civil Servants Who Responded to the Questionnaire

Ministry and Grade	Total No. of Civil Servants	No. of Civil Servants Interviewed	Per Cent Interviewed
Agriculture—*Total*	*129*	*39*	*30*
Grade 2	9	2	22
Grade 3	26	9	30
Grade 4	94	28	29
Education—*Total*	*687*	*64*	*9*
Grade 2	140	27	19
Grade 3	309	27	9
Grade 4	238	10	4
Finance and Economy—*Total*	*602*	*107*	*18*
Grade 2	57	21[a]	37
Grade 3	147	39	27
Grade 4	398	47	12
Municipal and Rural Affairs—*Total*	*138*	*39*	*28*
Grade 2	21	11	52
Grade 3	33	9	27
Grade 4	84	19	24
Grand Total	*1,556*	*249*	*16*

[a] Includes 3 respondents who were in grade 2 when asked to be interviewed but who had been promoted to grade 1 by the time the interview was conducted about a month later. They are included throughout this report among the respondents in grade 2.

The aim was to interview about 15 per cent of the civil servants in each grade in each ministry. A somewhat larger proportion, therefore, were sent a letter[2] addressed to them by name, from the minister (or some other official in authority), describing the nature of the survey, identifying its director, and asking for the cooperation of the civil servant. Of the 616 who received such a letter, 274 agreed to be interviewed. In January and February of 1954, interviews were completed with 249 of these higher civil servants, comprising a 16 per cent sample of the 1,556 in grades 2, 3, and 4 in the four ministries mentioned above.[3] The interviews, each taking from an hour and a half to two hours and a half, were conducted in private, during office hours, by twenty-seven experienced interviewers and social workers employed in the Ministry of Social Affairs and the Ministry of Education. The interviewers, most of them trained at the Cairo School of Social Work and all members of the Egyptian Association of Social Workers, were given six hours of special instruction on the aim of the entire project, the purpose and nature of the questionnaire, and the interviewing and reporting procedure. They conducted the interviews orally, writing in Arabic as the respondent spoke in Arabic. The coding of the replies was done from the original questionnaire sheets, in Arabic, by experienced coders selected from the interviewing staff, augmented by other Egyptians familiar with this process, and supervised by this writer and a trained Egyptian statistician.

This procedure did not yield a perfectly representative sample of the Egyptian civil service. First, a sample of higher, rather than all, officials was sought. Second, the sample had to be limited to officials in a manageable number of ministries. Third, the respondents volunteered to be interviewed; we have no reliable knowledge of whether they differ (and if so, how) from those who did not volunteer. These 249 senior officials who make up our sample, however, do constitute a substantial (although a varying) proportion of those in their grades and ministries; a first study of such a social group is valuable even if not perfectly representative.

Who Are the Respondents?

Who, then, are the civil servants who responded to the questionnaire—the group whose characteristics, attitudes, and opin-

[2] Appendix 2.

[3] For further details of the total population and the sample, see Appendix 3.

ions are reported in this study? In later chapters we shall frequently refer to various types of civil servants: the older and younger, the administrative and the technical, those born in rural areas and those in urban, those educated in Western universities and those in Egyptian, and so on. To enable us to compare responses from these differing types of Egyptian higher civil servants, we shall at the outset describe these background and career traits. Having these data before us will also help us to understand the scope and relevance of the survey because they will tell us a great deal about those who are its subjects. Finally, this sort of information can be compared with similar data about the higher civil servants of other countries where such studies have been made.

Age. The respondents, as Table 2 shows, range in age from

TABLE 2
Age of Respondents

Age	Number	Per Cent
31-35	6	2.4
36-40	57	22.9
41-45	62	24.9
46-50	51	20.5
51-55	49	19.7
56-60	24	9.6
Total	249	100.0

31 to 60, at which retirement is mandatory. Almost 90 per cent, however, were between 36 and 55. Although a high proportion of Egyptian government workers enter the service in their twenties, our respondents, being in the higher grades, are of course older than the average. The age-groups we shall refer to most are 31-45, in which there are 125, or 50.2 per cent, and 46-60, in which there are 124, or 49.8 per cent. The respondents are thus evenly divided between the "older" and "younger." A study of 234 administrative workers in the higher civil service of the United States in 1940[4] showed a somewhat higher proportion in the older group. Thirty-nine per cent of this sample of American senior officials were between ages 30 and 44, and 61

[4] Reinhard Bendix, *Higher Civil Servants in American Society*, University of Colorado Studies, Series in Sociology, No. 2, University of Colorado Press, Boulder, 1949, Table II, p. 23.

per cent were 44 and older. Although these officials were all in administrative rather than technical or professional posts, their positions in the service are roughly similar to those of the Egyptian respondents. A study of British higher civil servants, involving somewhat higher levels than those in the American or the Egyptian surveys, shows a larger proportion of older incumbents of the highest ranks in 1950. Of 332 persons in the ranks above that of assistant secretary, 82 per cent were 45 and older, but among 713 persons holding the lowest post in the higher civil service of Great Britain, that of assistant secretary, 59 per cent were 45 or older.[5] Thus, to judge from the basis of such data as are available, the higher civil servants of Egypt are probably somewhat younger than those of Britain or the U.S.

Grade. Our sample of Egyptian senior officials was confined to those in grades 2, 3, and 4, that is, the three grades just below the highest, grade 1; in and above grade 1 are the directors-general or department heads, and the immediate aides to the cabinet ministers. As Table 3 shows, one quarter of the

TABLE 3

Grade of Respondents

Grade	Number	Per Cent
2	61	24.5
3	84	33.7
4	104	41.8
Total	249	100.0

respondents are in grade 2, the highest of the three grades sampled, while a third are in grade 3, and two fifths in grade 4, the lowest one sampled. Grade is difficult to compare from one civil service system to another. Although the American and British studies just referred to do not present information about grade in a way that permits us to make even a limited comparison, the American study does offer the "salary level" of the respondents. If we take the American "salary level" as roughly comparable to the Egyptian grade, it appears that the sample of American higher civil servants, relative to the total higher civil service in the U.S., is considerably higher in rank than are

[5] R. K. Kelsall, *Higher Civil Servants in Britain*, Routledge and Kegan Paul, London, 1955, Table 31, p. 200, and Table 29, p. 198.

the Egyptian respondents relative to the entire group from which they come. For only a quarter of the Egyptian respondents are in the highest rank of those sampled, whereas about half of the respondents covered in the American study are in the highest of the three "salary levels." In addition, whereas only 7 per cent of the American respondents were at the lowest "salary level," more than 40 per cent of the Egyptian respondents are in the lowest rank, grade 4.[6]

Both the American and the British studies thus refer to a group that is actually higher than our sample of the Egyptian higher civil service. But the two Western corps of senior officials are higher than the Egyptian sample in different ways. The British group are higher in rank and responsibility. The American group appear to be no higher in the American service than are the Egyptian group in their service, but the American sample includes a higher proportion of the upper grades, within the higher civil service itself, than does the Egyptian sample. It is important to remember the limitations to the comparability of these three national services, especially as it is so tempting to make comparisons.

Birthplace. The predominantly urban character of the respondents is shown in Table 4. Three quarters were born in

TABLE 4

Geographical Origin of Respondents

| | PLACE OF BIRTH | | PLACE LIVED UNTIL AGE 20 | |
	No.	Per Cent	No.	Per Cent
Urban	185	74.3	241	97.2
Rural	64	25.7	7	2.8
Total	*249*	*100.0*	*248*	*100.0*

urban areas, which is approximately the converse of the ratio for the entire nation, of whom three quarters are in agricultural pursuits. The weight of urban influence becomes even greater when we look at the place where the respondent lived up to the age of 20, irrespective of his birthplace. As Table 4 shows, 97 per cent are urban in this sense, no doubt mainly because of movement to urban secondary schools and universities. The influence of birthplace persists nevertheless, as we shall see later,

[6] Bendix, *op.cit.*, note 4 above, computed from Table XIII, p. 37.

in that it establishes the limit of the Egyptian's exposure to Western modes of life. The American sample has a higher proportion, about two fifths, born in rural areas.[7]

Education. As might be expected in a group of highly placed government officials, the vast majority of respondents have a bachelor's degree. Table 5 shows that three quarters have this

TABLE 5

Educational Level of Respondents

	Number	Per Cent
Less than secondary	1	0.4
Secondary only	29	11.6
B.A. or equivalent	192	77.1
Higher than B.A.	27	10.9
Total	249	*100.0*

degree, and more than another tenth have taken higher degrees, while only an eighth failed to go beyond secondary school. Those who have the B.A. degree or higher thus constitute 88 per cent of the total sample. Among the American sample of higher civil servants in 1940, only three quarters had reached this educational level,[8] and among all the British higher civil servants in 1950 only 63 per cent had a university education.[9] The Egyptian sample thus has more formal education. This result may surprise readers accustomed to viewing Egypt as an "underdeveloped" country; but Egypt is among those non-industrial areas in which, by native tradition and emulation of the West, higher education has grown at a pace approximating that in Western countries. (We are not, of course, comparing the relative quality of Egyptian, American, and British university education.) The close relation between education and the government service in the Near East has already been mentioned and will be examined anew, in its contemporary aspect, in the next chapter. One further point, to be elaborated later, is that 217 of the 249 respondents have been graduated from college, and of these 217, the great majority, 84 per cent, attended Egyptian universities; only 35, or 16 per cent, took their bachelor's degree in a

[7] *Ibid.*, Table III, p. 23.
[8] *Ibid.*, computed from Table x, p. 33 and Table II, p. 23.
[9] Kelsall, *op.cit.*, note 5 above, Table 20, p. 136.

Western university, most of them in England and the United States.

Function. Unlike the American and British studies, which confined themselves to administrative officials, our survey of Egyptian higher civil servants includes both technical and administrative workers, as Table 6 shows. Among the Egyptian

TABLE 6

Function of Respondents

	Number	Per Cent
Administrative	38	15.3
Technical	211	84.7
Total	*249*	*100.0*

respondents, indeed, technical workers, comprising 85 per cent of the total interviewed, far outnumber administrative workers. This numerical superiority of the technical workers in our sample is probably itself an indication that they are more professionally oriented than administrators, are perhaps less secretive about their work, and are more likely to understand researches like this one and hence more willing to participate in them.

The distinction between technicians and administrators, however, is not always clear, for if administration itself is developing a body of principles that can be learned it can be considered no less technical a pursuit than those now classified as technical or professional. It is quite possible that different criteria have been used to classify by function the three national civil service corps we have been discussing. In any case, there seems to be a real difference between administrative and technical officials among the Egyptian respondents; later in this chapter we shall see briefly the nature of this difference, which will be further examined in Chapter 7.

Social origin. Table 7 shows the main occupations of the respondents' fathers up to the time the respondents reached 20 years of age. Nearly two fifths of the respondents are the sons of civil servants. Almost a quarter are the sons of landlords, another 16 per cent of peasants, and the remainder of small merchants, independent professionals, army officers, and white collar workers not in the civil service. In social origin these

TABLE 7

Occupations of Respondents' Fathers

Occupation	Number	Per Cent
Civil servant, white collar	94	38.8
Landlord	57	23.6
Peasant	39	16.1
Small merchant	21	8.7
Independent professional	14	5.8
Army officer	9	3.7
White collar, non-civil service	8	3.3
Total	242	100.0

higher civil servants of Egypt are thus predominantly an upper middle class group, for only about a quarter are the sons of peasants or merchants, while none had fathers who were urban laborers. How do these Egyptian senior officials compare with the American and British? Among 180 American higher civil servants in 1940, only 3 per cent were the sons of government workers, while 28 per cent were the sons of professionals, another 29 per cent the sons of farm owners, and 10 per cent the sons of laborers.[10] Among 331 British civil servants in ranks above that of assistant secretary in 1950, nearly 40 per cent had fathers in professional and technical pursuits, about a quarter clerks and salesmen, 17 per cent were owners of farms or businesses, and a like proportion were manual workers or domestic servants. About a tenth of these British senior officials had fathers in the civil service.[11] Recent data on the French civil service show that sixty-five per cent of all successful candidates in the examinations conducted from 1945 to 1951 by the Ecole Nationale d'Administration had fathers who were employers and independent professionals, or higher civil servants, managers, and technicians.[12] Thus the Egyptian higher civil servants in our sample were recruited from sons of civil servants to a much greater degree than the American or British. The lowest socioeconomic sources of civil servants in Egypt (the peasants and small merchants) provided about a quarter of our respondents,

[10] Bendix, *op.cit.*, note 4 above, Table v, p. 26.

[11] Kelsall, *op.cit.*, note 5 above, Table 24, pp. 150-151.

[12] T. B. Bottomore, "Higher Civil Servants in France," *Transactions of the Second World Congress of Sociology* (Belgium, 1953), International Sociological Association, London, 1954 (2 vols.), Vol. I, pp. 145-152.

whereas the lowest social group from which the U.S. sample is drawn (the manual workers) provided only a tenth of the sample of 1940 American higher civil servants. In Britain the comparable groups (manual workers and domestic servants) provided a sixth of the higher civil servants in 1950. The three main sources of the Egyptian senior officials in our sample are thus the civil service itself, landlords, and peasants. For the American corps in 1940, the three main sources were farm owners, professionals, and small businessmen. For the British corps in 1950, the three main sources were (1) professionals, clerks, (2) owners of farms and businesses, and (3) manual workers and domestic servants. Although the Egyptian higher civil service, it appears, draws more upon the lowest socioeconomic groups than do the American or British, it also draws somewhat more heavily from the landlord class. The American and British corps recruit mostly from the middle classes, the Egyptian more from the very top and the very bottom layers, and to the extent that it does recruit from the middle class it does so from the sons of civil servants. This is not surprising in view of the greater strength and relative numbers of the middle classes in Western countries than in less industrialized areas. In Egypt, the middle class has been weak in numbers and influence, and civil servants have comprised a large proportion of it.

We have further information on the social origin or milieu of the Egyptian respondents, this time on the educational level attained by their wives[13] and their parents. Among the wives, 13 per cent are illiterate or barely literate, 41 per cent completed primary school, 37 per cent completed secondary school, and 9 per cent had a bachelor's degree or higher. The extraordinary growth in women's education is revealed in the amount of schooling of the respondents' mothers compared with that of their wives. Of this older generation of women, 56 per cent are illiterate, another 20 per cent are barely literate, only 20 per cent completed primary school and 4 per cent secondary school, and none had a college education. The respondents' fathers, of course, had more formal education than the mothers, but not so

13 Among the 249 respondents, 16 are women, all of them in the Ministry of Education. They are included, without differentiation, among the men because of their small number and concentration in one ministry.

much as the respondents themselves. Of the fathers, 24 per cent are illiterate or barely literate, 23 per cent completed primary school and another 23 per cent completed secondary school, and 30 per cent had a college education.

Bureaucracy and Professionalism

We have reviewed the broad characteristics of our sample of Egyptian higher civil servants in order to see what sort of people they are as a group; and we have sought to compare them, in age, education, etc., with roughly similar senior officials in the U.S. and Britain. Now we turn to another type of description and comparison, this one within the corps of Egyptian senior officials themselves. Instead of comparing Egyptian government workers with those of the U.S. or Britain, we now compare some Egyptian officials with other Egyptian officials to see whether they respond differently to certain questions and situations. For example, how do the older civil servants compare with the younger? Do they have more education, or less? Do they like the civil service more, or less? Have they been more exposed to Western influences, or less? Are they more dissatisfied with government work, or less? The same questions may be asked concerning the more and the less educated respondents, or of those in administrative and those in technical posts. This type of comparison is of course more reliable than comparisons between Egyptian and American or British civil servants, since it does not involve data gathered in other cultures and on the basis of other criteria.

Egypt, like other Eastern and agricultural countries, is engaged in a mighty effort to transform itself. This effort began before the abolition of the monarchy but has been accelerated since the army seized control in 1952. The nation's leaders incessantly proclaim their goals to be elimination of corruption in government, creation of new industries, agricultural reform to increase the proportion of landowners among the tillers of the soil and to increase production, development of national power and prestige, and a rise in the general standard of living.[14] The means by which these goals are to be achieved display an at-

[14] See, for example, the article by Prime Minister Gamal Abdel Nasser, "The Egyptian Revolution," *Foreign Affairs*, Vol. 33, No. 2, January, 1955, pp. 199-211.

tempt to approach the technology of Western society in efficiency and pervasiveness. The governmental apparatus, the civil service, is one of the agencies of this vast transformation. Hence Egyptian leaders have emphasized the need for an efficient, loyal, highly skilled, and incorruptible corps of government workers. Efforts at civil service reform are, therefore, deliberately intended to change the government service in a Western direction. Since this is the goal of Egyptians themselves it is essential that we understand the relationship between their civil service today and what the nation's leaders (before and since the abolition of the monarchy) intend that it should become. We ought to understand, that is to say, what Western public bureaucracy is, to what degree its Egyptian counterpart now shares its characteristics, and which classes of Egyptian officials approach this model most closely. Our interest in the Westernization of the Egyptian civil service is not the result of Western feelings of superiority or of ethnocentrism, but of the fact that this is what the Egyptian national leadership and the leaders of the civil service themselves are striving to accomplish.

The Western model of the civil servant, to which the Egyptian leaders aspire, has been developed through several centuries of political and economic change. These changes, and the concomitant emergence of the model of the public bureaucracy (to which the reality, needless to say, does not always conform), have been chronicled and analyzed by Western social scientists until its general features are well known.[15] Bureaucracy has been analyzed from two related standpoints. First, studies of bureaucratic *structures* have examined the centralization of power and authority, the establishment of a hierarchy of offices with special requirements and prerogatives, and the existence of rules governing the exercise of function and authority. Second, studies of bureaucratic *behavior* have examined the institutional or behavioral concomitants of these structures, such as caution in interpreting the rules, self-interest among the corps of officials, conduct toward the public, and (more recently) informal relationships not envisaged in the prescribed system.

In the course of our efforts to compare the attitudes and be-

[15] See the comprehensive collection of discussions edited by Robert K. Merton and others, *Reader in Bureaucracy*, The Free Press, Glencoe, Ill., 1952.

havior of Egyptian and Western higher civil servants, we distilled three related components of bureaucratic behavior. Each element corresponds to a structural feature of bureaucracy.

1. Rationality and universalism: emphasis upon efficiency in getting a task performed, and recruitment based upon competence rather than other considerations such as need, loyalty to family or religion or community.

2. Hierarchy: emphasis upon the prerogatives of position, upon the authority of the superior official and the obedience of the subordinate.

3. Discretion: emphasis upon the official's area of free judgment and personal initiative, the willingness to accept responsibility and to exercise the full measure of discretionary powers permitted by the regulations.

As industrialization and urbanization have proceeded in more and more areas of the world, large organizations with these structural and institutional qualities have also grown. Accompanying this growth has been an extraordinary development of new professions to supply these bureaucracies with the technical skills they require. Professionalization has thus been characteristic of the recent occupational history of the West. This aspect of modern bureaucracy has likewise three related components:

1. Skill: emphasis upon technical competence as the chief characteristic of an organized group, and upon self-discipline and self-regulation in the group to maintain its standards of skill.

2. Self-protection: emphasis upon self-interest of the professional group through monopoly of function, secrecy, exclusion.

3. Service: emphasis upon service to the public or clientele as the main feature of professional activity, upon the protection of the public's interest.

In order to assess how closely the Egyptian higher civil service approaches this Western model, we have constructed several scales or indexes,[16] based upon appropriate items in the questionnaire. The details of their makeup are fully described in

[16] In a Guttman scale such as we use here, the component items are so related to one another that, given only a respondent's score, we know (within a small margin of error) how he replied to all the items in the scale. In an index the separate items are merely combined without being related to one another to the same degree.

Appendix 4; here they are summarized to enable us to use them throughout this study.

The degree to which a respondent approximates what we take to be Western bureaucratic norms is measured by a *Bureaucratic Scale* of three items. Of the 249 respondents, 37 gave no "Western" answers, 20 gave one Western answer, and 96 gave two such responses. These 153 higher civil servants, we say, are low on the Bureaucratic Scale. The remaining 96, who gave "Western" answers to all three items, we say, are high on the scale. The value of this measure is not that it enables us to say that these 96 Egyptian civil servants are "more Western" than, for example, the civil servants of other countries; we do not have the comparative data to justify such an assertion. Its value is that it permits us to compare those Egyptian senior officials who are high on the scale with those who are low. For example: Are the highs older or younger than the lows? Are they more or less educated than the lows?

The *Professionalism Index* provides a measure of the degree to which the respondents express adherence to the qualities we have just described as professionalism: emphasis upon skill, self-protection, and public service. This index is made up of four items in the questionnaire. Of the 249 respondents, 8 answered none in conformity with these professional values, 45 answered one item, and 118 answered two items this way. These 171 civil servants, we say, are low on the Professionalism Index. Seventy-one respondents answered three items in conformity with professional values and 7 answered all four items this way; these 78 respondents, we say, are high on the index.

In measuring the Egyptian civil servants' exposure to Western influences we use two devices, an *Exposure Scale* and the respondent's age. The Exposure Scale is composed of four items in the questionnaire. Of the 249 respondents, 143 have been exposed to either no Western influences or to only one such influence (as indicated, for example, by travel in a Western country, knowledge of a Western language, and so on). These 143 we say have low exposure. The remaining 106 respondents have been exposed to two, three, or four such Western influences, and we say they have high exposure. As is more fully explained in Appendix 4, there are several limitations to this scale as a measure of exposure to Western patterns of behavior. First, it tells us only about the respondent's physical exposure to the West but not about his personal predisposition toward what he sees in or from the West. The degree to which a Near Easterner absorbs Western influences depends not only upon exposure to them in the sheer physical sense but also upon his predisposition or the degree to which he is prepared to adopt Western behavior and attitudes. Thus one Egyptian educated in Europe or the United States may return with great admiration for everything Western, while another may go home rejecting all he has seen. Both are influenced in some way, but this study cannot say just how and why.[17]

The second limitation of the Exposure Scale is that it does not take adequate account of *duration* of exposure. Thus a young civil servant who has read Western newspapers and books for five years is, according to the scale, no less exposed in this respect than an older man who has been reading them for twenty or thirty years. Age, in other words, is itself a measure of exposure to Western influences.

Because of these limitations and because of the special relationship of age to the Exposure Scale (discussed at length in Appendix 4), we shall use age differences and the scale in referring to degree of exposure to Western influences.

The *Job-Satisfaction Index* tries to measure the degree to which the Egyptian civil servants in our sample are satisfied with their posts in the government service. It is made up of four items. Of the 249 respondents, 198 answered none, one, or only two of these questions in a manner indicating satisfaction; they are low on the index. The remaining 51 respondents answered three or all four items in such a way as to indicate satisfaction; they are high on the scale.

Differences among the Respondents in Degree of Westernization

We have now described some general characteristics of the 249 Egyptian higher civil servants who responded to the questionnaire; indicated the intention of Egypt's leaders to make this civil service an efficient corps more like the Western model of a

[17] Several researches have been begun on this question. For one report, see John and Ruth Hill Useem, *The Western Educated Man in India*, Dryden Press, New York, 1955.

civil service; described the Western model of public and private bureaucracy in terms of typically bureaucratic and professional attitudes; summarized the measures of bureaucratic tendencies, professionalism, exposure to the West, and job-satisfaction; and indicated that exposure to Western influences is closely related to age.

We are now in a position to compare the socio-economic characteristics of those respondents who are high and those who are low on the Bureaucratic Scale and the Professionalism Index, and to see the differences between those who are high on the one and those who are high on the other.

Let us first outline the factors in the experience of the respondents that make for high or low bureaucratic tendencies: exposure and age, grade, function, social mobility, and degree of satisfaction with one's job.[18]

Age and exposure. We have just discussed the combined influence of age and exposure. As Appendix 4 shows, age exerts the most influence, but we assume that exposure is closely related to age. In any case, the older are more highly bureaucratic, but there is no significant relationship between our Exposure Scale and degree of bureaucratic tendencies.

Grade. Since grade and age vary together, the influence of grade on bureaucratic orientation is the same as that of age. Civil servants in grade 2, the highest, are much more likely to display Western bureaucratic predispositions than are those in grades 3 and 4; and those in grade 2 are, of course, older than those in the lower grades.

Function. Administrative workers have a slight tendency to be higher in bureaucratic orientation than technical workers.

Social mobility. We measure social mobility by whether or not a respondent in the civil service is in a post that has more prestige and status than the occupation his father followed. Those who are upwardly mobile, whose fathers were in occupations lower in prestige and status than the civil service, tend

18 In measuring the strength of relationships between variables, such as age and exposure, exposure and professionalism, etc., the chi-square test is used. Where the chi-square value is significant at the .05 level or below, the relationship is taken to be so close that it can hardly be attributed to chance.

to be higher in bureaucratic orientation than those respondents who have not risen beyond their fathers in occupational status.

Job-satisfaction. How is job-satisfaction related to bureaucratic orientation? There is some indication that the more highly satisfied respondents are also higher on the Bureaucratic Scale. When we examine this relationship separately among the older and the younger civil servants, we find that among the older, who tend to be more bureaucratic in general, job-satisfaction has no effect; they are more bureaucratic whether they are high or low in job-satisfaction. Among the younger respondents, however, job-satisfaction does make a difference: the more highly satisfied tend to be more bureaucratic.

Having reviewed the effect of these factors upon Western bureaucratic tendencies, what can we conclude? We can say that high bureaucratic predisposition is more characteristic of the older respondents, of those in the higher grades, of those in administrative posts, of those whose fathers had lower socioeconomic status than they themselves have achieved, and of those who are more satisfied with their jobs. High bureaucratic orientation thus accompanies greater responsibility, a higher position in the service, and general satisfaction. With respect to exposure, its influence is bound up with that of age, to which exposure is itself related. Exposure is not the most significant influence upon degree of Western tendencies in the respondents; age (one's total experience, that is), and factors directly related to the job and one's position in the bureaucracy, are the most significant influences.

We can now turn to professionalism and see how this tendency is affected by the same factors we have just reviewed for the Bureaucratic Scale.

Age and exposure. Neither age nor exposure has a statistically significant effect upon degree of professionalism. There is only a slight difference in the degree of professionalism displayed by the older compared with younger respondents, and by those highly exposed to the West compared with those less exposed.

Grade. Since, as we have already seen, age and grade tend to exert influence in the same direction, it is not surprising to see that grade makes little difference to professionalism. A closer inspection reveals a matter of interest. Among the respondents with lower exposure to the West, grade does not matter: the higher and lower grades show little difference with respect to professionalism. But among those with higher exposure, the highest grade has a larger proportion of respondents displaying a high degree of professionalism. This group with both higher exposure and higher professionalism is not only in the highest grade but is composed of the older civil servants as well; this gives us another indication of the way age and grade tend to exert their influence in the same direction.

Function. The relationship between function and professionalism is much more marked than any of the others examined in this section. It will be recalled that we have divided the 249 respondents into two groups, 38 in administrative posts and 211 in technical posts. Among the technical workers, the proportion of high professionals is much greater than among the administrative workers; the two proportions are 36 per cent and 8 per cent respectively. As we shall see later in this chapter, not only are the technical workers more oriented to professionalism, but the administrative workers are correspondingly more oriented toward bureaucratic tendencies. That this difference is a genuine one is supported by the fact that it persists even when age and exposure are taken into account.

Social mobility. Professionalism is not materially affected by social mobility. Among the upwardly mobile—that is, those respondents whose status as civil servants is higher than that of their fathers' occupational status—23 per cent are high on the Professionalism Index, whereas among those who have not risen beyond their fathers' status, 31 per cent show a high degree of professionalism.

Job-satisfaction. The influence of job-satisfaction is very weak. The highly satisfied respondents have a slightly (but not significantly) higher proportion of high professionals. If we take out the influence of exposure to the West, however, a more marked relationship emerges; among those with low exposure, the more satisfied have a much larger proportion of high professionals than do the less satisfied respondents. This relationship is not unexpected, since, as we shall see in the next section, the respondents in technical posts tend to be both more highly professional and less critical of the civil service in general.

What can we conclude about the factors that influence professionalism? The relationships here are, in the first place, not so marked as in the case of bureaucratic tendencies. Also, the very factors that seem to be most influential with respect to bureaucratic orientation are rather weak when it comes to professionalism. Exposure, age, grade, social mobility, and job-satisfaction are all closely related to bureaucratic orientation but none of these has much effect upon professionalism. On the other hand, function has little effect upon bureaucratic orientation but is the only factor that markedly affects professionalism; it affects professionalism in the expected way—that is, those in technical posts have a much greater proportion of respondents high on the Professionalism Index than do those in administrative posts.

The difference between bureaucratic and professional tendencies is further seen when we briefly compare the characteristics and attitudes of the respondents who score high on the Bureaucratic Scale with those of the respondents who score high on the Professionalism Index. Such an analysis gives further insight into the differences between these two Western tendencies among Egyptian higher civil servants.

We saw a moment ago that bureaucratic orientation and professionalism are influenced by quite different factors. This suggests that these two attitudinal or behavioral complexes are not related to one another, but rather that a high degree of either one will not be accompanied by an especially high proportion of highs or lows in the other. And this is precisely the case, as Table 8 shows. Among those high on professionalism, 38.5

TABLE 8

Relation between Bureaucratic Scale and Professionalism Index

BUREAUCRATIC SCALE Position	PROFESSIONALISM INDEX POSITION	
	High Per Cent	*Low Per Cent*
High	38.5	38.6
Low	61.5	61.4
Total	*100.0*	*100.0*
(Cases)	(78)	(171)

per cent are high on the Bureaucratic Scale; among those low on professionalism, 38.6 per cent are high on bureaucratic orientation. Thus those high on the Bureaucratic Scale come in equal proportions from the high and low professionals.

To explore further this broad difference between the bureaucratic and the professional orientation among our respondents, we have noted the responses to 39 items of the questionnaire that were given by those respondents who score high on the Bureaucratic Scale and those high on the Professionalism Index. It must be stressed that we are *not* directly comparing the civil servant high in bureaucratic orientation with the one high on professionalism. We are trying to see whether those high on professionalism show the same traits when compared with those low on professionalism that those high on the Bureaucratic Scale show when compared to those low on it. This kind of comparison will be clearer in the following review of the socio-economic background of the two types of civil servant.

Socio-economic background. (1) *Age*: the proportion of highly bureaucratic respondents is much greater among the *older* than among the younger; but the proportion of high professionals is slightly greater among the *younger*. (2) *Exposure*: the proportion of the highly bureaucratic with low exposure is greater than the proportion with high exposure; high professionals—same. (3) *Birthplace*: the proportion of high bureaucratic who are rural-born is greater than that of low bureaucratic; but the proportion of high professionals who are rural-born is about the same as that of those born in urban areas. (4) *Place of higher education*: the proportion of highly bureaucratic is slightly greater among those educated in the West than among those educated in the East; highly professional—same. (5) *Grade*: the proportion of high bureaucratic respondents is significantly greater among those in grade 2 (the highest) than among those in grades 3 and 4 (the lowest in our sample); the proportion of high professionals in the highest grade is only slightly greater than that in the lowest two grades. (6) *Educational level*: the proportion of the highly bureaucratic is higher among those who have not graduated from college than among those who have; the proportion of high professionals is greater among the respondents who have graduated from college. (7) *Function*: the proportion of highly bureaucratic is somewhat greater among administrative than among technical workers; but the proportion of highly professional is much greater among technical workers. (8) *Social mobility*: the proportion of highly bureaucratic is considerably higher among those upwardly mobile than among the stable; but the proportion of high professionals is slightly greater among the stable. (9) *Job-satisfaction*: the proportion of highly bureaucratic among the more satisfied is somewhat greater than among the less satisfied; highly professional—same.

On each of these nine important background characteristics we have thus seen the traits that distinguish those civil servants who stand high and those who stand low on the Bureaucratic Scale and the Professionalism Index. These traits are not always the same as between the bureaucratic and the professional types; more often they are different. Of the nine characteristics just reviewed, the difference between high and low on the Bureaucratic Scale is the *same* as the difference between high and low on professionalism in only three cases; in one (grade) the difference is only one of degree; and in five the differences are *not* the same. This is another indication of the gulf between the professional and bureaucratic orientation among the higher civil servants of Egypt.

Further evidence appears in an analysis of responses to other types of questions, including the following subjects: (1) how the respondent obtained his first civil service job, what he likes about the service, when and why he decided to become a government worker; (2) matters relating to professional standards; (3) fair treatment of the public and of other civil servants; (4) matters of personal initiative and responsibility on the part of civil servants; (5) judgments of the conduct of civil servants, especially supervisors; (6) estimates of the public's attitude toward the civil service. Of the 30 questionnaire items in these six groups, the traits marking off the highly bureaucratic respondent from the low are the *same* as those distinguishing the high professional from the low in only 9 items; in the other 21, the traits distinguishing high from low in bureaucracy and professionalism are *not* the same. In most of the cases, therefore, bureaucratic and professional predispositions appear again to be rather different qualities; the respondents in each group tend to differ in their socio-economic background, their job experience, and their attitudes and opinions. The things that distinguish high bureaucratic orientation are in most cases different from those that distinguish high professionalism.[19]

How the Respondents Differ in Background

Thus far we have presented the socio-economic background of the 249 higher civil servants in our sample, the kind of scales and indexes used to measure their degree of exposure to Western influences, the degree to which the respondents reveal Western norms of bureaucratic and professional predispositions, and the differences between the qualities that seem to make for high degree of bureaucratic orientation and of professionalism. In some of these summaries we have referred to the respondents' ages, their exposure to Western influence, their functions, social mobility, and degree of job-satisfaction. Now let us briefly examine some of these same factors to see what differences they produce among the higher civil servants.

Age. Throughout this study we refer to the differences between the older and younger respondents. Age is a highly significant factor, for it includes the whole life-experience of the individual. The older have had more years of service in the government than the younger, and this is, of course, important. The older have also higher proportions in the top grade and in administrative posts (22 per cent, compared with 9 per cent for the younger). Among the older a significantly higher proportion have taken their higher education in Western countries— 28 per cent, compared with 11 per cent for younger respondents. The older have also been significantly more exposed to Western influences. At the same time, their level of education is significantly below that of their younger colleagues; among those aged 31 to 45, 98 per cent have at least a college degree, but only 78 per cent of those aged 46 to 60 have one. Perhaps because of their higher grades, the older show a slightly higher proportion with high job-satisfaction than do the younger. In social and geographical origin, the differences are likewise interesting.

---

[19] Statistical significance has not been referred to in this analysis of differences between those high and low on bureaucracy and those high and low on professionalism. We consider here the relevance of the accumulation of many differences in the same direction irrespective of the size or significance of each difference. For a recent statement of the rationale of this procedure, see Samuel Stouffer, *Communism, Conformity and Civil Liberties*, Doubleday, N.Y., 1955, Appendix D.

Among the older there is a lower proportion whose fathers were also civil servants; the fact that the younger tend more to follow their fathers into government work is a reflection of the vast increase in the number of civil servants during the last several decades. The older, naturally, have a higher proportion than the younger who were born in rural areas; and since they had further to go, socially, the older have a higher proportion of persons who, as civil servants, have risen in occupational and social status beyond the level of their fathers.

With respect to entrance into the service, the differences are less impressive but still noteworthy. The older learned about and obtained their first government job to a less extent through the mediation of influential persons than did the younger. The older decided, in higher proportion, to enter the service at age 21 or earlier. They entered the service, too, more for personal and material reasons than did the younger.

Differences among these age groups on professionalism and professional standards are rather slight, as also on matters of fair treatment of the public. Although the older seem to be more willing to defend the civil servant's right to act on his own initiative, they are also quicker to defend disciplinary action by superiors under any circumstances. They are also consistently more defensive about the civil service; that is, they are more likely to say the civil service is run properly and to expect proper behavior in office.

These differences between older and younger respondents will be referred to frequently in later chapters. We might add one more point about the influence of age; it often significantly affects other relationships, such as that between Western exposure and dislike of some aspects of the civil service, but its influence on many responses is seldom significantly changed by the introduction of another factor.

Function. As might be expected, the respondent's type of post is closely related to the degree of his orientation to his profession. The civil servants in technical jobs are much more likely to be higher on the Professionalism Index than those in administrative work. Among the 38 administrative workers in our sample of 249, only 8 per cent are high on professionalism; among the 211 technical workers, 36 per cent are high in this respect. The situation is reversed on the Bureaucratic Scale.

Although the differences are not so strong here, they do suggest that the administrative workers are more likely to be highly bureaucratic than the technical; 47 per cent of the administrative workers but only 37 per cent of the technical are high in bureaucratic orientation. Thus the technical worker is more oriented toward professional values, the administrative worker (although less markedly) toward bureaucratic values.[20] Two other relationships are interesting, although not very marked. The administrative workers have a higher proportion than the technical—32 per cent compared with 24 per cent—who have risen in social status beyond their fathers. Such a finding is understandable in view of the findings that the administrative workers are also more oriented to the bureaucracy, and are older and hence higher in grade and more likely to be the sons of men whose status was lower than that of the higher civil servant. Despite their greater age and responsibility, however, the administrative workers have a somewhat lower proportion who are highly satisfied with their jobs—only 13 per cent, as against 22 per cent among the technical workers. Although not statistically significant, this difference is suggestive. It may be that administrative workers tend to be more critical of the civil service in general, and hence less satisfied; they may be concerned with a wider vista of affairs than the technical workers, and therefore find more to be critical about. There is some evidence, to be discussed in Chapter 7, that the technical workers are indeed less critical about civil service affairs.

Social mobility. There is a very strong relationship, as Table 9 shows, between rural origin and upward social mobility.[21]

[20] For more detailed analyses of this difference in orientation, see Wilbert E. Moore, "The Nature of Industrial Conflict," in *Industrial Conflict and Dispute-Settlement*, Industrial Relations Centre, McGill University, 7th Annual Conference, Montreal, 1955, pp. 1-15; and Dwaine Marvick, *Career Perspectives in a Bureaucratic Setting*, Michigan Governmental Studies No. 27, University of Michigan Press, Ann Arbor, 1954, especially chapter IX.

[21] We distinguish here only between those respondents who are upwardly mobile and those who are stable, rather than establishing three categories of upward, stable, and downward. It is quite clear that a peasant's son in the higher civil service has reached a position of higher social status than his father. Because of Egyptian tradition, however (not unlike that of Western nations) a wealthy landowner's son in the higher civil service has not so clearly declined from his father's social

TABLE 9

Social Mobility and Place of Birth

| | | PLACE OF BIRTH | |
| | | URBAN | RURAL |
		Per Cent	*Per Cent*
Upwardly mobile		18.9	41.9
Stable		81.1	58.1
	Total	*100.0*	*100.0*
	(Cases)	(180)	(62)

Note: Significant at .001 level.

Among the rural-born, 42 per cent have risen to an occupational status beyond that of their fathers, whereas only 19 per cent of the urban-born have done so. Of course, those of rural origin come from families lower in social status and thus had to make less of an advance to achieve higher status in their own lifetimes. It is more difficult for the urban dweller to rise above his father's status because it was probably relatively high to begin with. As we saw earlier in this chapter, 40 per cent of the civil servants are the sons of civil servants and hence stable in social status compared to their fathers; and this group is, of course, largely urban in origin. Since the rural-born civil servants are those who are the most upwardly mobile, it is not surprising to find that the respondents less exposed to the West are also more mobile—for the rural naturally tend to be less exposed than the urban. In Table 10 we see that only 16 per cent of the more exposed, but 31 per cent of the less exposed, are also upwardly mobile.

TABLE 10

Social Mobility and Exposure to the West

| | | DEGREE OF EXPOSURE TO THE WEST | |
| | | HIGH | LOW |
		Per Cent	*Per Cent*
Upwardly mobile		15.7	31.4
Stable		84.3	68.6
	Total	*100.0*	*100.0*
	(Cases)	(102)	(140)

Note: Significant at .01 level.

---

status—he himself, after all, still expects to be a landowner if he is not yet one.

The various ministries. Although it is hard to evaluate such data, it may be intrinsically interesting to see how the four ministries differ from one another in certain respects. On exposure to the West, as Table 11 shows, there are marked dif-

TABLE 11
Exposure to the West, by Ministry

	AGRICULTURE Per Cent	EDUCA- TION Per Cent	FINANCE Per Cent	MUNICIPAL AND RURAL AFFAIRS Per Cent
High exposure	51.3	56.3	31.8	41.0
Low exposure	48.7	43.7	68.2	59.0
Total	*100.0*	*100.0*	*100.0*	*100.0*
(Cases)	(39)	(64)	(107)	(39)

Note: Significant at .01 level.

ferences. The Ministries of Agriculture and Education have a considerably higher proportion of civil servants with high exposure as compared with the Ministries of Finance and Economy and of Municipal and Rural Affairs. As to bureaucratic orientation, Table 12 shows that the Ministries of Educa-

TABLE 12
Bureaucratic Scale, by Ministry

	AGRICULTURE Per Cent	EDUCA- TION Per Cent	FINANCE Per Cent	MUNICIPAL AND RURAL AFFAIRS Per Cent
High bureaucracy	23.1	45.3	44.9	25.6
Low bureaucracy	76.9	54.7	55.1	74.4
Total	*100.0*	*100.0*	*100.0*	*100.0*
(Cases)	(39)	(64)	(107)	(39)

Note: Significant at .02 level.

tion and Finance and Economy have the highest proportion high in bureaucratic orientation, while the lower proportions are in Agriculture and in Municipal and Rural Affairs. In respect to professionalism, the differences among the four ministries are minor, although the Ministry of Municipal and Rural Affairs has a much larger proportion of highs than the other ministries. On job-satisfaction the differences are again significant; Agriculture and Municipal and Rural Affairs have a lower proportion of respondents highly satisfied.

Religion. A final difference among the ministries is interesting in view of the traditional Coptic Christian stronghold in the Ministry of Finance. Traces of this position remain in the Egyptian civil service today, as Table 13 shows. There are 30 Coptic

TABLE 13

Respondents' Religion, by Ministry

	AGRICULTURE Per Cent	EDUCA- TION Per Cent	FINANCE Per Cent	MUNICIPAL AND RURAL AFFAIRS Per Cent
Muslims	92.3	93.8	84.1	84.6
Coptic Christians	7.7	6.2	15.9	15.4
Total	*100.0*	*100.0*	*100.0*	*100.0*
(Cases)	(39)	(64)	(107)	(39)

Note: Not statistically significant.

Religion was not asked on the questionnaire. The respondents' religion was determined from their names by a group of Egyptians, Muslim and Coptic, in and outside the civil service. They agreed unanimously on all but a few of the identifications.

Christians among our 249 respondents, a proportion larger than they constitute in the total population. The Ministry of Finance has the highest proportion of Christians, 16 per cent, with Municipal and Rural Affairs close behind it with 15 per cent. Put another way, the Ministry of Finance accounts for only 43 per cent of *all* the respondents but for 57 per cent of those who are Coptic Christians. But a disproportion of this size, which is not statistically significant, hardly indicates domination of the ministry, a claim that one still frequently hears in Egypt and which was recently advanced in a widely-read defense of Islam against "modernist" inroads. "In a very few years," the author says, "the percentage of government offices occupied by Copts has risen to the following astounding figures: sixty per cent of the common posts, ninety per cent of all higher posts, and one hundred per cent of certain special posts, as in the Department of Finance."[22] The author gives no data or sources to support this claim. An echo of this attitude may be heard in the comment of one respondent who, replying to question 20, said the gov-

[22] Muhammad al-Ghazzali, *Our Beginning in Wisdom*, translated by Ismail R. el Faruqi, American Council of Learned Societies, Washington, D.C., 1953, p. 97. (Originally published in 1950.)

ernment ought to take religion into account in making appointments to the civil service:

"So that the minority may not dominate the majority by means of its fanaticism. The majority is never fanatically self-centered because of its feeling of power but the minority becomes fanatically self-centered to compensate for its numerical weakness." (No. 421, 50 years old, agricultural technician in grade 3.)

As we shall see in Chapter 6, however, only a very few respondents expressed the same opinion.

The influence of religious differences, indeed, appears to be rather weak among the higher civil servants in our sample. The proportion of Muslims and Copts is virtually the same among the older, as it is among the younger respondents. In grade, the differences are minor. The two groups are equally represented in grade 2, the highest from which our sample is drawn. In grade 3, the Muslims have a higher proportion than the Copts —35 per cent, compared with 23 per cent. In grade 4, the Copts have a higher proportion—53 per cent, against 40 per cent for the Muslims. Such a distribution hardly supports the notion of Coptic domination. In exposure to Western influence, where one might expect a considerable difference, the Copts have only a slightly higher proportion highly exposed. With respect to bureaucratic predispositions, the difference is larger but still not statistically significant. Among the Muslims, 40 per cent are high on the Bureaucratic Scale, while among the Copts only 27 per cent are. As to professionalism, the difference is rather small, although the Copts have a few percentage points more among those high on this index. A difference between the two groups which comes near to being statistically significant is in degree of job-satisfaction. Among the Copts, 33 per cent say they are highly satisfied, but among the Muslims only 19 per cent say so. This may be the result of the Copts' reluctance to criticize and register dissatisfaction in this way.

This absence of important distinctions among our respondents on the basis of religion confirms a recent study of the relative influence of religion and nationalism in the Near East.[23]

[23] See E. Terry Prothro and Levon Melikian, "Social Distance and Social Change in the Near East," *Sociology and Social Research*, Sept.-Oct., 1952, Vol. 37, No. 1, pp. 3-11.

✗ *Summary and Conclusions*

In order to introduce the questionnaire results and their place in this whole study of the present higher civil service of Egypt, we have summarized several kinds of data (which will be treated in greater detail in the following chapters).

1. *Background of the respondents.* What are the characteristics of the 249 respondents to the questionnaire? About half are from ages 31 to 45, and half from 46 to 60. This equal division makes our sample somewhat younger than groups of senior officials studied in the United States and Britain. About a quarter of the Egyptian respondents are at the highest level we studied, grade 2; a third are in grade 3, and about two fifths in grade 4. The United States and British studies have been about civil servants somewhat higher in grade than this Egyptian sample. About three quarters of our respondents were born in urban areas, and virtually all of them have lived in cities since their youth. Nearly nine out of ten have a college education, a higher proportion than prevails among the United States and British groups. Of the 217 who attended college, 35, or 16 per cent, did so in the West (mainly in England and the United States). Fifteen per cent of our sample are in administrative jobs and the large majority in technical posts. As to social origin, our 249 respondents come chiefly from fathers who were also civil servants, from landlords, and from peasants. They are thus mainly an upper middle class group in origin, but a higher proportion of these Egyptian higher civil servants comes from the lower socio-economic classes than is the case in the United States and British groups on which we have evidence. Almost 40 per cent of the Egyptian senior officials are sons of civil servants, a vastly higher rate of inbreeding than that reported in the United States and British corps.

2. *Degree of Westernization.* Egypt, it was shown, is engaged in an intensive drive to industrialize, to promote social welfare and eliminate traditional patterns of corruption in government. Since Egypt is thus trying to develop what have been known as Western bureaucratic patterns, it is important to determine how far the Egyptian higher civil servants already display such patterns and what groups among them do so to the greatest degree. After reviewing the nature of Western

bureaucratic and professional norms, we described the techniques devised to measure them among our respondents. What are the background characteristics of those high on the scale measuring Western bureaucratic patterns? They are the older respondents, in the top grade, more in administrative posts, more upwardly mobile, and more satisfied with their jobs. The relationship between exposure to the West and degree of bureaucratic orientation is not significant. This finding led us to reconsider the nature of our measure of exposure and to the conclusion that age is itself an indication of exposure among a group so Westernized as this one compared to the total population of Egypt. What factors make for high professionalism among our respondents? The factors just reviewed are not significant determinants of professionalism. But function, that is, administrative or technical work, which is not so important with respect to bureaucratic orientation, is rather significant here. Those in technical posts include a much larger proportion high in professionalism than do those in administrative work.

3. *High bureaucratic and high professional orientation.* Professionalism and bureaucratic attitudes are influenced by different socio-economic and job factors. As might be expected, these two predispositions or tendencies are not related to each other. Thus, among the respondents high on professionalism, an equal proportion is in turn high and low on bureaucratic orientation. The two are totally unrelated. Further evidence of this absence of relation appears in a comparison of the differences between the respondents high and low on the Bureaucratic Scale with the differences between those high and low on the Professionalism Index.

4. *The influence of certain socio-economic traits.* How do certain important characteristics divide our respondents? Age, again, is highly significant. The older are more exposed to the West, higher in grade, have a lower level of education but a higher proportion of Western university graduates, and are more rural and more upwardly mobile. Function has strong influence in a limited area. Those in technical posts, besides being more professional, are also less critical of the civil service and the government in general. Religious affiliation makes little difference among our respondents; Muslims and Coptic Christians do not differ much in most respects.

66

The factors that seem to determine the differences among the Egyptian higher civil servants are thus age and exposure taken together, and such job factors as function and grade. The two aspects of Westernization with which we are most concerned in this study—bureaucratic and professional tendencies—are rather different qualities that respond to different influences.

Having seen the method and the summary results of the questionnaire study, we are now ready to consider it in further detail and to relate its findings to the historical and contemporary data gathered in other ways. In the following chapters we shall examine the reasons why the civil service has been so attractive to educated Egyptians, the status and prestige of the service and how they have been changing, the problems of loyalty to different kinds of groups, and questions involving initiative and discretion.

Chapter 4. The Attraction of the Educated Man to the Civil Service

In countries with relatively little private industrial enterprise a government job has been the goal of a large proportion of the educated youth. With fewer outlets for their talents than are found in areas that are more advanced technologically, young people have looked to the government to provide both the income and the prestige or status they expect as the reward for their educational achievement. In many such countries, including Egypt, technological and economic underdevelopment has not seriously hindered educational advancement. As we saw in Chapter 3, indeed, the 249 Egyptian higher civil servants in our sample have a higher proportion of college graduates than even the groups of more senior officials in the United States and Britain. Where formal higher education has developed beyond the capacity of the economy to satisfy the expectations of those who obtain it, the problem of unemployment among intellectuals arises. Unemployment among such a middle class group of articulate, alert, and politically-minded young men is less easily disguised or settled than, for example, underemployment in agriculture, a problem likewise found in non-industrial areas. In the case of countries under the domination of other powers, a great deal of the nationalist passion for independence takes the form of agitation for turning over more and more government posts to the "natives"—a process that has given birth to the terms "Indianization," "Egyptianization," and "Sudanization."

It has been easier for "underdeveloped" areas to expand their educational facilities, especially in liberal arts and law, than to expand the economic opportunities for those who use those facilities. The resultant pressure for government jobs has swelled the ranks of the civil service far beyond the point of real need. This is true in Egypt. Secular education has in fact been identified, since its introduction by Muhammad Ali in the early nineteenth century, with government posts. Seeking to make Egypt a powerful industrial and military state, he sent promising young men to schools in Europe at government expense and built special schools in imitation of the West in order to produce a corps of trained technicians who could engineer and sustain the profound transformation he wanted. Free, secular education made a sharp break with the existing tradition-bound religious schools that had no connection with government except in religious affairs. From its very beginning, therefore, secular education was associated with government posts. Why would anyone attend a school other than the traditional religious ones except in order to become a state employee?

This connection between education and government service is, of course, not peculiar to Egypt or the Near East. In Europe public higher education was, early in the modern era, used to train officials of state and church. Even in England, the famous Northcote-Trevelyan report of 1854, from which the present British civil service developed, argued that competitive examinations as a means of recruitment would have important effects upon the educational system. If proficiency in such tests were made the key to the success of applicants, the authors claimed, it "would probably do more to quicken the progress of our Universities, for instance, than any legislative measures that could be adopted."[1] In the United States, of course, the connection has not been so strong. Despite the existence of many courses in schools of public administration, there has been less direct connection between the civil service of the federal government, which neither supports nor controls liberal higher education, and the universities, which are supported by private funds or by local governments.

In Egypt, however, the connection between education and government service seems to have been much more intimate, especially since 1892 when, as we saw in Chapter 2, Lord Cromer made the school certificate not only a requirement for a civil service job but also a guarantee of one. The certificate became the goal of the student and his parents. Cromer was well aware that establishing this requirement might encourage Egyptians to acquire it; he even hoped it would. In his report of 1903 he said that the second "main object" of the government's

[1] *Report on the Organization of the Permanent Civil Service*, Great Britain, House of Commons, Sessional Papers 1854-1855, Vol. xx. This report, submitted to Parliament in February, 1854, is reprinted in *Public Administration* (London), Vol. 32, Spring, 1954, pp. 1-16. See p. 9.

educational policy was "to create an efficient Civil Service." He asserted that there was a lack of Egyptians qualified for government posts. "The object of the Government, therefore," he went on, "is to encourage young Egyptians to work for the Secondary Certificate." Previously there was little incentive for them to do so, since the primary school certificate was enough to get one a government job; but in 1901 it was ruled that this certificate would entitle its holder only to a post paying a very low salary. The ruling had the effect of ending the decline in the number of students seeking the secondary school certificate. That Cromer knew the harmful results of such a policy is evident in his bland comment in the same discussion: "An educational policy which aims wholly at the production of Government servants, and nothing else, would, indeed, be unjustifiable."[2]

It has been thus an irresistible combination of need, tradition, and deliberate planning that has directed the educated Egyptian's ambitions toward a government job. The need has been apparent in the oversupply of educated youth in certain fields in an agricultural society. The tradition was created early in Egypt's modern era when secular education was established to train skilled civil servants. The deliberate planning cemented these effects by the creation of special job incentives to acquire formal education.

Why They Enter the Civil Service

Our questionnaire survey throws some light on the way in which these influences operate to attract recruits to the Egyptian civil service today. It asks questions concerning the reasons the respondents entered the civil service, what they like and dislike about it, their opportunities for other kinds of jobs, and their attitudes toward leaving government employment.

Question 14 asks: "Why did you select the civil service instead of some other kind of work?" Table 14 shows the replies. A majority of 53 per cent entered because of limited opportunities elsewhere or for security. Another 21 per cent entered for what we may also call mainly economic reasons—they lacked the

[2] Great Britain, Egypt, No. 1 (1903). *Report by His Majesty's Agent and Consul-General on the Finances, Administration, and Condition of Egypt and the Sudan in 1902* (Cd. 1529), pp. 54-55.

TABLE 14

Respondents' Reasons for Entering Civil Service

	No. of Respondents	Per Cent
Limited opportunity elsewhere	75	30.2
Security	56	22.6
Inadequate funds for own business	37	14.9
Only place for educated person	22	8.9
Father's orders	17	6.9
To serve community	17	6.9
Qualifications not good enough elsewhere	16	6.4
Government paid for education[a]	8	3.2
Total	248	100.0

[a] This group therefore had to enter the government service for a specified minimum period.

money to set up their own businesses or their qualifications were not good enough for other jobs. If we add the 3 per cent who were obliged to enter because the government financed their education on that understanding, then about three quarters entered mainly for economic reasons. Next in size is the group, 9 per cent, who became civil servants because they felt the government was the only place for an educated man. Another 7 per cent entered because their fathers insisted on it, and an equal proportion did so to serve the community or out of some impulse to perform a public service.

Here are two comments indicating the kind of mixed motives —economic, and prestige or familial—which impelled some of our respondents to become civil servants.

"Because any young man used to want, at that time, a government post because of its reputation for respectability." (No. 120, 57 years old, administrative worker in grade 2, civil servant since age 21.)

"Because I imitated many of my relatives, who are government officials." (No. 254, 59 years old, administrator in grade 2, college graduate.)

The only data at all comparable to these are for two groups of U.S. civil servants. One study, made in 1949, covered 335 scientists who had already left government jobs in 1948. More than a third took other jobs in the civil service, about a third went to work in private industry, and the remaining third left the labor market temporarily or permanently.[3] When they were asked why they had entered the government service, the reasons given by the largest proportion, 52 per cent, concerned the opportunity to do work that would be interesting, important, or make them more competent. The next largest group of answers, 43 per cent, mentioned chiefly economic reasons; 13 per cent mentioned some personal convenience; and 12 per cent a wish to aid the nation's war effort. (The total of the replies is more than 100 per cent because some respondents gave more than one reason.)

Another study, made in 1947, covered 730 U.S. civil servants in medium and high grades in professional and administrative posts.[4] Asked their reasons for entering the service, 701 respondents gave 1,042 reasons. The largest proportion of reasons, 48 per cent, was economic. A third mentioned some professional interest, such as in a special task or program. Ten per cent were personal reasons and 4 per cent a wish to aid in the war effort.

Any comparison of our Egyptian survey with these two American studies must be viewed with considerable caution because of the differences in method, the subjects, and the conditions of the research; but broad differences may be viewed as at least indicative. Among the Egyptian higher civil servants, three quarters say they entered for economic reasons. Among the two groups of American officials, the proportions citing these reasons were 43 and 48 per cent. Among the Egyptians none differentiated professional or task-oriented reasons from what we are calling economic reasons, whereas among the two groups of Americans about half and a third did so. The American studies tend to support one another because the results are not too dissimilar even though the two groups of subjects are different. Each resembles the other much more than either of them resembles the Egyptian group in regard to their reasons for entering the civil service. The comparison shows that the Egyptians were strongly motivated by economic considerations. So too

[3] Syracuse University, Maxwell Graduate School of Citizenship and Public Affairs, *Attitudes of Scientists and Engineers about their Government Employment* (2 volumes, mimeographed), Syracuse, N.Y., July, 1950, Vol. 1, pp. 15, 24.

[4] Frances T. Cahn, *Federal Employees in War and Peace*, Brookings Institution, Washington, D.C., 1949, pp. 175-178, 195.

were the Americans, but they were also impelled by professional concerns, of which the Egyptians, free to offer any reason they wanted to, made no mention whatsoever. These results conform to the facts of economic life in the two countries. Suitable employment opportunities for educated people are more available in the United States than in Egypt and other non-industrial societies.

Let us return briefly to the Egyptian respondents to see how they differ among themselves in their responses. Table 15

TABLE 15

Reasons for Entering Civil Service, by Age

	AGE 31-45 *Per Cent*	AGE 46-60 *Per Cent*
Economic, material	50.8	74.2
Inadequate funds for own business	24.2	5.6
Other	25.0	20.2
Total	*100.0*	*100.0*
(Cases)	(124)	(124)

Note: Significant at .001 level.

shows the proportion of younger and older respondents who gave various kinds of answers. Roughly equal proportions of both groups say they entered mainly for economic and material reasons such as financial return or security. The main difference between them, however, is in the *kind* of economic reason they give. Among the younger respondents, 24 per cent say they entered the government service because they lacked the money to set up their own business, but only 6 per cent of those 46 to 60 gave this as a reason. This significant difference indicates that the younger civil servants contemplated another kind of career more seriously than did the older, or that at least, in retrospect, they thought they did. In either case, the data reveal an interesting difference in outlook. The older appear to have been much more committed to government service right at the start of their careers. This point is further substantiated by the response to another question (to be dealt with in greater detail in Chapter 5), showing that older respondents decided at an earlier age to enter the service.

Seeking also the Egyptian higher civil servants' attitude toward their occupational choice today, we asked what they like about the service. Question 22 asks simply: "What do you like about government work?" Table 16 shows the replies. The

TABLE 16

What Respondents Like about Government Work

	Number	Per Cent
Performing a public service	83	33.9
Security	81	33.1
Just a source of income	32	13.1
Nothing at all	28	11.4
Opportunity to reach high position	16	6.5
Feeling of independence	5	2.0
Total	*245*	*100.0*

largest proportion, about a third, say they like performing a public service of some kind. An equal proportion mention economic security. Thirteen per cent say merely that it is their source of livelihood. Only 7 per cent see the service as a means of acquiring power or reputation. Only 2 per cent like the feeling of independence that goes with government employment; it is significant that so few expressed the "security" idea in this particular way. Finally, 11 per cent say they do not like anything at all about it.

The responses to a similar question, however, were somewhat different. The civil servants were asked, in question 43, to complete a sentence beginning with the following words: "The best thing about holding a government post is . . ." Table 17

TABLE 17

Sentence Completion: "The best thing about holding a government post is . . ."

	Number	Per Cent
Economic advantages	171	69.2
Chance to do public service	54	21.9
Less work, easier	13	5.3
Nothing good about it	9	3.6
Total	*247*	*100.0*

shows that on this question the proportion mentioning the chance to perform a public service was only 22 per cent compared with 34 per cent when the question was put more directly.

Who are the civil servants who, in their responses to the

more direct question, stress public service and who are those who stress security?

Public service is stressed more by those who, in several ways, have greater contact with Western patterns. *Age*: Among respondents in the age-group 31 to 45, about a third say they like the opportunity to do some kind of public service; among those 46 to 60, the proportion is about the same. But some differences in response emerge if we consider the proportion who mention public service among three age groups:

Age 31-40   29.0 per cent
41-50   32.7
51-60   39.7

Exposure: Among those highly exposed, as measured by the Exposure Scale, 39 per cent mention public service, but among the less exposed only 31 per cent do so. *Place of higher education*: Among the respondents educated in the West, 41 per cent mention public service, whereas among those educated in Egypt, only 36 per cent do so. *Level of education*: Among the respondents who have graduated from college, 36 per cent mention public service, but among those who have not gone beyond secondary school, only 19 per cent do so. Only the last of these four comparisons is statistically significant but it is relevant that all these differences point in the same direction: public service is mentioned by a higher proportion of the respondents with greater Western contact as revealed by these four indications.

With respect to the differences between the civil servants who stress security, three of the following four comparisons are statistically significant. All of them point in the same direction and indicate that those who most stress security have had less contact with the West. *Age*: The proportions who stress security are as follows:

Age 31-40   50.0 per cent
41-50   29.1
51-60   24.7

Thus as age rises, the proportion stressing security falls. One explanation may be that the oldest are furthest in time from their original decision to enter the service and hence, having enjoyed security for many years, are less concerned with it at the moment. *Exposure*: Those with low exposure have a higher proportion stressing security—40 per cent, compared with only 23 per cent among the civil servants low on the Exposure Scale. *Place of higher education*: Of those educated in Egypt, 35 per cent mention security, but only 15 per cent of those educated in the West do so. *Level of education*: Of those who did not get a college degree, 39 per cent mention security; of those who did get a degree, only 32 per cent do so (this is the only one of the four differences that is not statistically significant).

Thus, the respondents who say they like working for the government because it gives them a chance to do a public service of some kind are quite different from those who stress the economic security of a government post, as the following summary shows:

Public Service	*Security*
older	younger
more exposed to West	less exposed to West
higher education in West	higher education in Egypt
more educated	less educated

One further comment ought to be made on this point. Whether a civil servant stresses the public service or the security aspect of his occupational position ought to be related in some way to his income. Surveys of American groups generally reveal that people give greater weight to the things they lack than to those they possess. This study of Egyptian higher civil servants demonstrates this point too. As Table 18 shows, the

TABLE 18

What Respondents Like about Government Work, by Possession of Independent Income

	INDEPENDENT INCOME Per Cent	NO INDEPENDENT INCOME Per Cent
Like chance to do public service	39.0	21.9
Like economic security	29.6	41.1
Like other things	31.4	37.0
Total	100.0	100.0
(Cases)	(172)	(73)

Note: Significant at .05 level.

respondents with an independent income have a higher proportion who like the chance to perform some kind of public service, whereas those who have no income but their government salaries have a higher proportion liking the economic security of a public post. Those who depend less on their civil service jobs for their livelihood are freer to look upon their employment as a way of serving the public.

The Quality and Size of the Civil Service

The emphasis upon economic factors in the motivation of those attracted to Egyptian civil service and as the aspect of government work that most appeals to those in it, indicates that much is at stake when a young Egyptian decides upon a career as a public official. The sacrifices a youth and his family must make in order to get him through secondary school and university are so great that there is considerable pressure upon him to acquire the formal certificates that will qualify him for the civil service with its moderate salary and relative security of tenure.

External tokens of achievement have taken precedence over genuine learning and a spirit of inquiry at all levels of the Egyptian educational system. This has been the observation of many Egyptians as well as of foreign observers. Where formal education has been so closely bound up with vocational goals, rote learning and verbalization have been the methods encouraged by a centralized administration and too eagerly followed by an anxiety-ridden student body. The effect of this educational weakness upon the civil service has been recently emphasized by the director of the Civil Service Commission. In his annual report for 1952, he commented:

"The attention of the Commission was drawn—as a result of the reports of the examiners—to the fact that the applicants' standard is weak in the general knowledge that every citizen should have . . . —weak from two sides, the professional and the social. The Commission also noticed that they lack originality and skill in applying what they are taught in school to the situations and problems that were put before them in the personal tests, and that most of what they absorbed in their studies is mere mechanical memorization and the ability to recite the facts stored in their minds, without the ability to relate them to each other and without truly understanding them. . . . The Commission sees that it has the duty to point out the necessity for broadening practical studies in the faculties and institutions to meet the needs of the public service."[5]

This was not the first time an Egyptian government agency has made this criticism of the educational system. The same complaint was made in 1920 by a British adviser in the Egyptian Ministry of Education to a commission empowered to recommend reforms in the civil service system. Opposing the requirement of a school certificate for admission to civil service examinations, he remarked: "Such conditions tend to maintain the exaggerated importance of the Secondary Certificates (Part I and Part II) and of the Primary Certificate. . . . The present system which makes certain examinations of a not very advanced nature the be-all and end-all of a student's scholastic career tends to produce rigidity in the curriculum and to foster the memory rather than the brain."[6]

The rote method is the legacy of the old religious pedagogy perfected in Al Azhar, the center of Islamic learning in Cairo (itself considerably reformed in recent years). It was applied to the very first secular schools built by Muhammad Ali in the early nineteenth century.[7] The effects of this method of education and the importance attached to uniform examinations are revealed in a recent study of the interests and wishes of Egyptian school children as compared with those of American school children. Consistently higher proportions of Egyptian pupils expressed a wish for self-improvement—that is, to become more intelligent, to be promoted in school, to pass scholastic examinations. The author, an Egyptian educational psychologist, attributes these differences to the emphasis upon examinations in Egypt.[8] Since 1952, especially, the government has tried to

[5] Republic of Egypt, Civil Service Commission, *Annual Report, 1952* (in Arabic), Government Press, Cairo, 1953, p. 14, and *Annual Report of the Commission on Budgetary Proposals for the Fiscal Year 1954-1955* (in Arabic), 1954, pp. 53-55.

[6] *Report of the Cadre Commission*, May 24, 1921, Government Press, Cairo, par. 12, p. 3.

[7] Abu Al-Futouh Ahmad Radwan, *Old and New Forces in Egyptian Education*, Teachers College, Columbia University, New York, 1951, pp. 88-89; and J. Heyworth-Dunne, *An Introduction to the History of Education in Modern Egypt*, Luzac and Co., London, n.d. (*ca.* 1938), p. 227.

[8] El-Demerdash Abdel-Meguid Sarhan, *Interests and Culture. A Comparative Study of Interests, Concerns, Wishes, Likes, Dislikes, and*

deemphasize formal examinations. An official account of the first year of the Republic lists among four "fundamental principles" of the new educational policy: "Alleviation of the burden of public and private examinations at all educational stages and especially the first one."[9] Indeed, uniform national examinations at the completion of primary schooling have already been abolished.

The connection between education and the civil service has led to what Egyptian authorities believe is undue support for higher education at the expense of primary education. Table 19

TABLE 19

Percentage of Funds Allocated for Various Levels of Education in Academic Years from 1948-1949 to 1952-1953

	1948-1949	1949-1950	1950-1951	1951-1952	1952-1953
Primary	44	35	34	46	48
Secondary	42	45	50	39	38
Universities	14	20	16	15	14
Total	*100*	*100*	*100*	*100*	*100*

Source: Computed from Egyptian Ministry of Finance and Economy, *Budget of the Egyptian Government 1953-1954* (in Arabic), Government Press, Cairo, 1953, tables on pp. 228, 1008-1009, 1048-1049, 1074-1075. For 1948-1949, 1949-1950, and 1950-1951 these proportions are based upon actual expenditures. For 1951-1952 and 1952-1953 the proportions are based on estimated expenditures.

shows the proportions of the total budget for public instruction that were allocated for the various levels of education. In a country in which three quarters of the population of school age and older are said to be illiterate, higher education has enjoyed an unusually favorable position. Primary education in recent years has actually been receiving a higher proportion than before. In 1920, according to a leading Egyptian educator, it received only 15 per cent of the total education budget, and by 1945 its pro-

---

Happiest Days of Egyptian and American Children, Teachers College, Columbia University, Contributions to Education, No. 959, N.Y., 1950, pp. 83-88.

[9] Hassan Khadr and Amin Hassouna, *Egypt's Republic in Its First Year,* Department of Public Relations of the Egyptian Armed Forces, Cairo, 1954, p. 85.

portion had risen to 39 per cent.[10] Since then, as Table 19 shows, this proportion has risen even more.

Earlier in this chapter we referred to the great stake the educated young Egyptian has in his effort to obtain a civil service post. The evidence from the questionnaire confirmed this notion of the motivation of the civil servant. There is, unfortunately, however, only scattered evidence on the actual proportion of secondary school and university graduates who enter the civil service or other occupations. With respect to secondary school graduates, the government has published statistics showing the number who entered government jobs and other types of employment at the end of several academic years; this material is summarized in Table 20. In six academic years between 1942

TABLE 20

Type of Employment Obtained by Graduates of Secondary Schools

	Government Posts	Other	Per Cent in Government Posts
1942-1943	145	314	32
1943-1944	59	122	45
1945-1946	93	250	27
1946-1947	293	410	42
1947-1948	355	562	39
1948-1949	402	547	42

Source: Gouvernement Egyptien, Département de la Statistique Générale et du Recensement, *Statistique Scolaire, Année Scolaire 1951-1952* (French and Arabic), Imprimerie Nationale, Le Caire, 1953, Table xxxii, p. 303.

and 1949 the graduates who took government posts comprised from 32 per cent to 45 per cent of the total number who obtained employment, according to these official records.

For university graduates and those who received higher diplomas, the evidence is more scanty, covering only the academic years 1948-1949 and 1949-1950. In the earlier year, 485 graduates took government jobs and 89 other kinds.[11] In the

[10] A. H. El-Koussy, in *The Year Book of Education 1952*, University of London and Evans Bros., London, chapter on Egyptian education since 1945, pp. 445-457; see p. 447.

[11] Gouvernement Egyptien, Département de la Statistique Générale et du Recensement, *Statistique Scolaire, Année Scolaire 1951-1952* (French and Arabic), Imprimerie Nationale, Le Caire, 1953, Table xxxiii, pp. 306-307.

later year 206 entered the government and 66 took other employment. Thus in 1948-1949, 85 per cent entered the government and in 1949-1950, 72 per cent, both considerably higher proportions than for the secondary school graduates.

How does this Egyptian rate of entrance into the civil service compare with others on which there are relevant data? For the United States, it was reported in 1952 that of the 475,000 who annually receive the bachelor's, master's, and professional degrees, two to four per cent enter the federal civil service; this proportion is roughly equal to the proportion that federal employees constitute of the total labor force in the United States.[12] This is a much lower proportion than for Egypt. Although the U.S. rate of entrance into the civil service by university graduates is probably among the lowest of the technologically advanced countries, the difference between it and the Egyptian rate is at least indicative of the serious problem facing Egypt and similar countries. Evidence for Ceylon, likewise a technologically underdeveloped country, shows a similar situation. A survey was made in 1950 of the occupational choices of 1,365 boys in four provinces who sat for the secondary school certificate examination, constituting a 10 per cent sample of all who did so. The proportion selecting government service varied from 75 per cent to 99.9 per cent.[13]

To discover the number of civil servants employed by the central government of Egypt is not an easy task. Published estimates vary considerably. One of the reasons for the wide discrepancies often found is that some estimates are of the number of posts covered in the annual budget, whereas others estimate the number of officials, that is, the number of posts actually filled. Even when they cover the same categories, however, estimates vary widely. The Statistics Department of the Ministry of Finance and Economy publishes a periodical review on the civil service, but so many government departments fail to report in time for publication that the final survey is useless for our purposes.[14] To give a clear and concise picture

[12] John J. Corson, *Executives for the Federal Service*, Columbia University Press, New York, 1952, p. 43.

[13] T. L. Green, "Vocational Problems in Education in S.E. Asia," *Journal of Educational Sociology*, April, 1953, Vol. 26, No. 8, pp. 384, 388.

[14] For example, *Statistics of Officials and Employees in the Govern-*

it is necessary to see how many civil service posts the budget provides for, how many civil servants there are actually in such posts, and the proportion they constitute of the Egyptian population.

The Civil Service Commission itself, apparently using budget data on the number of posts rather than civil servants, has reported that in 1954-1955 there were 381,615 posts, an increase of 61 per cent over 1940-1941. The categories of post in which we are interested, requiring at least a primary education, totaled 170,345 in 1954-1955 (these are called permanent and temporary grades); in 1940-1941 there were only 47,480 such posts provided for in the budget. They thus increased more than two and a half times in this period.[15]

The actual number of civil servants in these permanent and temporary grades was for some time unknown. In 1953, however, estimates were being made in two ways, first by counting the number of officials with pension records, and second by counting heads in the various government buildings. This second method, under the supervision of the army, yielded a total of 152,334 civil servants in permanent and temporary grades in 1954.[16]

What proportion of the total population do government workers constitute? On the basis of budget allocations for civil service posts in 1950-1951, a British civil service official who studied personnel problems in the Egyptian government estimated that 2.2 per cent of the population were in the government's employ, and that 35 per cent of the government's expenditures went for their salaries. In contrast, he pointed out, the British civil servants were only 1.3 per cent of the total population and their salaries accounted for only 9 per cent of the government's annual outlay.[17] In the last decade or so the proportion of the budget allocated for government workers has been growing. In 1940-1941, ac-

ment and Public Services on January 1, 1951 (in Arabic), Government Press, Cairo, 1953, see notes to summary table, p. 1.

[15] Egyptian Government, Civil Service Commission, Annual Report, 1952 (in Arabic), Government Press, Cairo, 1953, table on p. 16, and Annual Report of the Commission on Budgetary Proposals for the Fiscal Year 1955-1956 (in Arabic), 1955, p. 49.

[16] From a summary table kindly provided by Major Omar Abaza, Egyptian Army, March 21, 1954.

[17] Egyptian Government, Ministry of Finance, Report on the Personnel Questions of the Egyptian Civil Service, by A. P. Sinker, Government Press, Cairo, 1951, pp. 44-46.

cording to the Civil Service Commission, it was 34.9 per cent. By 1952-1953, it had risen to 40.6 per cent, but even this latter figure, high as it seems, does not tell the whole story; for the Commission points out that a detailed reckoning shows that fully 46 per cent of the 1952-1953 budget was marked for salaries, wages, and certain other incidental expenses in connection with the civil service.[18]

One further indication of the size of the Egyptian civil service is illuminating. For the year 1947, when the most recent census was taken, all the information is available to determine what proportion of the population with a primary education or higher the government was prepared to hire under the 1946-1947 budget. The 1947 census showed a total of 366,639 persons with a primary education or higher.[19] From this total we must exclude 81,781 students in the secondary schools in that year, because they were not in the labor market.[20] The remainder, 284,858, were the source from which civil servants could be recruited for the permanent and temporary grades. Now in 1947 the budget provided for approximately 92,000 such posts (excluding the army but including teachers and the police).[21] Thus the government was at least ready to employ in posts requiring a primary education or higher 32 per cent of all Egyptians who had such education. If we make the reasonable assumption that there is no serious difference between the number of posts and the number of civil servants, we can say that in 1947 about one third of all Egyptians, male and female, with a primary or higher education and not in school, were employed by the government. Since 1947, and especially since 1952, this proportion has probably declined because the civil service has not increased in size as much as education has expanded.

[18] *Annual Report, 1952* (see note 15 above), pp. 16-17.
[19] Computed from Egyptian Government, Ministry of Finance and Economy, Statistical Department, *Statistical Pocket Year Book 1952*, Government Press, Cairo, 1953, Table 10, pp. 20-21.
[20] Computed from Arab League, Cultural Office, *Yearbook of Arab Culture. First Year* (in Arabic), Press of the Authorship, Translation and Publication Committee, Cairo, 1949, p. 356. This figure is lower than the one obtained by computation from data in Egyptian Government, Ministry of Public Education, Statistical Office, *Educational Statistics from 1882 to 1952* (mimeographed, in Arabic), Cairo, n.d.
[21] Computed from Egyptian Government, Ministry of Finance, *Egyptian State Budget 1946-47* (in Arabic), Government Press, Cairo, 1946.

83

In spite of the increase in public services since 1952, the government has sought to reduce the size of the civil service or at least to keep it from expanding at the old pace. One means has been to keep down requests for appropriations. Another has been by not filling certain vacancies created by retirement.[22] The government for a time encouraged retirement by allowing full pension rights before the age-limit of 60. The success, as well as the cost, of this policy appears in the rise in pension payments for the following three fiscal years:[23]

1952-1953	£.E.	4.9 million
1953-1954		8.7
1954-1955		10.4

The Commission reports considerable pressure against reductions on the part of those already in the service as well as by university graduates who would like to be in it.[24] A third method has been to refuse to increase civil service salaries at the pace of the increase in the cost of living and, moreover, to reduce such cost-of-living adjustments as had been made. It was only in June of 1955 that this policy was reversed.[25]

Partly as a result of their financial hardships, the civil servants grumble a good deal. They seem to feel that they no longer occupy the high place they once did in the Egyptian social structure. We shall deal with this matter of status and prestige in the next chapter. Here, meanwhile, we can examine what the questionnaire survey tells us about the things civil servants dislike about government work and their attitude toward leaving it entirely.

Question 23 asks: "What do you dislike about the government service?" Table 21 shows that the largest number mention the

[22] Decision of the Council of Ministers, July 21, 1953, carried out in Circular Letter No. 45/1953 of the Civil Service Commission, in *Collection of Circular Letters Issued by the Commission since Its Establishment in 1952* (in Arabic), Government Press, Cairo, 1954, p. 62; and Civil Service Commission, *Report of the Commission on Budgetary Proposals for the Fiscal Year 1953-54* (in Arabic), 1953, pp. 4-6.

[23] National Bank of Egypt, *Economic Bulletin* (English edition), Vol. VIII, No. 2, 1955, table on p. 103.

[24] Civil Service Commission, *Annual Report, 1952* (see note 15 above), p. 3; *Report of the Commission . . . 1953-54* (see note 22 above), p. 3; *Annual Report of the Commission . . . 1954-55* (see note 5 above), p. 42; *Annual Report of the Commission . . . 1955-56* (see note 15 above), p. 8.

[25] Text of law in *Al Ahram* (Cairo), June 30, 1955, p. 9, col. 4.

TABLE 21

What the Respondents Dislike about the Civil Service

	Number	Per Cent
Routine, monotony	91	36.5
Favoritism	60	24.1
Wrong use of personnel	36	14.5
Low salary	28	11.2
Absence of initiative	20	8.0
Nothing	9	3.7
Instability	5	2.0
Total	249	100.0

routine and monotony of government work, to which we may add those who speak of the absence or killing of initiative in the service. The next largest group are those who complain about favoritism, and to it we may add the group disliking wrong use of personnel. Only 28, or 11 per cent, complain of low salary, but it must be remembered that all our respondents are in the higher grades and that about 70 per cent have income other than their civil service salaries.

The differences in what the older and younger respondents dislike about the civil service are shown in Table 22. It is clear

TABLE 22

What the Respondents Dislike about the Civil Service, by Age

	AGE 31-45 Per Cent	AGE 46-60 Per Cent
Favoritism and wrong use of personnel	25.6	54.6
Routine and lack of initiative	52.9	39.5
Instability and low salary	21.5	5.9
Total	*100.0*	*100.0*
(Cases)a	(121)	(119)

a Excluding 9 who say they dislike nothing.
Note: Significant at .001 level.

that the older complain mainly about favoritism and the wrong use of personnel, while the younger are more disturbed by the monotony of the civil service and its discouragement of initiative. Among the younger, too, a higher proportion complain about instability and low salaries; they are, of course, in the lower grades and earn less.

To get further indications of their attitudes toward the service, the respondents were asked, in question 17: "Do you think that you might leave the civil service entirely for some reason?" If the answer was yes, the official was asked: "Under what circumstances would you leave?"

Of 248 who replied, 140, or 56 per cent, said they might leave, while 108, or 44 per cent, said they would not. (Unfortunately we have no data on actual turnover.) Table 23 shows

TABLE 23

Circumstances under Which 140 Respondents Would Leave the Civil Service

	Number	Per Cent
For better-paying job	74	52.9
To enter own business or independent profession	30	21.4
For a job more suitable to qualifications	15	10.7
To take advantage of rules encouraging retirement	15	10.7
For a job in a specific field	6	4.3
Total	*140*	*100.0*

the circumstances named by the 140 who said they might leave. The first thing this table tells us is that 74 officials say they would leave for a better-paying job. We saw in Table 21, however, that only 28 said they dislike the low salaries in the civil service. It may be that low pay does not bother very many but is a cause of deep resentment in those whom it does affect.

Let us return to the earlier question, in response to which 56 per cent said they might leave the service entirely under some circumstances. How do the older and younger groups differ in their replies? Table 24 shows that the younger are much more

TABLE 24

Attitude toward Leaving the Civil Service, by Age

	AGE 31-45 Per Cent	AGE 46-60 Per Cent
Would leave	64.5	48.4
Would not leave	35.5	51.6
Total	*100.0*	*100.0*
(Cases)	(124)	(124)

Note: Significant at .02 level.

willing to leave than the older. The reasons for this difference are easy to imagine. First, the older are in the higher grades and are therefore less likely to feel the pinch of low salaries or to resent other aspects of employment in a bureaucracy. Second, they are much more committed to the civil service as a career, have less recent experience of anything outside of it, and have a greater stake in the retirement pension system.

It might also be expected that attitudes toward leaving the service would be affected by a respondent's opportunity to command a job outside. Question 18 asks: "Since becoming a civil servant, have you been offered any opportunities for employment outside the civil service?" Of the 249 officials, 59, or 24 per cent, had received such offers and 190, or 76 per cent, had not. How do these two groups differ in their attitude toward leaving the service? Table 25 shows there is no significant difference in

TABLE 25

Attitude toward Leaving the Civil Service, by Whether or Not Other Offers Have Been Received

	OFFERED JOB Per Cent	NOT OFFERED JOB Per Cent
Would leave	60.3	53.8
Would not leave	39.7	46.2
Total	100.0	100.0
(Cases)	(58)	(184)

Note: Not statistically significant.

their response. Among the respondents who have received offers of other jobs, 60 per cent say they would leave, while among those who have not had such an opportunity, almost the same proportion, 54 per cent, likewise say they would leave under certain conditions. Thus the possibility of another means of earning a living has little effect here. It is not the respondents' confidence in their ability to get other employment that impels more than half of them to say they would leave the service. Rather, it appears to be a generalized resentment and annoyance that leads them to respond this way. Their replies are more an indication of their morale than of their actual intention.

That this is so is supported by another set of figures. Question 39 posed the following problem to the respondent: "Suppose you were asked to advise an intelligent young man—say, a young cousin of yours—on his career. What sort of a career would you advise him to follow?" Of the 248 who replied, virtually all, 244, advised a career other than the civil service. Yet, as we have just seen, only 140 would themselves consider leaving the civil service. A civil servant who says he would leave is only revealing the depth of his dissatisfaction; his declaration is probably not a reliable guide to his action.

Summary and Conclusions

The documentary and questionnaire data presented in this chapter indicate the great stake the civil servant has in remaining one and that the educated young Egyptian has in becoming one. This has been true to such a degree that Egyptian and other observers have charged that the public schools have become mere factories, as it is usually phrased, for the production of government servants. We saw how, historically, the connection between secular education and government employment developed under Muhammad Ali in the early nineteenth century. This connection was supported near the end of the century by Lord Cromer's policy of virtually guaranteeing a public post to every graduate of a secondary school; and, all along, the scarcity of employment opportunities for secularly educated youth in an agricultural but transitional society intensified their desire to raise their economic and social status by obtaining a government job.

The results of the questionnaire, as we saw, conformed with these historically and economically determined conditions. Three quarters of the 249 respondents say they entered the civil service for economic reasons, in contrast with a smaller proportion among two groups of U.S. government workers. Asked what they like about the civil service, a third of the Egyptian respondents mentioned economic security and another third the opportunity to perform a public service. Those with more Western contacts (the older, those more highly exposed to the West, those more highly educated, and those who took their higher education in the West) stressed public service; those with fewer such contacts stressed security. Likewise, the respondents with an independent income were more likely to say they liked the chance to perform a public service, while those who rely entirely on their government salaries tended to stress security.

The intense pressure for government posts has led to considerable emphasis upon obtaining a school certificate, with consequent neglect of learning for other than directly vocational reasons. The Civil Service Commission has been moved to comment on the low level of ability, except in rote learning, displayed by applicants for government jobs. Egyptian governments have found it impossible, or at least difficult, to resist the pressure to make the government service a haven for educated youth. In 1947, as we saw, the state was prepared to (and probably did) provide a post for about a third of all Egyptians with a primary or better education not then enrolled in a secondary school. Recent efforts, since 1952, have reduced this proportion somewhat.

The present regime's efforts to reduce the attractiveness of civil service employment seem to have had the effect, in conjunction with trends which began at least a decade earlier, of increasing the resentment of those in it and of discouraging others from entering it; but it has not led to any voluntary drift out of the service. More than half of the respondents to the questionnaire said they would leave the service under certain conditions (mainly for a better-paying job); but this is more an indication of their morale than of their real intentions.

In this chapter we have occasionally alluded to the unfavorable attitude of the senior officials toward the civil service. This appears to be the result of their own and the more articulate public's awareness that the service has declined in status and prestige. The data on and the reasons for this decline will occupy our attention in the next chapter.

Chapter 5. Changes in Status and Prestige

Attitudes toward the civil service, in "advanced" as well as in "underdeveloped" countries, are somewhat contradictory. Like other symbols of power, the public bureaucracy evokes fear, respect, opposition, and even ridicule in mixtures that depend upon the national tradition, the nature of the political system, the economic opportunities available, and the kind of civil service the nation has devloped. In Egypt these contradictory attitudes are freely expressed. Many Egyptians speak of the high status of the government official but disparage the man who values the shabby security of public employment. A special paradox, too, has existed in Egypt since the advent of the military regime in 1952. On the one hand, the relative status (and remuneration) of the civil service has been reduced by the increasing prominence of military men and by the identification of all forms of civilian government with the old regime. On the other hand, the military rulers have instituted social and political changes and a program of economic development that will enhance the higher civil servants' control over life in Egypt.

Attitudes toward Government

Hostility to the public bureaucracy does not, of course, imply disrespect or a low status for it. There are sources of hostility to government representatives in all kinds of society, for they are the agents of the repressive power of the state. They prevent citizens from doing what they want to, require them to do other things they do not want to do, and collect taxes—for all this the public also has to pay them. In doing these things the agents of government are also protecting the public and enabling them to do things they want to do, but such permissive features of the bureaucratic achievement do not erase frustrating ones from people's memories. Moreover, government is the greatest monopoly (even if a necessary one) in a world familiar with monopoly, and there is no appeal from it save to one of its own creatures.

In the United States hostility toward the government apparatus has been accompanied by low prestige for its personnel. One observer summarizes the studies of the prestige of the civil service in this way: "The prestige of government employment as a whole has never been high and, outside of certain elective positions, government jobs rank low in the public esteem when compared with similar positions in private employment."[1] These studies, however, do not tell the whole story. It is probable that the prestige of the federal civil service has risen since the 1920's. The further application of the merit system and increasing public awareness of it has perhaps evaporated some of the atmosphere of "pull" and the "clubhouse" surrounding government employment. Another factor may be the growth of welfare functions at the various levels of government, which causes its representatives to be seen in a better light by the public. In addition, the New Deal era brought a feeling of excitement and adventure with its Brain Trust and the highly educated and often brilliant young men it attracted to Washington. Finally, the relative prestige accorded to businessmen seems to have declined in recent decades and that of professionals seems to be greater— and the civil service has had to enlist a growing number of technical and professional workers. However, the last few years, with evidence of corruption and subversion, may have halted or reversed the trend.[2]

Such changes notwithstanding, it is probably still true that a comparable post in private industry is both more coveted and more highly regarded by Americans than one in the government. In a society that stresses individual initiative, business values, and endless change, it is not likely that "safe" government jobs can be of high status. These posts are not sought after by the upper socio-economic groups; except for a few families, the United States, unlike England, has little or no tradition of public service as a career for those already highly placed in society.

In Egypt (and most of the Near East), as we have seen to

[1] Sidney Mailick, "Public Service Prestige: Problem and Paradox," *Public Personnel Review*, Vol. 10, No. 3, p. 155. See also U.S. Government Commission on Organization of the Executive Branch (Hoover Commission), Personnel Policy Committee, *Report, Appendices*, October, 1948, Appendix C.

[2] These observations are supported by recent research reported by Morris Janowitz and Deil Wright in "The Prestige of Public Employment: 1929 and 1954," *Public Administration Review*, Vol. 16, No. 1, Winter 1956, pp. 15-21.

some degree, the situation is quite different. Egypt has no recent tradition placing business particularly high in socio-economic status. Moreover, as we have seen in Chapter 4, government service has been the goal of educated youth, and Egypt, as an Islamic country, accords especially high status to the well-educated. And opportunities outside the civil service have not been numerous.

There is an even more profound reason why the civil service in Egypt has relatively higher status than its counterpart in the West. Throughout the Arab world the government is still the dominant source of power. Unlike the West, where private economic power and the political system have built up competing power groups, in the Near East men have had relatively little leverage against government except revolt, indifference, or flight into the desert (and even these latter escapes are now severely limited). Political and economic power have thus been more closely connected in the Arab world than in the West, and this connection has enhanced the influence and status of those who possess them. Government in general is more feared and esteemed as more powerful; as a consequence, its agents, the civil service, share this position in Egypt. The civil service has been further elevated by virtue of its connection for long periods in Egypt, especially, with the vastly superior scientific, technological, and military apparatus of Western conquerors and rulers. In the West, government has more functions and performs more services, but its power is narrower in the sense that it is checked by other groups and institutions and that it can add functions only by following a certain constitutional course. In the Near East and in Egypt through most of its history, the situation is the opposite. Consequently, any connection with government—even the post office clerk's in a largely illiterate nation—confers status. Further, the fact that corruption is known to exist detracts from status in the West but less so in the Near East, where indeed the respect and fear on the part of the public may be all the greater because the abuses are demonstrations of arbitrariness and power.

The place that sheer power has in the relationship between governors and governed in Egypt is illustrated in the answers the higher civil servants gave to two questions regarding their impression of the average Egyptian's attitude toward government officials. Question 49b asks: "Does the man in the street respect the civil servant?" Of 247 who replied, 82 per cent said yes. The nature of this respect is specified in the answers to the further question: "Why do you think so?" The 202 who said the public respects the civil servant gave three reasons: 24 per cent said because of the traditional high status of the civil servant; 35 per cent said because the civil servant is educated and performs a public service; and the largest proportion, 41 per cent, said because the civil servant can exert power over the ordinary citizen.

A similar question followed: "Does the man in the street fear the civil servant?" and again the respondents were asked why they answered as they did. Of the 248 who replied, a majority of 59 per cent said yes. Of this group of 146 respondents who said the public fears the civil servant, 113, or 77 per cent, gave the same reason given most often to the previous question: because of the power of the civil servant as an agent of government. Significantly, then, this large number of respondents were probably thinking of government as a regulating and restricting force rather than as a service to the community. Although there are no comparable data for the West, it seems reasonable to say that higher civil servants there probably do not see their own power as the main determinant of public respect for the service, nor, probably, do so high a proportion think they are feared by the ordinary citizen.

Irrespective of the impressions of the Egyptian civil servants themselves, there is some evidence that their traditionally high status and prestige has somewhat declined in recent years. The questionnaire results also suggest that the senior officials themselves think so too, and even say so when not asked about it directly. And, as noted earlier in this chapter, events and tendencies are now taking shape that will probably have the effect of raising the status (and certainly the power) of the higher officials. The Egyptian public bureaucracy is thus now in a period when it is subject to strong forces acting in opposite directions. Just how the civil service will emerge will depend upon the political future of Egypt and upon the outcome of its efforts at technological advance. In any case, this study comes at a time when certain long-range effects upon the status of the civil service are already apparent but before the full effects of the new military regime are clear.

Decline in Status and Prestige

In assessing the changes in the socio-economic status and the prestige of the higher civil service of Egypt, we come up against a difficulty that often bedevils us in this study. We have ways of assessing the status of the service today by means of information which the 249 respondents have provided us and of certain opinions and attitudes which they have expressed. But to compare our judgment of their status today with what it was in the past, we should have to refer to similar studies for earlier periods. Unfortunately, there are no such studies. There are primary sources and analyses based upon them that show the civil service has had high status. Just how high we cannot say in reliable comparative terms. All we can do is to accept the conclusion, already validated, that the status was high and to see whether current data, including all that our questionnaire has elicited, give the impression of change, and if so, in what direction.

The nature of the questionnaire study constitutes a second limitation upon any assessment of the status and prestige of the civil service. This is not a survey of public opinion about the service. It is a study of the service itself. Consequently, all our conclusions about its social position must be inferences from the information, opinions, and attitudes provided by the respondents. We judge that position through an analysis of the civil servant's self-image, his estimation of himself and his impression of the way others estimate him, and through a consideration of his economic position today.

In response to several kinds of question, the Egyptian higher civil servants reveal a difference between the way they view their own status and the way in which they think the general public sees it. They express considerable dissatisfaction with their economic position and the prestige now accorded to them, yet when asked directly what their public reputation is they give what appears to be a high estimation. The implication of their replies is that they, as civil servants familiar with their own social position, are aware of its deterioration while the public, yet unaware of this change, still sees the government official as the lofty personage he once was. The civil servant seems to think he is living on accumulated prestige.

Several questions touch the civil servant's self-image. Question 39 (briefly referred to in the previous chapter) asks: "Suppose you were asked to advise an intelligent young man—say, a young cousin of yours—on his career. What sort of career would you advise him to follow?" Of the 248 who replied, only 4 said they would recommend the civil service. The remaining 244 respondents were asked, after they had named the career they would recommend, about the government service: "What do you think of the civil service as a career for an intelligent young man?" Of the 241 who replied, only 21, or 9 per cent, had something favorable to say about such a career. The vast majority unequivocally rejected it with varying degrees of intensity. There is, of course, a tendency among professional workers to belittle their careers as unrewarding, unappreciated, or even futile, and to warn others not to make the same mistake. How much of such an attitude is merely modesty or self-pity and how much is a solid opinion that determines behavior is hard to assess. Yet, the near unanimity with which Egyptian higher civil servants reject their own careers must be an indication of something deeper than conventional professional modesty.

Here are the reasons for the career recommendations of four civil servants, the first of whom recommends the engineering profession and the others employment in private business. Two point out that their recommendations are to the advantage not only of the individual but also to that of the nation as well, the third advocates "Egyptianization" of private business, and the fourth stresses the stultifying effect of government work.

"Because the country is about to carry out great engineering projects." (No. 104, 44 years old, administrative worker in grade 4.)

"I think that the opportunities in private business are better for his country and for himself." (No. 19, 43 years old, technical worker in grade 3.)

"Because there are only a few Egyptians working in this field [private business]; foreigners monopolize the representation of foreign firms in Egypt, and we should do this in order that Egyptians may gradually replace them." (No. 107, 34 years old, technical worker in grade 4.)

"He may have a future but government service curtails creativeness, activity and the personal motive for work." (No. 225, 50 years old, administrative worker in grade 3.)

This low estimation of the government service as a career is supported by the replies the respondents made to question 17: "Do you think that you might leave the civil service entirely for some reason?" Of the 248 who answered, well over half, 56 per cent, said yes. As we saw in the previous chapter, in Table 24, the proportion of the younger respondents who said they might leave was about two thirds; and, as Table 25 showed, there was no important difference, in the answers to this question, between those civil servants who had been offered other employment and those who had not ever had such an opportunity.

The Egyptian civil servants' rejection of the civil service as a career has an interesting sidelight. In answer to another question (to be considered in detail later in this chapter), 125 respondents gave as the most important determinant of occupational prestige the opportunity to serve the state or the public. Of these 125, 123 replied to the question asking what career they would recommend to an intelligent young man; and of these 123 who place so high a value upon the opportunity to serve the state or the public, only one recommends the civil service.

Further indications of the low self-image of the Egyptian servant appeared in two other comparisons of answers. First, of 82 respondents who say that what they like best about the civil service is the opportunity to perform a public service, 47, or 57 per cent, say they might leave the service under certain conditions. This is about the same proportion of the entire sample who answered this way, indicating that among the civil servants most anxious to serve the public interest the proportion who might leave the government entirely is no smaller than among those to whom the idea of public service is not so important.

Second, let us look at the degree of job-satisfaction among those respondents who entered the civil service primarily for reasons of personal economic advancement and among those who entered mainly to serve the public or for reasons of prestige rather than material advantage. Table 26 shows that among those whose stated motives were primarily economic, 24 per cent are highly satisfied with their jobs as revealed by the Job-Satisfaction Index, whereas among the respondents who entered

TABLE 26

Job-Satisfaction, by Reason Respondent Entered Civil Service

	ECONOMIC REASONS *Per Cent*	STATUS OR PUBLIC SERVICE REASONS *Per Cent*
High job-satisfaction	24.0	8.9
Low job-satisfaction	76.0	91.1
Total	*100.0*	*100.0*
(Cases)	(192)	(56)

Note: Significant at .02 level.

to serve the nation or because their fathers insisted or because the civil service was the only career acceptable to them as educated men, only 9 per cent are now highly satisfied. The rewards of public service in terms of status and prestige are thus not high today in Egypt, according to the testimony of our sample.

In the effort to learn the higher civil servants' notion of the status of their own occupations, they were asked to rank ten occupations, including government bureau chief and government clerk. Before we consider their assessment of these ten occupations, however, it will be useful to examine a related matter, the respondents' opinions as to what determines occupational prestige, the characteristics of a job that in their judgment give it high status. Question 35 asks: "As you know, people have different reasons for thinking highly of a certain post or occupation. Here are some of these reasons. Please arrange them in what you think is the order of their importance. Call the most important reason number 1, the next in importance number 2, and so on." The five elements compared are: good salary and working conditions, skill required to do the work, opportunity to meet important people, opportunity to serve the public, and opportunity to serve the state. Table 27 shows the proportion designating each element as the most important. The highest proportion, 38 per cent, selected "chance to serve the state" as the most important basis of job prestige. Next came "good salary and working conditions," "skill," "chance to serve the public"; no respondent gave first place to "chance to meet important people." The civil servant's emphasis upon service to the *state* is not surprising, although one would suppose that the vast difference

TABLE 27

Most Important Basis of High Occupational Prestige

	Number	Per Cent
Chance to serve state	94	37.8
Good salary and working conditions	77	30.9
Skill required to do the job	47	18.9
Chance to serve public	31	12.4
Chance to meet important people	. . .	. . .
Total	249	100.0

between the number selecting this factor and the number emphasizing service to the *public* is larger than would be found among Western government workers. The low proportion emphasizing skill is perhaps likewise different from what might be found in the West. There have been few studies on this matter anywhere. A recent summary[3] mentions only two. One, reporting the opinions of U.S. college students, shows that they consider the economic return of an occupation to be just as important as its social contribution. The other, reporting the opinions of a sample of the total U.S. population, shows equal emphasis upon economic return, social contribution, and skill. The only significant difference thus appears to be the one with respect to skill.

To obtain another indication of the Egyptian civil servants' ranking of these five elements of job prestige, we weighted the place given to each of them by each respondent—5 points for first rank, 4 points for second, and so on. The total point scores and relative indexes are given in Table 28, which shows, again, that "chance to serve the state" is still clearly considered the

TABLE 28

Relative Ranking of Elements of Occupational Prestige

	Weighted Score	Index
Chance to serve state	983	100.0
Good salary and working conditions	829	84.3
Chance to serve public	826	84.0
Skill required to do the job	822	83.6
Chance to meet important people	253	26.0

[3] A. F. Davies, "Prestige of Occupations," *The British Journal of Sociology*, Vol. 3, No. 2, June, 1952, pp. 134-147, especially p. 146.

most important. There is not much difference in the respondents' ranking of the next three features: economic rewards, public service, and skill. Finally, "chance to meet important people" is by far the least important. In both of these types of measure, shown in Tables 27 and 28, there were no significant differences among the respondents according to age, exposure to the West, or place of higher education.

Having summarized the respondents' views as to what lends high prestige to an occupation, we may consider the way in which they rank ten specific occupations, including two in the civil service. Question 42 asks: "People rate various posts and occupations differently. Here is a card listing several occupations. Just place number 1 alongside the occupation the general public thinks most highly of, number 2 for the next, and so on." The following ten occupations were listed: factory worker, small merchant, doctor, government clerk, landowner, bank director, lawyer, factory owner, peasant, and government bureau chief. Table 29 shows the weighted score for each one, obtained by

TABLE 29

Ranking of Ten Occupations

	Weighted Score	Index
Doctor	2,252	100
Bank director	1,953	87
Lawyer	1,779	79
Factory owner	1,692	75
Landowner	1,619	72
Government bureau chief	1,333	59
Government clerk	919	41
Small merchant	885	39
Factory worker	569	25
Peasant	475	21

counting a ranking of first place as 10, second place as 9, and so on, and then totalling the points accumulated for each occupation. There are some interesting results. First we must recall that the question asked the respondents to give not their own but the general public's ranking. In surveys, this type of question usually brings out the respondents' own views anyway; so we may take these rankings as being at least close to those of the civil servants. It is noteworthy that an independent professional calling, that of doctor, is clearly rated highest. In second place is bank director; after him come the lawyer, factory owner, and landowner, with but a few index points separating them from one another. Thus the landowner, traditionally of highest status, is rated by civil servants below two professional occupations and two highly urban ones. After landowner there is a large gap, and then comes government bureau chief in sixth place. After another large gap comes the government clerk, only slightly above the small merchant. Another large gap separates the latter from the factory worker and peasant, in ninth and tenth places respectively.

The two civil service occupations—bureau chief and clerk— thus are given sixth and seventh places. This rating, indeed, is not unlike what one would expect from a sample of well-educated persons in Western countries, which is one indication of the degree of change that has occurred in Egyptian social values. There are no significant differences between the ratings given to both of these civil service occupations by younger and older respondents, or by those more and less exposed to the West. This would suggest that the apparently low self-ranking pervades the civil service and is not concentrated among one or another group within it. The high status accorded the professional and financial-industrial callings is probably symptomatic of the growing industrialization and professionalization of Egyptian society. An interesting piece of complementary evidence appears in a study of changing attitudes of adolescent girls in Alexandria, by an Egyptian student at the Institute of Sociology and Social Science of Alexandria University.[4] In 1953 he reported the results of his questioning 90 schoolgirls about the occupation which they would like for their husbands. The majority said engineer; doctor received the next largest vote; then teacher, lawyer, and merchant. It is significant that civil servant *as such* was not mentioned (although, of course, most teachers are government employees, and engineers, doctors, and lawyers may likewise work for the government).

We have just reviewed the data showing that the self-image of the civil servants is rather lower than one would expect from

[4] Muhammad A. S. Mito, "The Social Change of Daughters' Position in Egyptian Middle Class Families in Alexandria," thesis at The Institute of Sociology and Social Science, Alexandria University, 1953, p. 37 of typed manuscript.

the innumerable accounts in the remote and recent past. Despite this unexpectedly low self-estimation, the respondents seem to believe that the general public does not yet share this viewpoint. To the civil servant, the man in the street still retains the old mixture of fear and respect toward the government official, according to the responses to four questions dealing with this subject.

Question 49a asks: "Do you think that the man in the street has enough appreciation of the job that the civil servant does?" Of 248 who replied, 79 per cent said no. This is probably not an unduly high proportion when we recall that government workers are generally unappreciated group, and that in a society like Egypt, with so much illiteracy and isolation in rural areas, there is likely to be little awareness of what the government does.

Question 49b asks: "Does the man in the street respect the civil servant?" As we saw earlier in this chapter, 82 per cent of 247 respondents said yes.

Question 49c asks: "Does the man in the street fear the civil servant?" Of the 248 who replied, 59 per cent said yes.

Question 49d asks: "Does the man in the street consider the civil servant difficult to approach, or does he consider the civil servant as a servant of the people and therefore easy to approach?" Of the 248 who replied to this question, 40 per cent said the public considers the civil servant difficult to approach.

The replies to the last three questions indicate that the higher civil servants still see themselves as the objects of respect, fear, and awe among the masses of the population. These senior government officials thus no longer privately consider themselves awesome, but appear to believe that no similar disenchantment has yet penetrated the general population. Just how long it will be before this public attitude of respect and fear becomes diluted by indifference and even contempt is hard to say. Some respondents, indeed, believe the public already approaches this point. One higher civil servant says that the government worker's status has fallen considerably; he is himself ambivalent about this change, for he calls it "democracy," perhaps in justification of this public attitude. The public does not respect the civil servant, he says,

"Because the government official's income is much less than that of those working in private companies and private business,

101

in addition to the fact that high officials are almost entirely stripped of the authority which they used to enjoy—this is democracy." (No. 405, 47 years old, administrator in grade 3.)

Among educated Egyptians the government worker has become an object of sympathy spiked with ridicule. There are several reasons for the decline in the veneration for the civil service: the waning of foreign rule, the spread of education, the development of new opportunities for educated youth, and the oversupply of government job-holders and the decline in their economic status.

Reasons for the Decline in Status of the Civil Service

Government in the Near East, as we saw earlier in this chapter, has traditionally been less restrained than in the West. Those connected with it have had both economic and political power, whereas in the West the identification has been much less intimate. In the Near East, consequently, a government connection has conferred high status and prestige. In areas like Egypt, which were controlled by Western powers, the status and prestige of a government connection has been even higher, because the Westerner has represented a technologically more advanced society and a state with a formidable military apparatus far beyond the capacity of the local population to achieve. In such an area the civil servant has had two abundant sources of high status: his position as a representative of government, and his proximity to the foreign ruler in whose status and prestige he therefore shared.

With the growth of resistance to foreign rule, one of these sources began to run dry. As the movement for national independence in Egypt gained momentum after World War I, the prestige an Egyptian enjoyed through his association with the resented alien power began to decline. More and more, such influence as Great Britain had in Egypt was exerted in less obvious ways; the number of Englishmen in the civil service began to decline until they became rare in the government offices. Their virtual disappearance after World War II followed the increase of self-government in Egypt and the withdrawal of British armed forces to a smaller area until in 1954 agreement on full evacuation was reached. The Egyptian civil servant has thus lost one important source of status in recent decades; his prestige became that of an Egyptian in a certain position among Egyptians, and no longer did he in any way share in the high status of the more powerful Western rulers.

Another aspect of the high status of civil servants in Egypt has been the fact that education, so highly regarded in Arab-Muslim culture, was the hallmark of the government employee to a degree matched in few other major career lines. With the spread of education, especially since World War I, the civil service is now less outstanding in this respect. At the same time, the increase in the number of educated youth seeking government posts produced an oversupply of civil servants; the fear of an educated unemployed population was a main consideration in the government's policy of swelling the ranks of its employees.

The result has been that the civil service is no longer the economically attractive career it used to be. A survey by the International Labor Organization concludes that in underdeveloped areas "government service is remunerated more highly relative to private industrial employment," while in "industrially advanced countries" the opposite holds true, at least for the lower grades in the civil service.[5] This generalization probably no longer holds for Egypt. Wage and salary data available do not permit a reliable comparison between the civil service and private industry, since for the latter, salaries of clerks are lumped with those of administrative and technical workers.[6] But during the steep climb in the cost of living, which is now nearly three times what it was in 1939 according to the official index,[7] salaries in private industry have been able to hold their own better than have the highly controlled government salaries.

These policies have reduced the relative economic advantage of government employment to the point where the civil servant is probably not as well paid as technical and administrative experts in private industry. As early as 1950, a British civil service expert who was asked to study personnel practices in the

[5] "Salaries and Hours of Work in Government Service: An International Comparison," *International Labor Review* (Geneva, International Labor Organization), Vol. 68, nos. 4-5, Oct.-Nov., 1953, pp. 413-414.

[6] Republic of Egypt, Ministry of Finance and Economy, Statistical Department, *Statistical Pocket Year-book, 1953*, Government Press, Cairo, 1954, Table 30, pp. 40-41.

[7] National Bank of Egypt, Cairo, *Economic Bulletin* (English edition), Vol. IX, No. 2, 1956, p. 209.

Egyptian service observed that: "A comparison between the salaries paid by certain commercial firms in Egypt, including banks, to their employees and those paid by the Egyptian Government to civil servants shows that as a general rule salaries are somewhat higher in outside employment."[8] What seems to have happened is that industrial and commercial development in Egypt during 1920-1940 and then during and after World War II created many openings for managerial, technical, and clerical workers. A large proportion of Egyptian youth, however, were still attracted to the civil service by tradition, for family reasons, for relative security of tenure, or out of political partisanship, and so produced an oversupply not only of aspirants but also of appointees. Meanwhile, salaries in private industry had to be raised in order to attract suitable workers. Had more Egyptians been willing to work outside the government, the results might have been quite different.

Although the civil service is still a very attractive career in Egypt, there is evidence in the responses to the questionnaire that it is not so popular as it used to be. We saw in Table 15, Chapter 4, for example, that there is a significant difference between the proportions of the older and younger respondents who say they became civil servants because they lacked funds to set up their own business. Among the respondents of ages 46 to 60, only 6 per cent give this reason, but among those 31 to 45, 24 per cent did so. In recent years, it appears, young Egyptians are at least giving more consideration to other careers before deciding to go into government service. This conclusion is supported by the answers to question 13: "How old were you when you first thought of a career in the civil service?" Of 249 respondents, 43 per cent said their decision was made before they were 22 years old, and 57 per cent at that age or afterward. But, as Table 30 shows, there are significant differences between the older and younger respondents with respect to the age at which they decided upon the civil service as a career. Among those now 46 to 60 years old, about half decided before they were 22 and about half afterwards, but among the younger respondents, those now 31 to 45, nearly two thirds decided after

[8] Egyptian Government, Ministry of Finance, *Report on the Personnel Questions of the Egyptian Civil Service*, by A. P. Sinker, Government Press, Cairo, 1951, p. 23.

TABLE 30

Age at Which Respondents Decided on Civil Service Career, by Age

	AGE 31-45 Per Cent	AGE 46-60 Per Cent
Decided at age 21 or lower	34.4	50.8
Decided at age 22 or higher	65.6	49.2
Total	100.0	100.0
(Cases)	(125)	(124)

Note: Significant at .02 level.

they were 22. It appears from our sample, therefore, that the decision to enter the civil service is now made later in a young man's life than formerly. In part, this change may merely reflect the longer years of schooling today and the consequent postponement of career choices among younger men. But even if we exclude the respondents who have not taken at least the bachelor's degree, the marked difference between the older and younger men persists, as Table 31 shows. Of 219 respondents who earned

TABLE 31

Age at Which College Graduates Decided on Civil Service Career, by Age

COLLEGE GRADUATES WHO DECIDED ON CIVIL SERVICE	AGE 31-45 Per Cent	AGE 46-60 Per Cent
At age 21 or lower	32.8	45.4
At age 22 or higher	67.2	54.6
Total	100.0	100.0
(Cases)	(122)	(97)

Note: The chi-square value of this table just misses significance at the .05 level.

the bachelor's degree, 122 are between 31 and 45 years of age and 97 between 46 and 60. Among the younger officials about two thirds decided upon the government service when they were 22 or older, whereas among the older officials only a little more than half did so.

Regardless, therefore, of the prolongation of education, the younger civil servants decided on their ultimate career at a later age. The reason may well be that the civil service, no longer exerting the attraction it used to, has not been so automatically the choice of educated youth in recent years. They may end up

105

as civil servants but at least they do not make up their minds so soon and they perhaps give more thought to other possible careers than did their older colleagues.

How much of the decline in the civil servant's status is attributable to the fact that it is economically no longer so attractive a career as it used to be? Several questions touch this problem, although, of course, the responses to them do not conclusively tell us just how important a part the decline in real income has played in the decline in status as a whole.

We saw in Chapter 4 that 140 respondents out of 248, or 56 per cent, said they would leave the civil service under certain circumstances. Table 23 showed that of these 140, more than half, 53 per cent, said they would leave for a better-paying job. Another indication of the importance of income to the civil servants appears in the responses to question 51, which asked them to complete a sentence beginning with the following words: "The worst thing about being a government official is. . . ." Of the 226 who did so, 48, or 21 per cent, mentioned low pay and lack of future. Further light is incidentally thrown on the civil servant's low self-image by the fact that 15 per cent complained that the government official is not appreciated, liked, or respected. Thus more than a third of the respondents, in this free answer, mentioned features of government employment that indicate declining socio-economic status and prestige.

Some questions deal directly with the adequacy of salaries in the government service. Question 31 asked: "It is often said that salaries in the civil service are inadequate. Are you able to live on your salary as a civil servant?" Of the 249 who replied, 133, or 53 per cent, said no. The response to such a question must be interpreted carefully, since everyone would like to be making more money. For this reason the question asked was not whether the respondent wanted more money or thought that he deserved more or could use more, but specifically whether he could live on his salary. It is symptomatic of grave dissatisfaction with salaries when more than half of a sample of *higher* civil servants, receiving the largest incomes in the service, say that they cannot live on what they earn as government workers. To meet living costs, a large number of civil servants supplement their salaries with income from property or from other employment.

Among our 249 respondents the proportion who have such

other resources is high. Question 32a asks: "Do you have other resources such as buildings or land or investments of any kind?" In reply, 174, or 70 per cent, reported that they do have such assets. They were asked further: "Do you use some of this income for your living expenses?" Of the 174, 159, or 91 per cent, said they do draw upon these resources to meet living costs. Such a high proportion of civil servants with outside resources should not be surprising, since so large a proportion, as we saw in Chapter 3 and will see again in the next section, come from middle and upper class families. It may very well be that the enjoyment of this additional income makes it possible for them to remain in the civil service. If this is so, and if this situation persists, the service will be comprised of an ever larger proportion of persons who either have additional income or live in respectable shabbiness on their government salaries. The Egyptian civil service may indeed not be far from this situation already.

The inadequacy of government salaries generates pressure among the civil servants to obtain other employment after hours (which, conveniently, means after 2 p.m., at the latest, in a country where most private businesses remain open in the late afternoon or evening following a mid-afternoon closing). This the government forbids, except with special permission rarely granted. Yet one hears from articulate Egyptians in general and from the civil servants themselves that many government workers seek and engage in outside employment, either without applying for permission or in violation of a refusal to grant it. That the government workers feel strongly on this point is apparent in the answers to question 33a, which asks: "As you know, civil servants are not permitted to hold other jobs except under certain circumstances and with special permission. Do you think that the government should permit all civil servants to hold other jobs without exception?" Of the 249 respondents, 51 per cent said yes, taking a rather extreme position. Since many of the respondents are in general aware of the ethical problems involved in government employment, such a high proportion is a significant indication of the intensity of their dissatisfaction with salary levels. This conclusion is further supported by the reasons given by the 127 respondents, who say the civil servant should be allowed to take on any other employment too; 59 of them, or 46 per cent, say this would enable the government worker to supplement his low salary. As one respondent puts it, he should be free to obtain outside employment

"To spend his leisure time in a useful way, for himself and others, and so that it will be additional source of income which would fortify him against bribery." (No. 226, 58 years old, administrator in grade 3.)

On this point, concerning freedom to engage in other employment, the respondents with income-producing assets agree with those not so fortunate; among the former, 51 per cent say the government should give the civil servant absolute freedom to take on additional employment, and among the latter 51 per cent likewise say so. Thus the apparently most needy civil servants are not especially the most disgruntled on this score; the dissatisfaction goes beyond differences in income to a profound resentment against the policy of restricting the freedom to work after hours.

Social Mobility among the Civil Servants

We have just reviewed the decline in civil service status and prestige, as revealed in the self-image of the respondents and in the drop in their salaries relative to those in private industry. One type of evidence regarding socio-economic status remains to be explored—the social origin of the civil servants. Table 7 in Chapter 3 listed the occupations of the respondents' fathers. We saw there that the three largest social groups from which our respondents come (accounting for nearly four fifths) are civil servants (39 per cent), landlords (24 per cent), and peasants (16 per cent). Each of these three groups is probably the most important component of the social class of which it is a part: the middle, upper, and lower class, respectively. The question presents itself: Are the social sources of the higher civil service changing? Is an increasing proportion of senior officials coming from the lower, higher, or middle socio-economic levels? Table 32 provides the answer by showing the fathers' occupations of the younger and the older respondents, enabling us to see the changes in recent decades. Although the differences are not statistically significant, they are nevertheless strong. Among the older respondents, only 34 per cent are the sons of

TABLE 32

Occupations of Respondents' Fathers, by Age of Respondents

FATHERS' OCCUPATIONS	RESPONDENTS AGED 31-45 Per Cent	RESPONDENTS AGED 46-60 Per Cent
Civil servant	43.9	33.6
Landlord	21.9	25.2
Peasant	11.4	21.0
Other	22.8	20.2
Total	100.0	100.0
(Cases)	(123)	(119)

Note: Not statistically significant.

civil servants, whereas among the younger ones 44 per cent are. Thus the civil service itself has provided an increasing proportion of the government workers in recent years. There is little change in the proportion of civil servants coming from the landlord class, but the proportion coming from the peasantry has declined. Thus the middle class has been providing a higher proportion of our respondents as time has passed, the upper class about the same as formerly, and lower class somewhat less. Does this mean that the Egyptian civil service is on its way to becoming more and more a preserve of the upper and middle classes?

This question can be answered only by considering what has happened to the distribution of socio-economic groups in the entire Egyptian society. If the proportion of our respondents who are sons of civil servants has increased, it is not surprising in view of the great increase in the number of civil servants in the last few decades. The same holds true, conversely, for the peasantry. This class has provided a decreasing proportion of our respondents, but it has also constituted a decreasing proportion of the total male employed population. Census data show that the males in agricultural pursuits constituted 64 per cent of the total number of employed males in 1907. This proportion has steadily declined each decade, until in 1947, the year of the most recent census, it was only 50 per cent.[9]

It appears, then, that the civil service has been the career-line

[9] Computed from Egyptian official census reports published decennially by the Egyptian government: 1907 census, p. 283; 1917 census, p. 379; 1937 census, p. 184; 1947 census, p. 282.

for upper and middle class sons but that it is not becoming any more difficult for others to gain entrance into it. Indeed, if education continues to spread down through the social classes and if the civil service itself is really declining in status and prestige, then it may become more and more the career-line for lower-class youth able to take advantage of the public education system.

To some extent, the government has always provided openings for a rise in social status. Among our 249 respondents about a quarter, as civil servants, enjoy higher status and prestige than their fathers. Most of these upwardly mobile officials naturally come mainly from the lower socio-economic groups, for whom the civil service meant an advance. For the rest, it meant either staying on the same social level as their fathers or going down somewhat. Table 33 shows, consequently, that among the re-

TABLE 33
Social Mobility, by Age

		AGE 31-40 Per Cent	AGE 41-50 Per Cent	AGE 51-60 Per Cent
Upwardly mobile		21.0	20.2	35.2
Stable		79.0	79.8	64.8
	Total	*100.0*	*100.0*	*100.0*
	(Cases)	(62)	(109)	(71)

Note: The chi-square value of this table just misses significance at the .05 level.

spondents aged 51-60 we find the highest proportion of the upwardly mobile. Similarly, Table 9 in Chapter 3 shows that a much higher proportion of the rural-born officials have risen beyond their fathers' socio-economic status; they are, of course, the peasants' sons to whom a government career has meant both higher income and higher status. One would expect to find that the upwardly mobile would be highly pleased with their advanced status, but the proportion among them who are highly satisfied with their jobs is not significantly greater than the proportion among those for whom the civil service did not mean an advance in socio-economic status. As Table 34 shows, among the upwardly mobile 25 per cent are highly satisfied with their jobs and among the socially stable 18 per cent are. This difference is not a marked one. Thus the upwardly mobile are

TABLE 34

Social Mobility and Job-Satisfaction

	UPWARDLY MOBILE *Per Cent*	STABLE *Per Cent*
High job-satisfaction	25.0	18.1
Low job-satisfaction	75.0	81.9
Total	*100.0*	*100.0*
(Cases)	(60)	(182)

Note: Not statistically significant.

not especially more satisfied with the civil service than others to whom this career was not an advance in status. This confirms in part all our other evidence as to the decline of the Egyptian civil service in status and prestige. Even those for whom entrance into the awesome ranks of the government officials was a step upward socially are not especially pleased with what they find. They have been disenchanted.

Summary and Conclusions

The vast gulf in the Near East between the power of the rulers and the weakness of the masses of the ruled has been the social setting in which the civil service, as the representative of governmental power, has enjoyed higher status and prestige than in the West, where political responsibility, democratic institutions, and private economic power have diminished the awe in which the trappings of the state are viewed by the ordinary citizen. Our account of the status and prestige of the higher civil service of Egypt has shown that they have declined as notions of democracy spread, foreign rule declined, education became more general, other opportunities appeared for educated youth, and the standard of living a government salary can bring fell.

The higher civil servants themselves so little esteem their own calling that only 4 of 248 recommend it as a career and few of them see it as bringing more prestige than others open to educated young men and women. Despite this low self-image, however, the Egyptian higher civil servants still believe the general public stands in awe of them. The officials themselves know better. In recent years, a significantly higher proportion of them seriously consider other careers before entering the service. In addition, they express profound dissatisfaction with the economic status that a government salary can buy. Most of those who say they would leave the service give as the reason the need for a better-paying job. More than half of these relatively highly paid government workers say they cannot live on their salaries; and about half also believe the government should place no restriction whatever upon their taking on other employment after hours.

In social origin, the higher civil servants in our sample are drawn largely from the three main elements of the middle, upper, and lower social classes: the civil servants themselves, the landlord class, and the peasantry. Although the proportion supplied by the peasantry has declined in recent years, this does not mean that the service is becoming the preserve of the middle and upper classes. It is simply that the proportion of peasants in the entire society has declined with urbanization and the growth of industry and commerce. There is still considerable opportunity in the Egyptian civil service for the poor rural or urban youth who can take advantage of the public education system. In our sample, indeed, we found that a quarter of the senior officials are upwardly mobile socially, that is, as civil servants they are in an occupation of higher status and prestige than their fathers enjoyed. This group, one would expect, would find service in the government highly gratifying. Yet they do not seem to be significantly more satisfied with their jobs than do those respondents for whom entrance into government employment did not mean social and economic advancement. This is the full measure of the change in the status and prestige of the higher civil service of Egypt: even those for whom it has meant entrance into a higher social class have become disenchanted. What is happening in Egypt in this respect is, of course, not unique. A recent summary of reasons for the decline in status of the higher civil servants of France mentions (1) the creation of new professional occupations and the decline in the importance of the state relative to private industry, (2) the change in "social values" attendant upon industrial capitalism "so that wealth and income came to predominate over rank and official position as the main determinants of social status," and (3) the fall in the real income of the civil servants.[10] These developments apply with varying degrees of influence to Egypt too.

[10] T. B. Bottomore, "Higher Civil Servants in France," in *Transactions*

The effect of the present military regime upon the civil service has been at first to accelerate its decline in status and prestige. The civil service was one of the first targets for reform and suffered by its identification with the "old regime," which was regarded as corrupt and feudalistic. But the long-range effects of the regime may be quite the opposite. As the effort to industrialize and to promote technological progress goes on, the role of government must become greater. This development will increase the power of the government officials over the economy and will make their functions even less understandable and controllable by the general public or even by the special interest groups affected by the myriad operations of a state seeking to induce technological and economic growth at the same time as it makes formal provision for social welfare. If some system of genuine representative government evolves, public control may counter these influences tending toward greater prestige and power of the civil service. Another factor that may enhance its position is the military regime's reduction of the influence and reputation of other social classes or groups: the big landowners, the old political parties and their leaders, and their allies in journalism and the law. Finally, the status and prestige of the government service may be raised by the present government's effort to eradicate corruption, institute personnel practices designed for efficiency and impartiality, and increase the services which government employees perform for the nation. If the status and power of the civil service should indeed begin to rise again, the question of the role of the bureaucracy in the state will again present itself, as it has done in Egypt before and in other countries also. We have seen that our sample of higher civil servants form a homogeneous group; nearly three quarters are drawn from the middle and upper classes and about two fifths are sons of civil servants. Can they form so cohesive a social group as to bar certain policies and to promote others merely because they operate the government machinery? This is a question which, along with others touching on the various loyalties of the service, we shall consider in the next chapter.

---

of the Second World Congress of Sociology (Belgium, 1954), 2 volumes, International Sociological Association, London, 1954, Volume 2, p. 147.

Chapter 6. Loyalties: The Professional and Private Worlds of the Civil Servant

Among the most persistent issues raised about public bureaucracy everywhere are those of corruption and red tape. Although the civil service in many countries is accused of both at the same time, these characteristics are in a sense at opposite poles. For red tape—the accumulation of procedural regulations rigidly and uniformly applied—is usually the means by which large organizations seek to prevent the special considerations and individual interpretations that lead to graft and favoritism.[1] Bureaucracies seem destined to move between these unsatisfactory extremes.

Varying Loyalties

The Western world has slowly developed a profession of public administration with standards of recruitment and models of performance in office. With characteristic emphasis upon the individual's responsibility, these standards and models have been viewed as moral issues in the West. The result has been that Western observers have generally lost sight, in their increasing contact with the government and administration of other areas, of the fact that their notions of honesty, fairness, and efficiency are the outgrowth of peculiarly Western developments in science and technology, religion, and economic organization. As such, these notions cannot be easily transferred to other societies with different traditions and a different line of social evolution. In the field of administration, public or private, questions of corruption and favoritism become, when we consider other cultures, not matters of individual morality but of varying loyalties. The West has evolved a form of loyalty to a given task, irrespective of one's economic relationship to it, which is still somewhat novel in the Near East, where religious traditions and economic organization have not combined to produce this

---

[1] Red tape and graft converge, of course, when an official sets up procedural barriers that he easily surmounts upon receiving a bribe.

type of moral commitment to a job. Nor has the Near East as yet developed the combination of nationalism and democracy that goes beyond loyalty to a state apparatus and encompasses loyalty to the public.

It is easy to generalize from the Western experience and to raise its relatively new loyalties to the level of universal moral imperatives. Primary loyalties differ, and it can bring only confusion to judge one group of persons by the standards of another. It is probably true, as a U.S. Senate subcommittee put it several years ago, that the "moral standards of the country . . . provide the ethical environment which in turn conditions the standards of behavior of public officials." The significant point, however, is whether or not specific standards for official behavior are elaborated by a society. The subcommittee went on to say that: "Low standards in the conduct of public affairs are a symptom of low standards in the country generally."[2] This is true only if the standards are similar or grow out of the same traditions. If, as so often happens in non-Western lands under Western political influence, the official standards of government are developed or imposed with little regard for the nature of the loyalties that command the general public, then immorality in the government does not imply immorality in the society. The measures are simply different.

Another common misconception is that the present Western civil service system is the only kind in which recruitment is based on merit and in which corruption can be reduced to harmless proportions. This is far from the truth. In tenth-century China, for example, as a student of the period points out, a system of controlled sponsorship prevailed under which promotion in the government came "on the recommendation of a superior officer, who thereafter was legally answerable for the quality and acts of his protégé." Recruitment, moreover, was through a system of controlled nepotism which gave higher civil servants "the privilege of nominating for entrance into the civil service one or more of their sons or other family members, and on occasion even dependents not related by blood." Although

[2] U.S. Government, *Ethical Standards in Government*, Report of a Subcommittee on Labor and Public Welfare, U.S. Senate, Committee Print, 82d Congress, 1st Session, Government Printing Office, Washington, D.C., 1951, p. 7.

115

these methods did not work perfectly, they were congenial to the values and expectations of the society and did enjoy some degree of success in bringing capable people into office and enabling them to advance in the government service. They harmonized with the prevailing Confucian system in which personal ties rather than abstract principles commanded loyalty. Thus the government "could make constructive use of the peculiarly strong social bonds that controlled the relationships of individuals and families: bonds of kinship, of friendship, of beneficiary and benefactor, enforced by the sanction of the ethical code and of public opinion. Where a man might venture to risk punishment for himself, he could not do so for another to whom he owed an obligation."[3]

In other countries and eras, similar systems have produced reasonable efficiency in government. An account by a European observer of sixteenth-century Turkey points out that in the central administration "the Sultan himself assigns to all their duties and offices, and in doing so . . . he only considers merit. . . . Thus . . . offices are filled by men capable of performing them."[4] In England during the same period, the interest of the crown in having its realm efficiently run enabled Thomas Cromwell to initiate what one scholar has called a "revolution in government."[5] In our own day, too, an observer has reported that during the absolute monarchy in Siam, up to 1932, minor government posts were filled by the relatives or protégés of the department heads. This arrangement is said to have had its merits, for the recruit felt a gratitude and loyalty to his chief which he would not have felt had he obtained his job in some impersonal way such as by competitive examination.[6]

All these are administrative systems in relative harmony with the social values and social structure in which they developed. They drew upon existing loyalties and adjusted civil service affairs to them; personal obligation was harnessed to the service

[3] E. A. Kracke, Jr., *Civil Service in Early Sung China, 960-1067*, Harvard University Press, Cambridge, 1953, esp. pp. 2, 74, 24, 197, 168.

[4] *The Turkish Letters of Ogier Ghiselin de Busbecq*, tr. by Edward Seymour Forster, Oxford University Press, London, 1927, pp. 59-60.

[5] See G. R. Elton, *The Tudor Revolution in Government*, Cambridge University Press, Cambridge, 1953.

[6] W. D. Reeve, *Public Administration in Siam*, Royal Institute of International Affairs, N.Y., 1951, p. 61.

of the state, which was itself seen in its personal embodiment, the emperor, sultan, or king. Loyalty to the state as an agency of the community, or to the nation, or to the "people" was not characteristic of these societies and has indeed developed only in the modern era in the West. As Sir Ernest Barker has remarked, the European state in 1660, for example, was not yet considered a "legal association, united in a common scheme of rights and duties. . . ." It was not yet fully disengaged (1) from the family, for there was no clear-cut distinction between royal income and government revenue, (2) from property, for the king actually owned much of the domain he ruled, and public offices were freely bought and sold, and (3) from society, for the nobility and the army enjoyed, by virtue merely of social position, special privileges from the state, and the state officials had a special position in society.[7]

The administrative problems of many non-Western areas today are the result of changing values: the penetration of Western notions of efficiency and loyalty in government, and the persistence of personal, familial, and communal loyalties in the population from which the administration is recruited. Anomalies are bound to follow when the formal governmental structure is based upon the expectation of responsibility to a remote abstraction called the government or the administration, while the responsibilities that are meaningful to the people are to friends (including political associates), relatives, and others, in their personal roles rather than as citizens or civil servants or elected officials. It is not that these two ways of looking at people—in their personal roles or in their relationship to a nation-state—entirely exclude one another. Rather, it is a matter of the degree to which the more formal roles of citizen, state employee, and elected official have evolved from traditional relationships and the degree to which these newer social roles are supported by other institutions and popular expectations.

Different bureaucracies require different kinds of personalities to man their many levels, depending upon the standards erected for them. A Western public bureaucracy demands (not always successfully) a certain impersonal attitude on the part of the

[7] Sir Ernest Barker, *The Development of Public Services in Western Europe, 1660-1930*, Oxford University Press, London, 1944, pp. 4-6.

official toward all who come before him, whether in person or by means of a formal document. In the Near East, people are not yet accustomed to looking upon others impersonally in any situation. Their tendency to look upon others as individuals, with families, friends, and communities behind them, is carried over into realms where recent changes have established different formal requirements.

Historical Influences upon the Egyptian Civil Service

The two most important recent historical influences upon the Egyptian civil service of today have been the Ottoman administration in the sixteenth to nineteenth centuries, and the British occupation during the nineteenth and twentieth centuries. In Chapter 2 we reviewed the general characteristics of these two streams of influence. Here we shall be concerned only with their effects upon the loyalties of civil servants and with questions of venality.

As we saw a moment ago, recruitment to high posts in the Ottoman Empire in the sixteenth century was based upon merit. According to the contemporary account of a European diplomat at the Sultan's court, de Busbecq, not birth but merit and personal achievement were the criteria for appointment and promotion in the Sultan's service. Beyond that point, however, bribery and corruption were rife, at least to the eye of the foreign traveler. De Busbecq observed that "a man who intends to go among the Turks must be prepared, as soon as he has crossed the frontier, to open his purse and never close it till he leaves the country. . . . Were it not for this expedient, their country would be as inaccessible to foreigners as those lands which are supposed to be condemned to perpetual solitude by excessive heat or cold." In the central administration, however, the Sultan exercised close control and considered only ability. De Busbecq contrasted this policy with the one prevailing in Europe: "Our method is very different; there is no room for merit, but everything depends on birth; considerations of which alone open the way to high official position."[8]

This situation was to hold good for only a short time, however, since this dependence on the character of the Sultan was

[8] De Busbecq, *op.cit.*, see note 4 above, pp. 25, 59-61.

one of its weaknesses, according to Gibb and Bowen.[9] The sultans themselves retired from active administration to the traditional but cloistered "pomp of monarchy." The military conquests of the sixteenth century, moreover, encouraged demoralization and a taste that could be satisfied only by further spoils. Since wars were not continuous, the ruling groups began to use their government positions for personal ends; bribery and corruption spread until the system changed the character of Ottoman officialdom. Although Egypt, as an outlying territory, was not subjected to a policy of Ottomanization,[10] the ill effects of corrupt foreign control could not be avoided. Egypt was ruled, as was the rest of the empire, by representatives of a central administration whose "ruling idea," as Gibb and Bowen put it, "was distrust—fear of treachery or of unregulated ambition on the part of the officers of the Empire. . . ."[11] From this policy of extreme centralization, suspicion, and quick turnover of provincial officials, developed an administration by men who saw their positions chiefly as an opportunity of limited duration to get as much as they could for themselves. It also encouraged the combination of subservience to one's chief and tyranny over one's subordinates which Lord Milner described as the legacy to the British when they occupied Egypt in 1882: "The fact is, that the rank and file of the Civil Service, like the rank and file of the Army, used to be ruined by ill-usage. They were ordered about like slaves, . . . yet they durst not for their lives breathe an objection to the commands of their superiors. . . . And as they were almost always penniless, . . . they dreaded dismissal like a sentence of death. . . . The members of each class of the official hierarchy revenged themselves for the maltreatment they received by maltreating, in their turn, the class beneath them. And they all maltreated the common people."[12] The tone was set by the Ottoman rulers and their chief representatives in Egypt, Turks who had intermarried with Egyptians. As Lord Cromer wrote, this group "occupied the principal

[9] H. A. R. Gibb and Harold Bowen, *Islamic Society and the West*, Vol. One, Part I, Oxford University Press, London, 1950, pp. 174-178.
[10] *Ibid.*, pp. 210, 225.
[11] *Ibid.*, p. 201.
[12] Alfred (Lord) Milner, *England in Egypt*, 2d edition, Edward Arnold, London, 1893, p. 401.

places under Government" when the English came in 1882.[13] Egyptian administration today is still based upon a decree of 1878 by the Khedive, the representative of the Ottoman Empire in Egypt, which he issued in response to pressure from a European commission established to inquire into the financial difficulties then facing the country.[14]

England, when it occupied Egypt in 1882, had already gone far in its efforts to establish its own efficient, non-political, and incorruptible civil service. Its representatives in Egypt were therefore shocked by the degree of official venality they found. They were not disposed to examine the problem historically or in terms of the functions which this easy bribery performed in Egyptian society. Most of them held the view that low salaries or immorality explained corruption. They were, however, concerned with improving the administration; at the close of a quarter-century of paternal rule Lord Cromer wrote that "it always appeared to me that the first and most important duty of the British representative in Egypt was, by example and precept, to set up a high standard of morality, both in his public and private life, and thus to endeavor to raise the standard of those around him."[15] This retrospective resolve is borne out by the contemporary evidence. A former civil servant in the Sudan, of Syrian origin, has written: "In Egypt and the Sudan, Syrians saw British rule at work, and were greatly impressed by the contrast between it and Turkish rule. Method, organization, justice and official honesty dazzled the Syrian mind hitherto accustomed to a corrupt and inefficient regime."[16]

Only three years after the beginning of the occupation, British representatives were already reporting on the progress of their efforts to reduce corruption. In 1885 Cromer sent word to London that in the high courts and in higher ranks of the government service "no corruption takes place." He added: "The lower Courts are not yet free from corruption, although in these

[13] The Earl of Cromer (Evelyn Baring), *Modern Egypt*, 2 vols. Macmillan, London, 1908, vol. 2, p. 171.

[14] *Ibid.*, vol. 1, pp. 61-63, and Government of Egypt, Civil Service Commission, *Annual Report, 1952* (in Arabic), Government Press, Cairo, 1953, p. 7.

[15] Lord Cromer, *op.cit.*, see note 13 above, vol. 2, p. 322.

[16] Edward Atiyah, *An Arab Tells His Story*, John Murray, London, 1946, p. 28.

also the standard of honesty has greatly improved. Little or no impression has as yet been made on the venal habits of the minor officials in the administrative services. . . ."[17]

The English example of administrative incorruptibility was doubtlessly not entirely lost upon Egyptians who knew it. Western efficiency and dispatch in governmental affairs were probably even more impressive to the Egyptian civil servant, because this aspect of British public bureaucracy touched less on his well-rooted loyalties and his economic necessities. But, the very fact that the British came to Egypt unwanted and remained there for nearly three quarters of a century in the face of opposition by the Egyptian articulate classes was not calculated to impress the lesson of honesty. In details of performance of duty, the British example indeed encouraged bureaucratic regularity and discouraged corruption or the application of irrelevant standards; yet in a larger sense the foreign rulers could not but encourage sycophancy, dissimulation, and distrust when their word was carried out ultimately by force although nominally by advice. The British administrators in Egypt set a noble personal example of moral rectitude, but they were Englishmen mindful of their role as representatives of the dominant power and tutors of "protected" Egypt, and they reacted to the Egyptian situation as their upbringing, education, and loyalties impelled them. Their Egyptian colleagues and subordinates, however, although they worked in the same offices, went home to Egyptian society, not to an Anglo-Saxon enclave transplanted to a pleasant island in the Nile. They came from a culture in which government had always, in the people's memory, been in the hands of foreigners, a power to be avoided or to be used to mitigate the harshness of cruel masters to whom corporal punishment came quickly and from whose whim there was little to protect even physical well-being. Ottoman despotism had at least had its weak spots; official corruptibility afforded a small margin of safety in certain ways. To combine moral rectitude with exploitation would have been to remove such small means of self-protection as still remained to a suffering population—unless, of course, genuine reform and reasonable humanitarian standards were advancing at the same

[17] Sir E. Baring to Earl Granville, from Cairo, February 10, 1885, in Great Britain, Egypt No. 15 (1885). *Reports on the State of Egypt, and the Progress of Administrative Reforms* (Cd. 4421), pp. 2-3.

time. But even if such mitigating circumstances were becoming more widespread, it would be generations before the population could accept new ideas in government when the old one of payment for services had been so long and severely tested. So despite the British example, Egyptian loyalties remained what they were. It was only by changing these loyalties in other ways, through education, the development of representative institutions, the growth of industry, the transfer of functions in the government and the economy, that the British helped to alter the conditions of life in Egypt and thus to alter the intensity of Egyptian loyalty to old symbols and to awaken a new set of loyalties to groups wider than the family, the village, or the religious community.

Conflicting Loyalties in the Civil Service

National differences are expressed in the most unexpected ways. In his well-known novel, translated into English as *Maze of Justice*, one of Egypt's leading belle-lettrists, Towfiq el Hakim, has the narrator describe the primitive and home-made weapons held by a prosecutor as exhibits in criminal cases. "I always think," the narrator continues, "that a single glance at a Legal Department store will immediately indicate the character of the village, its way of thinking and the degree of its civilization. I have no doubt, for instance, that the store of the District Attorney of Chicago would be quite innocent of sticks or home-made pistols."[18] Patterns of corruption in public life may likewise reveal the technological and political status of a society. Thus corruption in the United States typically involves offers of money and other gifts from private interests to government representatives in the letting of contracts, tax collection, lending of money, fixing of prices for goods and services, granting of franchises or licenses, allocation of raw materials, and granting of subsidies.[19] In other societies—less wealthy and less technologically advanced, where government performs fewer services

[18] Towfiq el Hakim, *Maze of Justice* (*Mudhakkirāt nā'ib fi al-Aryāf*, 1937), tr. by A. S. Eban, Harvill Press, London, 1947, pp. 92-93.
[19] These types of corruption occur in what are called "action-laden" areas of government activity by Senator Paul H. Douglas, in *Ethics in Government*, Harvard University Press, Cambridge, 1952, p. 23. See also George A. Graham, *Morality in American Politics*, Random House, New York, 1952, esp. chapter II.

(and performs them itself rather than paying private firms to do so)—these types of corruption may be found but are not typical. One observer, for example, points out that in China the main kinds of corruption are embezzlement, extra-legal taxation, and nepotism. In Mexico the chief device of the civil servant seems to be petty bribery and extortion.[20] In Egypt corruption means primarily the acceptance of small bribes by civil servants in return for some administrative favor, or improper appointment to and promotion in the government service itself. These are the charges most often made when Egyptians speak of corruption in government, or when leaders of the military regime refer to such matters in the trials of former political and governmental leaders and in press reports of changes in various ministries.

Reliable evidence of malfeasance in office anywhere is, of course, not easily obtained, and certainly not by interviewing civil servants. Evidence of abuses in the Egyptian civil service is abundant in the reports of the Egyptian Civil Service Commission and in the records of the Revolutionary Court.[21] Military leaders of the 1952 revolution, too, have often pointed to political abuses in the past which persist into the present. Thus Prime Minister Gamal Abdel Nasser, in a speech on the second anniversary of the revolution, stated: "We have inherited a heavy legacy: a ruined treasury, an unbalanced budget and corrupt Government. Indeed graft, favoritism, party conflict, personal interests, and the abuse of influence by Government officials were rife."[22] Our questionnaire made no attempt to elicit evidence of corruption or bribery but was intended to shed light on the civil servants' general attitudes toward government service, their conception of public service, their degree of professionalization, and some of their experiences that might bear upon these points. The value of the questionnaire data is that they give us some notion of the professional and administrative climate, and of the varying loyalties of Egyptian civil servants.

[20] On China, see Francis L. K. Hsu, *Americans and Chinese*, Schuman, New York, 1953, pp. 196-204. On Mexico, see Nathan L. Whetten, *Rural Mexico*, University of Chicago Press, 1948, pp. 545-554.

[21] See, for example, *Revolutionary Court* (in Arabic), Egyptian Press, Cairo, 1954, vol. 2.

[22] Reprinted in Hassan Khadr and Amin Hassouna, *Egypt's Republic in Its First Year*, Department of Public Relations of the Egyptian Armed Forces, Cairo, 1954, p. 69.

Any individual's loyalties are numerous—family, friends, nation, religious group, and so on. The higher civil servant has all of these, but his occupation and his sense of responsibility confront him with several more loyalties: to the public, the state, the particular administration in office, the civil service itself, his profession (law, medicine, engineering, economics, and so on), or the particular clientele his department is supposed to serve (for example, labor, farmers, villages, businessmen). In a civil service corps with a high degree of professionalism there is general understanding and agreement on the ranking of these loyalties; the official's education and training help him to develop the approved attitude toward these often competing loyalties. Even in a highly professionalized civil service, however, at least two possible competing loyalties remain: to the official's profession in the sense of his special skill, say medicine, or economics, or chemistry; and to his profession in the sense of the place where he applies his skill, that is, the public bureaucracy itself.

Professionalization and Public Service

How far has professionalization of administration gone in Egypt? What is the higher civil servant's conception of public service—to whom does he see himself obligated as a civil servant? The questionnaire provides some basis for answers to these questions.

It will be recalled from Chapter 3 (see also Appendix 4) that we have constructed a Professionalism Index of four items in the questionnaire: 27, 28c, and two parts of 35. The 78 respondents who answered three or all four in what we judged to be a "professional" or "Western" manner we graded as high on professionalism, and the remaining 171 as low. The value of this index, it was stressed, is not that it enables us to compare the degree of professionalism among Egyptian officials with that among officials of some Western government; it does not enable us to do this because there are no data of this kind for the West. What the index does permit is a comparison of the background of the high professionals with that of the low professionals. As we saw in Chapter 3, age, exposure, grade, social mobility, and job-satisfaction do not significantly affect the degree of professionalism among our 249 respondents.

Age. Among the officials 46 to 60 years old, 30 per cent are high on the Professionalism Index; among those 31 to 45, 33 per cent are high.

Exposure. Among those highly exposed to the West, 28 per cent are high professionals; among those not highly exposed, 34 per cent are high.

Grade. Respondents high in professionalism constitute 36 per cent of those in the second (or highest) grade and 28 per cent of those in the third and fourth grades.

Social mobility. The officials high on professionalism are 23 per cent of the upwardly mobile and 31 per cent of those whose occupational status is not higher than that of their fathers.

Job-satisfaction. The high professionals constitute 37 per cent of those high in job-satisfaction (as measured by the Job-Satisfaction Index described in Appendix 4) and 30 per cent of those low in this respect.

None of these differences is significant. There is only one important background characteristic, function, that significantly affects professionalism. Only 8 per cent of the officials in administrative jobs are high in professionalism, but 36 per cent of those in technical jobs are.

This absence of significant relationships between socio-economic background and professionalism is in great contrast to the strong relationships between background and degree of adherence to Western bureaucratic norms as measured by the Bureaucratic Scale. It would seem that bureaucratic orientation is a quality among the Egyptian higher civil servants that is more related to socio-economic background than is professional orientation. In general, socio-economic and job-experience traits such as age, social class, grade, and job-satisfaction appear to be more likely to differentiate a group with respect to some well-established and institutionalized pattern of behavior or opinion than with respect to patterns not so well-rooted in the culture. It may be concluded, therefore, that the failure of these traits to affect professionalism significantly is some indication of the relative weakness of this complex of attitudes and behavior among Egyptian civil servants. This is not surprising. Even in the West, where professionalization of many careers has been growing considerably in recent years, public administration is still one of the newer professions. Only twenty years ago, indeed,

Leonard D. White was able to say that the public gave no recognition to the career man in administration.[23] That these two decades have still left much to be desired in this respect in the United States is indicated in George A. Graham's insistence as recently as 1952 upon the need for a professional corps of high career administrators in the federal service, a point reiterated in 1955 in the report of a special study group under the second Hoover Commission on the organization of the executive branch of the federal government.[24]

Another index of the professionalization of an occupation is the extent to which universities give courses and degrees to prepare students for it. In the United States, for example, the federal government has done little to encourage universities to develop public administration courses as a means of providing trained civil servants, although it has offered various kinds of help to the universities for other purposes.[25] Yet the universities, on their own initiative, have established many courses in public administration, give advanced degrees in it, and have set up special institutes in this field.[26] In Europe, as we mentioned in Chapter 4, the universities themselves grew in response to the need of governments for trained officials. In Egypt, likewise, the universities have served as providers of civil servants; yet, even though they are state institutions, they have hardly touched the field of public administration. The field of administrative law is well developed in Egypt, but the field of government administration is not. The first course in what we know as

[23] Leonard D. White, *Government Career Service*, University of Chicago Press, 1935, pp. 85-86.

[24] Graham, *op.cit.*, see note 19 above, pp. 179-184; also *Personnel and Civil Service*. A Report to the Congress by the Commission on Organization of the Executive Branch of the Government, U.S. Government Printing Office, Washington, D.C., 1955, chapter III.

[25] See Richard G. Axt, *The Federal Government and Financing Higher Education*, published for the Commission on the Financing of Higher Education, Columbia University Press, New York, 1952, p. 11; and Richard Hofstadter, "The Development of Higher Education in America," Part One of *The Development and Scope of Higher Education in the United States* by Hofstadter and C. De Witt Hardy, published for the Commission on the Financing of Higher Education, Columbia University Press, New York, 1952, p. 133.

[26] See Roscoe C. Martin, "Political Science and Public Administration," in *American Political Science Review*, vol. 46, no. 3, September, 1952, p. 664.

public administration was given in Egypt only in 1954, at the American University at Cairo. In that year, too, the United Nations provided technical assistance in the creation of an Institute of Public Administration, which was opened in 1955, to train civil servants in various elementary procedures.

Further evidence of the weakness of professionalism among the Egyptian higher civil servants appears in their responses to several items in the questionnaire.

Item 35 asked the respondents to rate in order of importance the following five elements of job prestige: good salary and working conditions, skill required to do the work, opportunity to meet important people, opportunity to serve the state, opportunity to serve the public. It will be recalled from Chapter 5 that 38 per cent placed service to the state in first place and 31 per cent named good salary and working conditions as the most important, but only 19 per cent gave so high a rating to skill required to do the job and only 12 per cent to chance to serve the public. As Tables 27 and 28 in Chapter 5 show, the two determinants of job prestige most closely related to traditional professional values—skill and public service—are not rated as highly as those indicating a bureaucratic or a job orientation.

Not only are the respondents weak in orientation to these two aspects of professionalism, skill and public service, but they are correspondingly strong in the third aspect of professionalism (described in Chapter 3), self-protection of the corps. Several items in the questionnaire are relevant here.

Question 30 asks: "Do you think civil servants should have their own professional society, such as doctors, lawyers, and engineers have?" All were then asked: "Why do you think so?" Of the 249 who replied, 204, or 82 per cent, said they favored such an association. What is even more significant than this overwhelming proportion in favor of a professional association is the kind of reasons the respondents gave. Table 35 shows that most of them see an association primarily as a means of self-protection rather than as an expression of professional position, for 91 per cent of those advocating one say they do so because civil servants need an organization of their own to protect their economic interests. Only 4 per cent stress that an association's function might be related to raising the professional standing of government workers. This expression of need for self-protection

TABLE 35

Reasons for Favoring Professional Association

	Number	Per Cent
To protect interests	185	90.7
All workers should be in unions	10	4.9
To raise professional standing	9	4.4
Total	204	100.0

is undoubtedly influenced by the increase in public criticism of the civil service since 1952.

Another indication of the respondents' concern with self-protection emerges from their answers to question 44, which asks: "Do you think that the general public at present takes sufficient interest in the activities of the government?" Of 249 who replied, 233 or 94 per cent, said yes. This is a surprisingly large proportion when it is recalled that the 1947 census reported nearly 80 per cent of the population to be illiterate. It is difficult to resist the conclusion that these senior officials are not hospitable to greater public scrutiny of government. Question 45, following this lead, asks: "Do you think that the civil service would be improved if the general public took more interest in the activities of the government?" There were 179 replies, and every one said yes. Asked why they thought so, a clear majority, 58 per cent, said that greater public interest would make the government feel that it is being watched and that consequently it would improve. Thus, faced directly with a question as to whether government would be improved if public interest in it were greater, most of these senior officials assert that it would be, yet when asked, apart from this point, whether the public does take enough interest in government, they are virtually unanimous in saying yes.

It is in the light of these attitudes that we must interpret the fact that 70 per cent of the respondents report that they are in fact members of one professional association or another. It is probably an indication of the growth of professionalization that among the younger respondents a significantly higher proportion are members of such associations than among the older, as Table 36 shows.

That professionalism is rather a new type of loyalty among Egyptian civil servants is indicated in the answers given to the

TABLE 36

Membership in Professional Associations, by Age

		AGE 31-45 Per Cent	AGE 46-60 Per Cent
Members		76.8	63.7
Non-members		23.2	36.3
	Total	*100.0*	*100.0*
	(Cases)	(125)	(124)

Note: Significant at .05 level.

questions based on one of the imaginary situations. Question 28 tells of a government economist who is asked by his superiors to prepare a memorandum that he knows will contradict the views of professional economists. Ought he to yield to the bureaucratic superior or ought he to stand on his professional loyalty and refuse to prepare the memorandum? Of the 247 who replied, 129 said he should not prepare the memorandum. The reasons given by these 129 for their answer are interesting. They divided almost equally, 64 saying that the economist ought to follow his own notion of what is right, and 65 saying that he ought to refuse because he would otherwise have to contradict his professional colleagues in economics. One respondent, for example, stressed the priority of professional over bureaucratic identity; the economist should refuse to prepare the memorandum

"Because he is an economist before being a government official and his job doesn't justify ignoring his conscience." (No. 244, 52 years old, education administrator in grade 2.)

Another respondent presents an even more vivid picture of the distinct roles of professional economist and government worker. Asked what other economists would think if the civil servant prepared the memorandum, he says they would believe

"That he degraded his own personality as an economist and put on the dress of the government official who is interested in satisfying his superior." (No. 11, 43 years old, technical worker in grade 3.)

Further analysis shows that it is more the younger respondents and those educated in the West who adhere to the position that the economist ought to stick with his fellow economists and reject his bureaucratic superiors. Among the younger, 57 per

129

cent take this position, whereas among the older only 44 per cent do so. Among those who attended universities in Western countries, 64 per cent gave the more "professional" answer, whereas among those who went to Egyptian universities only 48 per cent did so. Because we are dealing with a relatively small number of respondents (only 129), these differences, while substantial, are not statistically significant. Yet it is suggestive that both differences point in the same direction: the group less inured to bureaucratic ways of the civil service and the group more exposed to the West, where professionalism is more highly developed, both show a greater tendency to argue from a more professional position.

Although their sense of professionalism seems to be less developed than that of their Western counterparts, the Egyptian higher civil servants are none the less sensitive to abuses in administration. As we saw in Chapter 4, there are many things they dislike about government employment. We saw in Table 21 that the second most numerous complaint, mentioned by 24 per cent of the respondents, was favoritism in personnel policy. This substantial proportion is especially significant because this response was offered spontaneously. Just how it compares with Western civil service corps is impossible to determine exactly because of the lack of comparable studies. There is, however, at least one piece of evidence to show that higher civil servants in the United States in 1947 did not complain of favoritism to this extent. In this study involving 730 government workers, only 17, or 2 per cent, voluntarily mentioned "politics" or favoritism in the federal service.[27]

What other evidence is there of this favoritism about which a quarter of the respondents complain? The same complaint abounds in the reports of the Civil Service Commission and in the evidence given in numerous trials of leading political figures of the period before 1952. The Commission in a recent report, charging that appointments are not made with sufficient regard for the requirements of the posts being filled, pointed out that in many departments "the number of those not qualified for their tasks has reached 40 or 45 per cent."[28] In his trial in 1953

[27] Frances T. Cahn, *Federal Employees in War and Peace*, Brookings Institution, Washington, D.C., 1949, pp. 237-238.

[28] Republic of Egypt, Civil Service Commission, *Report of the Com-*

Fuad Serag al Din, former Minister of Finance and a leader of the Wafd, Egypt's dominant political party until 1952, claimed: "Wafdist employees used to be dismissed in the days when the Wafd was out of power and they used to be transferred; so the [Wafdist] government was obliged to take care of them." He referred also to the practice followed by successful parties of not only reinstating their supporters but also giving them back "pay" for their time outside of government employment.[29]

Some of the items in the questionnaire bear upon these matters, but naturally reveal little supporting evidence. For example, question 40 asks: "If a young man wants to become a civil servant, what would be the best way for him to do so?" Under the circumstances of an interview, it is not surprising that most of the respondents, 94 per cent indeed, simply suggested a regular application or the acquisition of the proper education and training. Only 3 per cent suggested that an aspirant to a government job should get the support of an important person, and another 3 per cent mentioned that although this was the best way in the "old days," now it would be best to apply in the regular way. A clue to the overwhelming proportion's response is given in one civil servant's comment that

"The presumption is that he should present an application but the way things are actually done, he should seek someone to intercede for him." (No. 119, 52 years old, administrator in grade 2.)

Another respondent makes the same suggestion but in milder form:

"He should become qualified and seek mediation just to facilitate matters and not for special dispensations." (No. 230, 56 years old, education inspector in grade 3.)

A related question asked the respondents about their own experience in obtaining a government job. Question 12 asks simply: "How did you obtain your first civil service post?" An overwhelming majority of 89 per cent replied that they entered the service

mission on Budgetary Proposals for the Fiscal Year 1953-1954 (in Arabic), Government Press, Cairo, 1953, pp. 12-13.

[29] Verbatim testimony of Fuad Serag al Din, in _Al Ahram_ (Cairo), December 24, 1953, p. 8, col. 3. See also testimony of Makram Abayd before the Revolutionary Court on Dec. 31, 1953, in _Al Akhbar_ (Cairo), Jan. 1, 1954, p. 7.

131

through the regular procedure of application. The remaining 11 per cent stated plainly that their appointments were arranged or facilitated by some important person, or by a relative or friend. Here is still another situation in which we cannot judge exactly how Western civil servants would respond, but it seems reasonable to assume that, whatever the actual circumstances of their first appointments, not so high a proportion would flatly admit they entered through the mediation of sponsors, friends, or relatives. This means that our Egyptian respondents are either more willing to reveal such facts or that indeed more of them did obtain their first posts through some form of mediation. In view of the documentary evidence already presented and of the fact that examinations for government posts are a recent innovation in Egypt, the second conclusion appears to be the more warranted. None of the usual background traits, such as age, yields any significant differences among the respondents with respect to this question. Degree of professionalism, however, does significantly divide them. As Table 37 shows, 15 per cent

TABLE 37

How Respondents Obtained Their First Civil Service Posts, by Degree of Professionalism

	HIGH PROFESSIONALS	LOW PROFESSIONALS
	Per Cent	*Per Cent*
Regular procedure	96.2	85.4
Mediation	3.8	14.6
Total	*100.0*	*100.0*
(Cases)	(78)	(171)

Note: Significant at .02 level.

of those low in professionalism, as against only 4 per cent of those high in this respect, say they obtained their first government posts through the mediation of a sponsor, relative, or friend. This difference is not easy to interpret. It may mean that the more professionally oriented respondents were more qualified and hence did not need mediation to the same extent that others did; or it may reflect only their probably greater awareness that appointment through mediation is less "professional" than appointment as a result of a regular application.

In an effort to probe this experience, question 15 asks: "How did you first learn about the first civil service post that you obtained?" This time 36 per cent of the 249 respondents said through an important person or a relative or friend, and 64 per cent through some non-personal agency such as a newspaper announcement, the university, or the government itself. That so large a proportion should have learned through such personal means would not be surprising anywhere, for career guidance by friends and family is certainly frequent in Western societies too. There are, nevertheless, some revealing differences among the Egyptian senior officials on this point. First, as to age, this appears not to divide them significantly, but further inspection shows that age does play an important part in that it specifies the nature of other significant relationships.

One of these is exposure to the West. As Table 38 shows, of

TABLE 38

*How Respondents Learned about Their First Civil Service Jobs,
by Exposure to the West*

	HIGH EXPOSURE *Per Cent*	LOW EXPOSURE *Per Cent*
Through personal contacts	27.4	42.0
Through institutions	72.6	58.0
Total	*100.0*	*100.0*
(Cases)	(106)	(143)

Note: Significant at .02 level.

those highly exposed to Western norms, only 27 per cent learned through personal contacts, whereas 42 per cent of those not so much exposed to the West learned in this way. If we inquire further into this relationship to see if it holds among both younger and older respondents, we find that the significant difference appears only among those 31 to 45 and disappears among those 46 to 60. As may be seen in Table 39, the difference between high and low exposure is considerable in the 31-45 age-group. It is clear that the younger, less exposed group has the highest proportion, 48 per cent, who learned of their first government jobs through personal contacts. Exposure and age thus again work together; the more exposed and the older have the lower proportions learning through personal rather than more formal institutional contacts. (Incidentally, place of higher education has the same influence as the Exposure Scale; of those

TABLE 39

How Respondents Learned about Their First Civil Service Jobs,
by Exposure and Age

	AGE 31-45		AGE 46-60	
	HIGH EXPOSURE	LOW EXPOSURE	HIGH EXPOSURE	LOW EXPOSURE
	Per Cent		*Per Cent*	
Through personal contacts	27.1	48.1	27.6	34.8
Through institutions	72.9	51.9	72.4	65.2
Total	*100.0*	*100.0*	*100.0*	*100.0*
(Cases)	(48)	(77)	(58)	(66)

Note: Age 31-45 section is significant at .02 level; age 46-60 section is not statistically significant.

educated in the West, 80 per cent learned through the impersonal sources but this is true of only 63 per cent of those educated in Egypt; this difference is statistically significant.)

Degree of professionalism likewise divides the respondents into significantly different groups on this question. As Table 40

TABLE 40

How Respondents Learned about Their First Civil Jobs, by
Professionalism

	HIGH PROFESSIONALS	LOW PROFESSIONALS
	Per Cent	*Per Cent*
Through personal contacts	24.4	40.9
Through institutions	75.6	59.1
Total	*100.0*	*100.0*
(Cases)	(78)	(171)

Note: Significant at .02 level.

shows, among those high in professionalism only 24 per cent learned through personal contacts, whereas among those low in professionalism 41 per cent did so. Again age has the effect of specifying this relationship, this time among the older respondents. Table 41 shows that the difference between high and low professionalism is significant only in the older group. Here professionalism and age work together; the more professional and the older respondents have by far the lowest proportion, only 11 per cent, who learned about their first jobs through personal means.

TABLE 41

How Respondents Learned about Their First Civil Service Jobs, by Professionalism and Age

	AGE 31-45		AGE 46-60	
	HIGH PROFES- SIONALS	LOW PROFES- SIONALS	HIGH PROFES- SIONALS	LOW PROFES- SIONALS
	Per Cent		*Per Cent*	
Through personal contacts	36.6	41.7	10.8	40.2
Through institutions	63.4	58.3	89.2	59.8
Total	*100.0*	*100.0*	*100.0*	*100.0*
(Cases)	(41)	(84)	(37)	(87)

Note: Age 31-45 section is not statistically significant; age 46-60 section is significant at .01 level.

It thus appears that the questionnaire results do not unequivocally substantiate the documentary data as to favoritism and improper influence in appointments and promotions. Yet they do shed some light. We saw that when asked what they dislike about the government service, one quarter of the respondents voluntarily mentioned favoritism. We saw, also, that only 11 per cent reported that they themselves had obtained their first appointments through some form of personal mediation rather than through the regular procedure. When we turned to how the respondents learned of their first government jobs, we saw that 36 per cent mentioned a personal rather than an institutional source, and that these respondents tended to be more highly concentrated among younger ones less exposed to the West, among those educated in Egyptian universities, and among all those lower in professionalism and the younger ones even high in this respect.

Question 20 deals with the respondents' views about appointments to government posts. It asks: "As you know, the government, in employing people, considers their degree of education and experience. Do you think the government should consider other factors in making these appointments? For example—." The following "factors" were listed: social position, family connections, wealth, religion, and political belief.

Of the 249 who responded, 101, or 41 per cent, selected at least one of these five considerations, and 59 per cent rejected all of them, advocating only the criteria of education and experience. Some of these 101 respondents selected more than one of the five choices, so that a total of 150 choices was made, distributed as follows: social position, 59 per cent; wealth, 27 per cent; family connections, 7 per cent; religion, 5 per cent; political belief, 2 per cent.

Who are these 101 respondents who believe education and experience ought not to be the only qualifications for civil service employment? In age or in exposure to the West as measured by the Exposure Scale, they are no different from the other respondents. They do differ significantly in one respect: they are relatively more numerous among those educated in Egyptian universities rather than in the West. Table 42 shows

TABLE 42

Respondents' Opinion on Qualifications for Civil Service Posts, by Place of Higher Education

	EGYPT Per Cent	WEST Per Cent
Only education and experience	53.8	82.9
Other factors too	46.2	17.1
Total	100.0	100.0
(Cases)	(182)	(35)

Note: Significant at .01 level.

that among those educated in Western universities 83 per cent say there should be no criteria for government employment other than education and experience, while among those educated in Egyptian universities only 54 per cent take this position.

We have just seen how conflicting loyalties in the Egyptian higher civil service affect appointments to posts. Other aspects of government work are likewise affected by these loyalties that are none the less strong because they are extraneous to modern bureaucracy. Loyalty to family and friends is indeed still a powerful emotion in most of the world, where few others can compete with it successfully. And even where such loyalties to intimates have been supplemented by others of a broader and more abstract nature, as in the West, the primary-group loyalties remain very strong too. In the Near East the family, the village, and the religious community have much less competition for the fidelity of their members than do these associations in the West, where several of their functions have been assumed by other agencies such as the state, the schools, and commercial forms of recreation. The strength of the family in Egypt, for example, is exemplified in Towfiq el Hakim's novel, *Maze of Justice*, in which a village official tells the industrious government prosecutor:

"God bless the legal officer who was here before you. In a murder case he only required two witnesses, and nothing more. He would then close his report, turn to me and say: 'Well, the murdered man wasn't my father or brother. Come along, old man, let's go and have a drink.' "[30]

The Civil Service Commission has been aware of these conflicting loyalties among Egyptians. In a recent report the director refers to the shortcomings of the annual evaluation of government employees by their superiors, and observes: "It was found that that system . . . did not suit the requirements of the Egyptian environment." Consequently, several features of methods of evaluation in other countries were adopted but the resulting arrangement, "in its turn, did not suit our environment or our Egyptian society."[31] While the precise nature of the difficulties is not mentioned, it would seem that the requirements of secrecy, objectivity, and the exclusion of personal considerations were not congenial to the "environment."

Our questionnaire data throw some light on these conflicting loyalties regarding the relationship of the civil servants to the public and in personnel policy within the service.

Question 50 deals with the relationship of the government worker to the citizen: "Suppose that an ordinary citizen finds it necessary to go to a government official concerning legitimate official business. Which of the following ways would it be best for him to use in order to accomplish his purpose? (a) He should see a friend who knows the government official. (b) He should see a relative of his who is also a civil servant. (c) He should go directly to the official's office and state his problem." Following his selection of an answer, the respondent was asked why he chose as he did.

[30] See note 18, above, p. 32.

[31] Republic of Egypt, Civil Service Commission, *Annual Report of the Commission on Budgetary Proposals for the Fiscal Year 1955-1956* (in Arabic), Government Press, Cairo, 1955, p. 5.

Of the 249 who replied, 22 per cent selected (a) and (b) and 78 per cent chose (c). There were no significant differences among the respondents with respect to age, exposure, and so on. Again, we have little basis upon which to judge whether 22 per cent is a high or low proportion of civil servants who plainly recommend some form of mediation as the best way for an ordinary citizen to accomplish a legitimate purpose involving the government. That this figure somewhat underestimates the extent to which the respondents really believe in the advisability of mediation is indicated in their comments when asked why they made their selections. To this question, 11 per cent said that the direct method is best under the present regime; 18 per cent said that the direct approach would show the citizen knows his rights; and 71 per cent said merely that it is the "proper" way. Thus about nine tenths of the 193 who recommend the direct method do not say that it is an efficacious one, although this is what the question was asking. The respondents were asked for the "best" way, and they evaded this probing device by offering what they thought to be the "proper" way. Examples of this kind of reply appear in the following two reasons respondents gave for favoring the direct approach:

"Because this government official is there to do this job and there is no call for mediation." (No. 225, 50 years old, education administrator in grade 3.)

"To prevent mediation, which is the cause of corruption of character." (No. 218, 51-year-old woman, education supervisor in grade 2.)

One respondent, on the other hand, pointed out that mediation still gets results:

"Because the government machine doesn't carry out its duties as it should. Mediation is still the means for facilitating procedures." (No. 503, 36 years old, administrator in grade 3.)

A similar question, number 47, asks about favoritism in relations with the public: "Suppose a civil servant arrives at his office one morning and finds several persons waiting to see him. Among them is an acquaintance of his. Is it proper to keep this man waiting because others came before him?" Of the 247 who replied, 210, or 85 per cent, said it was proper to keep him waiting until his turn came. Most of the comments, like the two following ones, stressed the need for equality of treatment:

". . . order is supposed to be followed and people are supposed to be treated equally." (No. 408, 43 years old, agricultural technician in grade 4, Ph.D. in the United States.)

". . . he should treat all people on an equal basis, disregarding personal relations or position." (No. 436, 44 years old, agricultural technician in grade 3, A.M. in the United States.)

As to what the civil servant would actually do in such a situation, the replies are revealing. A further question asked: "What do you believe the average civil servant would actually do in such a case? Would he receive this man before the others?" Of 247 who replied this time 85 per cent said yes, that the average civil servant would take his acquaintance first and not make him wait his turn. Thus 85 per cent said it would be proper to keep him waiting and 85 per cent also predicted the average civil servant would *not* do the proper thing but that he would receive the acquaintance first. Let us go back a moment and consider the later replies of 210 respondents who said it was proper to keep the acquaintance waiting; of the 210, 177, or 84 per cent, predicted that the average civil servant would not keep his acquaintance waiting.

With respect to the first of these questions—the propriety of keeping the acquaintance waiting—there is only one statistically significant difference among the respondents, that is, between the 30 who went no farther than secondary school and the 217 who earned a university degree. Of the less educated group only 73 per cent said it was proper to keep the acquaintance waiting but of the more educated respondents 87 per cent took this position.

Some interesting relationships emerge, however, when we consider these two questions together, the respondents' opinion as to whether or not it is proper to keep the acquaintance waiting and their prediction as to what the average civil servant would actually do in such a situation.

Let us consider age first. There is no significant difference between younger and older respondents on the question of the propriety of keeping the acquaintance waiting. But as to what the average civil servant would actually do, the difference is statistically significant; among the younger officials 90 per cent say the civil servant would take his acquaintance first but only 80 per cent of the older ones make this unfavorable judgment. The older men, it appears, being higher in bureaucratic orientation and grade and in responsible posts, feel a greater commitment and loyalty to the service and hence are less willing to criticize it.

A comparable relationship appears in the answers to these questions when the respondents are divided according to place of higher education. On the question of propriety there is no significant difference between those educated in Egyptian universities and those in Western institutions. But on the prediction as to what the average government official would do, the difference is statistically significant. Of the group who took their college degrees in Egypt, 89 per cent say the official would take his acquaintance first but of the Western educated group only 68 per cent are so critical of the civil service.

Thus both the older and the Western educated respondents tend more to *expect* or predict proper behavior on the part of government officials. Not only do their notions of propriety in bureaucratic organizations seem to be affected by this combination of age and exposure to the West, but their *expectation* of official behavior is likewise closer to the Western model.

We may turn now to the questionnaire data that bear upon personnel policy within the civil service. One item deals with an imaginary situation, to be described below, in which a civil servant tries to avoid a transfer from Cairo to the provinces. This is a matter of considerable importance in Egypt, where few cities come even close to providing the physical conveniences and cultural amenities of life in Cairo or Alexandria. The pressure to obtain and hold a Cairo appointment is considerable, and the difficulty of finding trained, educated men and women to go out into the provinces is likewise overwhelming. Although life outside the two main cities has improved in recent years, it is still a problem to staff the outlying areas, especially in view of current attempts to decentralize administration. The pressure to live in Cairo or Alexandria, even if it means traveling a great distance twice daily to and from one's post, has led to the inclusion of a curious provision in the basic civil service law requiring an official to live in the area in which he works and forbidding him to live at a great distance, not precisely defined, except for urgent reasons and then only with the approval of the undersecretary of the ministry concerned.[32] Towfiq el Hakim has another relevant scene. A village legal officer remarks to a visiting colleague, "I think it's my turn to be posted to Cairo." The cynical visitor remarks, "Cairo postings don't come in turns, old man. Have you any influence?" The first officer answers, "None." The visitor then pronounces judgment: "Then you'll live and die in the provinces."[33]

One question, 52, is highly relevant to this colloquy. It describes an imaginary situation:

"A civil servant is officially informed that he is to be transferred from Cairo to a new post in the provinces. He has no objection to service in the provinces but he feels he must be near his aged parents, who cannot be moved away from Cairo, where they receive medical treatment. He therefore goes to the director general in the ministry, who is a close friend of his, and asks the director general to keep him in Cairo."

The situation was then slightly altered so that the civil servant and the director general are not friends but cousins. Following each situation the respondents were asked if the civil servant could expect the director general to grant him such a favor, and what they thought the director general would actually do. For the situation involving cousins, the respondents were also asked if the director general's relatives could expect him to grant this favor to the civil servant, and what these relatives would think of him if he did not keep his cousin in Cairo. This item was, of course, intended to test the strength of the respondents' loyalties to friends and family, also in the civil service, in the face of obligations to the government.

In analyzing the replies to these questions, we shall first consider the situation in which the director general and the civil servant are friends, then the one in which they are cousins, and finally we shall compare the two sets of replies.

To the question whether the civil servant could expect his friend the director general to keep him in Cairo, 73 per cent of the respondents said yes. This seems a high proportion, indicating a high degree of expectancy of such favors in the Egyptian civil service. The respondents divide significantly on this ques-

[32] Article 74 of *Law No. 210 of 1951* (in Arabic), as amended through 1954, Government Press, Cairo, 1954, p. 36.

[33] See note 18, above, pp. 117-118.

tion with respect to two background traits, grade and place of higher education, that is, one trait reflecting status in the hierarchy, the other exposure to Western influences.

As to grade, only 58 per cent in the second grade (the highest in our sample) said the civil servant could expect this favor, but 78 per cent of those in the third and fourth grades took this position. Those higher in the service thus show a significantly smaller proportion saying such a favor can be expected; having greater responsibilities and higher status, they apparently identify themselves more with the official image of the service and tend more to see it carried out in practice. A similar conclusion is suggested regarding those educated in the West compared with those who were graduated from Egyptian universities. Among the former, only 50 per cent said the civil servant could expect this favor, but among the latter 76 per cent did so.

The next question asked what the director general would actually do about the civil servant's request to remain in Cairo. To this question, 60 per cent of the respondents replied that the director would actually keep his friend in Cairo. It will be recalled that 73 per cent had said the civil servant could expect this favor; now we find only 60 per cent saying the favor would indeed be granted. This fact of a higher expectation than the prediction perhaps indicates changing values and growing awareness of responsibilities to position on the part of the higher civil servants; the subordinate, it is possible, expects more than he will get.

On this question, too, the only statistically significant differences among the respondents are those with respect to grade and place of higher education. As to grade, only 40 per cent of those in the second (or highest) grade felt that the director general would grant the favor but 66 per cent of those in the two lower grades took this position. As to place of higher education, only 35 per cent of those educated in the West believed the favor would be granted, as compared with 64 per cent of those educated in Egyptian universities. Thus again the respondents with higher status and those more exposed to Western patterns tend more to see the civil service as ignoring personal considerations in assignments; and again, as we saw in the replies to the question on keeping an acquaintance waiting until his turn came, these civil servants with higher status and greater exposure to the West not only *advocate* impartiality but also *expect* it and tend to see it prevailing in the practice of the Egyptian civil service.

Let us turn now to the altered situation, in which the civil servant and the director general are not merely friends but cousins. Do the respondents see this relationship as a stronger one? As a whole, they do not. Where the situation involved only friends, as we saw, 73 per cent said the civil servant could expect to be granted this favor, and in the present case, involving cousins, 75 per cent say so; this difference is negligible. As to what the director general would actually do about a cousin's request for such a favor, there is likewise no difference. Where only friends were involved, 60 per cent said the director general would grant the favor; in the case involving cousins, 59 per cent said the director would keep the civil servant in Cairo.

There are no significant differences among the respondents in their replies to the question whether the civil servant could in fact expect this favor. They do, however, divide significantly with respect to place of higher education on the question regarding what the director general would actually do; of the respondents who were graduated from Egyptian universities 61 per cent said he would grant the favor but only 38 per cent of those who attended Western universities took this position.

As in the first situation, there is a large difference between the proportion, 75 per cent, who said the civil servant could *expect* this favor and the proportion, 59 per cent, who said the director general would actually *grant* it.

One interesting difference emerges in the relative influence assigned to family connections as against the influence of loyalty to friends. We saw a moment ago that 73 per cent said the civil servant could expect the favor if the director general was his friend and 75 per cent if the director general was his cousin. A real difference appears, however, between the group educated in the West and the one educated in Egypt. Of the Western-educated group only 50 per cent said the friend could expect the favor but 65 per cent said the cousin could expect it. The Egyptian-educated group did not give more weight to the family connection; the corresponding proportions for this group are 76 per cent and 77 per cent.

To obtain a better idea of the influence of family ties in personnel affairs, we asked the respondents some questions about what the family of the civil servant and the director general might expect of the latter. They were first asked if the relatives could expect one cousin to grant the other the favor of helping him retain his Cairo post. Of 246 who replied, 81 per cent said yes. This is slightly higher than the 75 per cent who said the civil servant himself could expect the favor. Apparently a somewhat larger group of respondents believes the family is more likely to expect such favors than the civil servant himself, who after all is expected to be more aware of the difficulties involved in extending such special treatment. There is only one significant difference among the respondents in regard to this question, again in place of higher education. As in other phases of this question, the Western-educated group has a lower proportion, 65 per cent, than the Egypt-educated group, 84 per cent, who say that the favor can be expected, this time by the relatives. Many of the respondents who said the relatives could expect the director general to keep his cousin in Cairo pointed to the strength of family loyalties:

". . . the customs of the country favor relatives and friends." (No. 19, 43 years old, technician in grade 3.)

". . . the state of morality in Egypt as well as personal entreaties have much to do in these matters, contrary to the interest of the work." (No. 506, 48 years old, electrical engineer in grade 4.)

Even among those civil servants who replied that the relatives could not expect such a favor family loyalty was shown to be a powerful source of motivation. Thus one respondent who took this position added that the director general himself could take over the responsibility of caring for his cousin's parents, who after all are his own uncle and aunt. Here, paradoxically, the strength of family loyalty of one kind permits the ignoring of family loyalty of another kind:

". . . duty and the public interest make the transfer necessary. His keeping him in Cairo would be an act of nepotism, contrary to public interest. Moreover, the director general himself can take over his family obligations." (No. 32, 43 years old, technician in grade 3.)

A further question asked what the relatives would think if the director general did *not* keep his cousin in Cairo. Of 246 who replied, 56 per cent said the family would feel he is disloyal, 18 per cent that if the family was educated it would respect him for not giving special treatment to his cousin, 16 per cent that he is too strict in doing his job, and 10 per cent that he probably could not help it because he feared criticism. Consider for a moment the 18 per cent, 45 in number, who conceived the possibility that the family might respect the director general for *not* helping his cousin. It would be interesting to know how this group answered the question whether the relatives could expect the director general to do the favor for his cousin. Of the 44 who answered, only 59 per cent said the relatives could expect the favor to be granted. This proportion is significantly lower than the 81 per cent of all respondents who said the family could expect the favor.

The answers to the questions based upon this imaginary situation indicate the strength of family sentiment even among this group of higher civil servants and the apparently greater degree of such sentiment in the families from which they come, as reported by the respondents. Such powerful ties undoubtedly exert considerable pressure upon civil servants, as the answers analyzed above show, to put this older loyalty above the one to the government and the profession, a newer kind of loyalty now struggling to be born.

The Loyalty of Self-Protection

As the evolution of civil service systems in the West has shown, the creation of a profession of public administration, the transfer of loyalty from the individual ruler to the collective and changing government, from personal ties with groups outside the government to the obligation to serve the entire nation through serving the state, is a long process and an uneven one. As soon as a civil service corps begins to develop a professional aspect, however, the question of its proper function arises: will it go beyond administration to policy? This was the concern of a section of public opinion in England, for example, when the basic character of the civil service as now constituted was being formed. *The Economist* commented in 1855, during the public discussion, that the Northcote-Trevelyan plan "would amount to nothing short of an entire administrative revolution." That influential journal continued: "It would create a PROFESSION

145

—the members of which would be as exclusively entitled to practice the arts of government as are the members of the Royal College of Surgeons and Physicians to administer medicine. . . . It would hand over the whole Executive Government of the empire, except as regards its parliamentary functionaries, to a body of employees, trained in the same school, entering through the same gate, passing through the same ordeal, stamped with the same seal, imbued to a great extent with the same notions and traditions." In such a situation, *The Economist* feared, the career civil servants would be independent of the responsible ministers and all government business would have to be done through them.[34]

How much danger is there that public bureaucracies of a highly developed nature will trespass on the preserves of the policy-makers elected by the nation? This question used to be frequently debated in socialist circles; it was wondered whether a civil service accustomed to non-socialist procedures and goals would not "sabotage" truly socialist policy even if a socialist party should win an election. Recent history has in general shown that such fears are groundless. Clement Attlee, the Labor Prime Minister of England, recently pointed out that when he succeeded Winston Churchill as Prime Minister in 1945 he returned to the Potsdam conference "with precisely the same team of civil servants, including even the principal private secretary, as had served my predecessor." He observed also: "There were certainly some people in the Labor Party who doubted whether the civil servants would give fair play to a socialist government, but all doubts disappeared with experience."[35]

What of other countries? No one seriously charges the civil service of the United States with attempting to set policy through its administrative functions; indeed Bendix, who studied the background of a sample of higher civil servants in the United States, asserts that they vary so greatly that they lack the cohesion necessary to sabotage the policy of elected representatives of the nation.[36] The case of Germany under the Weimar

[34] *The Economist* (London), August 4, 1855, reprinted in August 6, 1955, Vol. 176, No. 5841, p. 456.

[35] C. R. Attlee, "Civil Servants, Ministers, Parliament and the Public," *The Political Quarterly*, Vol. 25, No. 4, Oct.-Dec., 1954, p. 308.

[36] Reinhard Bendix, *Higher Civil Servants in American Society*, Uni-

Republic is probably somewhat different. Bureaucratic sabotage seems to have been more successful in this period of German history than in the Third Reich, where according to a recent analysis the careerists in the foreign office opposed but did not resist Hitler's diplomacy; they clung to office and the semblance of power long after they had lost its essence. This observer concludes: "The bureaucratic instinct to survive proved far more potent than the bureaucratic impulse to shape policy according to its own desires."[37]

Do Egyptian higher civil servants form the kind of cohesive, homogeneous group that can, if it wants, "sabotage" the policy of the power-holders? In Chapter 3 we reviewed the socio-economic origin of the 242 higher civil servants for whom we had this information. We saw in Table 7 that nearly 40 per cent were the sons of civil servants, about 25 per cent the sons of landlords, and 16 per cent the sons of peasants; these three social classes account for about four fifths of all the senior officials in our sample. The largest group and probably the most homogeneous internally are the sons of civil servants. To obtain some notion of how similar they are to one another in other respects, we have compared them as a group with all other civil servants in our sample. They prove to be significantly different from the others in only two respects, exposure to the West and professionalism.

Being the sons of literate, educated urban dwellers, they are considerably more exposed to Western influences; 54 per cent of them are highly exposed, as compared with only 34 per cent of the other civil servants. With respect to age they differ somewhat but not quite significantly; 57 per cent of these sons of civil servants are in the younger age-bracket, 31 to 45, whereas only 47 per cent of the others in the sample fall into this age-bracket. As to professionalism, the sons of civil servants not unexpectedly have 40 per cent who are high on the Professionalism Index, compared with only 25 per cent for the other senior officials; this is a statistically significant difference. In

---

versity of Colorado Studies, Series in Sociology, No. 2, University of Colorado Press, Boulder, 1949, pp. 89-90.

[37] Paul Seabury, *The Wilhelmstrasse. A Study of German Diplomats under the Nazi Regime*, University of California Press, Berkeley and Los Angeles, 1954, pp. 162-163, 168-169.

other respects, however, such as bureaucratic orientation, degree of job-satisfaction, and religion, the sons of civil servants do not differ much from their colleagues.

From the answers to the items in the questionnaire and from the comments offered voluntarily, the impression is gained that Egyptian higher civil servants, except for a small number of extremists in domestic politics, are not a cohesive group that could exercise a united influence upon policy through their administrative functions. Their status in Egyptian society, moreover, does not give them the power to act in this way. The typical Western problem concerning the public bureaucracy seems to be to make it responsive to changes in government and even in economic systems. This preoccupation with reducing the political role of the civil service is not yet characteristic of Egyptian, or Near Eastern, government. The trouble in the past has been, indeed, that the civil service in Egypt was too pliable in the hands of the political party in power or of the throne.

The biggest problem of Egyptian and Near Eastern public bureaucracy is its diligence in self-protection. In this sense, as we have already seen, it is professionally advanced. We saw earlier in this chapter that the civil servants high in professionalism in general, not merely in the self-protection aspect, are so heterogeneous and inchoate a group that they do not differ materially from their colleagues in socio-economic background or in relation to certain job factors.

This concern with self-protection does not make the public bureaucracy of Egypt unique. Indeed, some observers insist that this aspect of professionalism is developing so rapidly in the West too that it has virtually destroyed the concept of public service. Narrow specialization has been accompanied by narrow self-interest.[38]

✗ Summary and Conclusions

We have seen, in this chapter, that honesty and efficiency in public administration assume the character of a moral issue in the West but are more a matter of varying loyalties, old and

[38] For example, Roy Lewis and Angus Maude, *Professional People*, Phoenix House, Ltd., London, 1952, pp. 8-9; and Sir A. M. Carr-Saunders, "Metropolitan Conditions and Traditional Professional Relationships," in

new, in the Near East and Egypt. Historically, there have been ways other than those prevailing in the West today to insure high standards of performance by civil servants. These methods include sponsorship, nepotism, and personal loyalty, all of which were in harmony with the values of societies in which they were used, but which would be considered improper in the contemporary West. The special problem facing the Arab countries and Egypt is the penetration of Western notions of honesty and efficiency in government at a time when personal, familial, and communal loyalties still persist in the population being governed and from which the administrators are drawn.

The clash of the two broad systems in Egypt was dramatic when the British occupied the country in 1882. Egypt had been ruled for centuries as an outpost of the Ottoman Empire, which combined indifference, brutality, and corruption with exploitation in administration. The main concern of the British was to improve administration and to eliminate corruption and favoritism. They did something by their personal example of honesty and efficiency but, as foreigners, their rule inevitably, and perhaps even against their will, encouraged sycophancy and distrust in both the civil service and the society.

Our questionnaire was intended to throw light on professionalism in the Egyptian higher civil service, and on the background of the frequent charges of corruption and favoritism made in reports of the Civil Service Commission and in the records of trials of political leaders under the monarchy before 1952. Professionalism, it was found, is not highly developed in the sense of public service or emphasis upon skill and competence but is considerably developed in the form of self-protection and self-interest. To meet these problems, Egypt in 1951 established a Civil Service Commission and codified the regulations governing civil service personnel (see Chapter 2).

The higher civil servants of Egypt do not appear to be homogeneous enough in socio-economic background, cohesive enough in social outlook, or strong enough as a body to control policy through their administrative functions. Their main cohesive quality is directed to self-protection. Far from trying to direct

Robert Moore Fisher, ed., *The Metropolis in Modern Life*, Columbia University Press, New York, 1955, p. 287.

policy, they are too subservient to take adequate initiative even in their proper sphere of administration, as the next chapter will show. Unlike the West, which is concerned with making the civil service responsive to changes in government and to new economic and social arrangements, the problem in Egypt is to make the civil service less pliable in the hands of those in power. To reach a reasonable level of efficiency and independence of politics that would make it the stable instrument of all kinds of government, the Egyptian public bureaucracy must move toward professionalization in a manner advocated by the Civil Service Commission; but before it can become such an instrument, there will have to be an expansion of economic opportunity for the educated population and a greater public role in political life for them. In other words, a Western type of civil service, such as Egypt is apparently aiming at, needs an institutional setting more like that of the West.

Chapter 7. Initiative and Subservience: The Range of Bureaucratic Behavior

In any group of persons among whom leaders are distinguished from followers and superiors from subordinates, the proper balance between initiative and obedience becomes a cardinal issue. In an army, to what extent should soldiers be encouraged to use their own discretion? Does their training in obedience weaken their capacity for personal initiative when they confront a problem not anticipated in all its complexity by the formal regulations? In a factory, should management welcome in the worker or minor supervisor a habit of thinking about the larger aspects of production, or should it require only the efficient performance of narrow tasks assigned from above? If initiative is to be encouraged, can it be kept within the bounds set for it? Finally, can initiative be cultivated by order, i.e., can subordinates be required to exercise initiative as they can be ordered to be obedient?

A public bureaucracy faces this broad problem, and still another involving not so much the relations between its senior and junior members but those of all of them together vis-à-vis the legislature and the public they are supposed to serve. As Bendix summarizes this dilemma: "Too great a compliance with statutory rules is popularly denounced as bureaucratic. Too great a reliance on initiative, in order to realize the spirit, if not the letter, of the law, is popularly denounced as an abuse of power, as interfering with legislative prerogative. Yet government administration cannot do without either compliance or initiative."[1]

In the previous chapter on professionalism, we have discussed the broader question of the responsibility of the civil service to the policy makers and the public. In the present chapter we shall consider the narrower one of the exercise of personal initiative by the Egyptian official within the compass permitted by the

[1] Reinhard Bendix, *Higher Civil Servants in American Society*, University of Colorado Studies, Series in Sociology, No. 2, University of Colorado Press, Boulder, 1949, p. 12.

regulations that govern his conduct. These two issues join at various points but for analytical purposes, at least, they may be treated separately.

Any discussion of the civil service in Egypt, indeed in the Near East generally, is almost certain to mention the unwillingness of high officials to delegate responsibility and the fear of subordinates to accept it. This writer's own experience has confirmed these accounts. One sees little initiative exercised on any level of the hierarchy. Responsibility is shifted whenever possible. An official tends to follow his superior slavishly, with virtually no range of personal choice even within a broad compass of agreement. More so than in the West, it appears, one can tell what sentiment is on top by testing it below; each official registers perfectly the attitude he sees above him. A common experience of this writer in his frequent meetings with civil servants on many levels is exemplified in the following series of events. The minister of a particular agency had approved a request and had instructed his personnel chief to supply certain information. The latter official first checked with another agency with which he was in liaison for its approval. Before actually giving the information, he checked further with still another agency which was involved only to the extent that the information was to be processed by some of its technicians. At two subsequent stages he checked again with his own minister, who had in the first place already approved all the steps, from first to last.

Incidents like this one are common in all bureaucracies; but precisely how common are they in any of them? There is practically nothing upon which to base a scientific answer to this question; there are only the impressions recorded by observers of several civil service systems. In this study we are trying to go beyond this type of evidence, which is not very reliable for comparative purposes. Red tape, after all, entwines all large organizations, and everyone probably has his favorite illustrative story. No civil service system escapes the charge of red tape in its own country. Unless we can validly distinguish important differences of degree, the characterization of a particular public bureaucracy as subservient, for example, can evoke evidence of a similar kind in others as well. Our questionnaire was intended to yield reliable quantitative data on just this subject. Our findings at present permit only rough comparisons, using these quantitative features, between the Egyptian civil service and what are widely accepted as the traits of Western public bureaucracies. More reliable and precise comparisons will become possible as such methods, improved and adjusted, are extended to other civil service corps.

Bureaucratic Orientations

It will be recalled that we have constructed a Bureaucratic Scale measuring the degree to which a respondent displays Western bureaucratic behavior (see Appendix 4 for details). This scale, constructed from items 23, 36d and 36f of the questionnaire, yielded four positions: no Western answers, one Western answer, two Western answers, and three Western answers. The 96 respondents who answered all three questions in the Western manner were placed high on the Bureaucratic Scale, and the remaining 153 respondents low. The value of this scale, as was pointed out, is not that it permits us to compare the proportion of Egyptian civil servants high on bureaucracy with the proportion in the public bureaucracies of other countries; for there are no comparable data. We do, however, infer that the average Western civil servant would score higher on the same scale than does the average Egyptian official. The real value of the Bureaucratic Scale, like that of the Professionalism Index used in the previous chapter, is that it enables us to compare the Egyptian civil servants high on the scale with those who are low. Are the more highly bureaucratic respondents older or younger, more educated or less, in administrative or technical posts? This is the kind of information our questionnaire results can supply.

The analysis of professionalism has just revealed that the usually important socio-economic characteristics and life-experiences do not significantly affect the degree to which this quality is present or absent among our respondents. Yet these traits and experiences do significantly affect bureaucratic tendencies.

Age and exposure. The degree to which respondents have been exposed to Western attitudes and behavior is indicated by a combination of their age and score on the Exposure Scale (see Chapter 3 and Appendix 4). There it was pointed out that age is significantly related both to the exposure and bureaucracy scales but that the two scales are not related significantly to each other. The reason is that, as shown in Tables A-6 and A-7 in Appendix 4, the oldest respondents, aged 51 to 60, are by far the lowest on the Exposure Scale and the highest on the Bureaucratic Scale. This position of the oldest group tends to weaken the relationship of exposure to bureaucratic orientation. But if we consider age and Exposure Scale score together as the more valid measure of degree of contact with Western patterns, then it is clear that the more exposed (that is, the older) are more highly bureaucratic in the Western sense: they are more willing to support the exercise of individual initiative. Table A-5 in Appendix 4 shows this plainly: among the younger respondents, aged 31 to 45, only 24 per cent are high on the Bureaucratic Scale, whereas among the older ones, 46 to 60, 53 per cent are high in Western bureaucratic tendency.

Grade. Since it is so closely related to age, grade has the same influence. Among those in the highest grade, the second, 49 per cent are high on the Bureaucratic Scale but only 35 per cent of those in grades 3 and 4 are high.

Function. On professionalism, function was the only important factor that significantly distinguished the highs from the lows. On the Bureaucratic Scale, interestingly, function has little effect. Among those in administrative posts 47 per cent are high, compared with only 37 per cent among those in technical posts. Although this is the expected direction of difference (that is, administrative officials have a higher proportion high on the Bureaucratic Scale than do technical workers) the extent of the difference is not statistically significant.

Social mobility. It will be recalled that we have distinguished between those respondents who, as civil servants, enjoy higher occupational prestige than their fathers, and those who do not. Among the upwardly mobile respondents 47 per cent are high on the Bureaucratic Scale, as compared with only 35 per cent among those not upwardly mobile. This difference is considerable but just misses statistical significance.

Job-satisfaction. As measured by the index described in Appendix 4, job-satisfaction does not significantly affect degree of Western bureaucratic orientation. Among those high on the Job-Satisfaction Index, 47 per cent are also high on the Bureaucratic Scale, as compared with only 36 per cent among those low

154

on the Job-Satisfaction Index. When, however, we consider the influence of job-satisfaction separately for younger and older respondents, a significant difference does emerge, as Table 43

TABLE 43

Bureaucratic Scale by Job-Satisfaction Index and Age

	AGE 31-45		AGE 46-60	
	HIGH SATIS- FACTION	LOW SATIS- FACTION	HIGH SATIS- FACTION	LOW SATIS- FACTION
	Per Cent		*Per Cent*	
High bureaucracy	40.9	20.4	51.7	53.7
Low bureaucracy	59.1	79.6	48.3	46.3
Total	*100.0*	*100.0*	*100.0*	*100.0*
(Cases)	(22)	(103)	(29)	(95)

Note: Age 31-45 section significant at .05 level; age 46-60 section not significant.

shows. Among the older respondents, job-satisfaction has no effect. Among the younger respondents, however, those with high job-satisfaction are significantly higher on the Bureaucratic Scale than others are; of those with high job-satisfaction 41 per cent are high in bureaucratic orientation, while among those low in job-satisfaction only 20 per cent are high in bureaucratic orientation. High job-satisfaction thus makes for high bureaucratic orientation among the younger respondents but has no effect among the older, who, as we already know and as Table 43 shows again, are already high on the Bureaucratic Scale.

High bureaucratic orientation, in summary, is more characteristic of the older respondents, those in the highest grade, those who are upwardly mobile in terms of occupational status, and those with higher job-satisfaction. Thus, exposure to Western patterns as measured by age and the Exposure Scale taken together, and greater commitment to the bureaucracy as indicated by higher grade and satisfaction on the job and social mobility, are what make for a high degree of Western bureaucratic qualities among the Egyptian higher civil servants.

The fact that these characteristics enable us to differentiate significantly between the respondents high on the Bureaucratic Scale and those low on it is evidence that bureaucratic orientation (or its absence) is a relatively well-developed pattern of

155

attitudes and behavior in Egypt. This is not the case, as we saw in the previous chapter, with regard to professionalism, on which the highs and lows are not significantly divided by these socio-economic characteristics and experiences on the job. Such a finding accords with historical sequence, for loyalty to the bureaucratic hierarchy in government has developed earlier than loyalty to a profession that is not confined to the public bureaucracy. It is only within recent decades that public administration itself has been moving toward the status of a profession.

Turning to the specific items in the questionnaire, we may begin with one whose replies indicate that the Egyptian higher civil servant is fully aware of the broad problem of initiative with which we are concerned in this chapter. Question 29 asks: "Here are several descriptions of civil servants. Who among them do you think is the best civil servant? (a) one who follows the regulations literally, (b) one who uses his own initiative in interpreting the regulations, (c) one who uses his own initiative without seriously violating the regulations."

Of 248 who replied, only 3 (1.2 per cent) selected the first type, the one who uses no personal initiative at all. Virtually all the respondents preferred some degree of initiative: 78, or 32 per cent, selected the second type, the one who uses some initiative, and a large majority, 167, or 67 per cent, selected the third type, which uses the highest degree of personal initiative. In this direct question, the respondents thus reveal their almost unanimous preference for the type of civil servant who uses his own initiative, and a considerable majority even prefers the one who uses a large measure of his own initiative. Their responses to other less direct questions do not, however, reveal such a widespread preference for the application of personal discretion.

Question 36 asks the respondent to consider the following imaginary situation: "A civil servant is assigned to factory inspection; his duty is to insure that factories conform to safety laws. In one factory he sees a floor that looks as if it might give way under the weight of a machine. According to the usual procedure, he telephones his superior but finds that he is away on official business and will not return that day. The inspector examines the floor again and is not certain that it will hold up for more than a few hours. He tells the factory owner of his fear. But the owner tells him that there is no ground for such fear, since the chief inspector had approved the factory only two weeks ago in the same condition. The owner shows him the certificate of approval, but the inspector is still doubtful and, taking the initiative, he orders the factory to be closed."

The following three questions are asked about this imaginary situation: "(a) Do you think that the civil servant acted properly in closing the factory? (b) Do you think the civil servant's superior will discipline him for taking such a step? (c) Do you think the civil servant's superior *should* discipline him for taking such a step?"

In this situation the result of the inspector's decision to close the factory is not given. In order to see how the respondents would be influenced by the knowledge of the consequences of the inspector's decision, we varied the basic situation in two ways, following each of which the same three questions were asked. In the first variation the inspector's judgment turned out to be wrong: "Now let us suppose, in the same situation, that the next day further inspection shows there was really no ground for fear. In fact, the factory owner is not required to make any repairs."

In the second variation the inspector's judgment turned out to be right: "Now, finally, in the same situation, let us suppose that a few hours after the factory has been closed on the inspector's order, the floor actually gives way, but no one is hurt because everyone had gone home."

The object of this series of situations and questions was to determine to what extent the respondents would defend the propriety of the civil servant's use of his own initiative, and to see whether their defense would be stronger when his judgment turned out to be right than when it turned out to be wrong. Before we compare the responses to the three phases of this situation, let us take each phase separately.

In the first situation, in which the outcome of the inspector's action was not specified, almost all the respondents, 90 per cent, said he acted properly in closing the factory; 26 per cent said he would be disciplined by his superior; and only 8 per cent said he *should* be disciplined. Thus there is little difference between the proportion, 90 per cent, who say the inspector acted properly and the proportion, 92 per cent, who say he ought not to be disciplined.

There is an interesting relationship in these figures. Only 24 respondents say the inspector did *not* act properly in closing the factory, but 62 say that he will be disciplined. How did these 62 respond to the first of the three questions? Forty-eight of them, the large majority, said that the inspector had acted properly. Thus 48 respondents, a fifth of the 239 who answered both the questions involved, defend the civil servant's exercise of personal initiative but assert that he will nevertheless be disciplined by his superior. This appears to be a large proportion of senior officials who lack confidence in the upper levels of the hierarchy and who clearly do not believe that the atmosphere of the civil service is congenial to the exercise of personal initiative.

In the second situation, it will be recalled, the inspector's judgment turned out to be wrong. Now only 74 per cent of the respondents say he acted properly in closing the factory (compared with 90 per cent when the outcome of his action was not specified); 47 per cent say he will be disciplined by his superior (compared with only 26 per cent in the first situation); and 22 per cent say he *should* be disciplined (as against only 8 per cent in the earlier phase). Again there is little difference between the proportion, 74 per cent, who say the inspector acted properly in closing the factory and the proportion, 78 per cent, who say he ought not to be disciplined. And again there is a big difference between the number of respondents, only 65, who say he did not act properly and the number, 115, who say he will be disciplined. Consider these 115; how do they answer the question as to whether or not the civil servant acted properly? Seventy-seven, about two thirds, say he acted properly. Thus 77 respondents, about a third of the 243 who answered both the questions involved, defend the civil servant's exercise of personal initiative but assert that it will only bring down disciplinary action upon him. Where the inspector's judgment was not indicated to be accurate or inaccurate, the proportion of respondents displaying this implied belief that the bureaucratic climate of the civil service does not encourage initiative was about one fifth. When the situation is altered to indicate that his judgment is wrong, this proportion rises to a third, implying that the respondents believe that personal initiative is more likely to be penalized in the Egyptian civil service if based upon an error of judgment.

Let us turn to the last of the three situations, in which the inspector's judgment is revealed to be correct. Now the proportion who think he acted properly in closing the factory rises again, to 88 per cent (virtually the same as in the first situation, where the outcome of the inspector's action was not specified); only 19 per cent now say he will be disciplined by his superior (a lower proportion than in the two previous phases); and only 4 per cent say he *should* be disciplined (again lower than in the other two situations). This time only 17 respondents say the supervisor will discipline the inspector, and of them 10 say the latter had acted properly in closing the factory. Thus only 10 respondents of the 244 who answered both the questions involved, or 4 per cent, now say that the inspector's proper use of personal initiative will bring on disciplinary action.

The following changes appear in the proportion of respondents who defend the civil servant's use of his own initiative but predict that it will only involve him in disciplinary action anyway. In the first situation, where the accuracy of his judgment was not specified, 20 per cent of the respondents implied in this way that the exercise of personal initiative is discouraged. In the second situation, where the inspector's judgment turns out to be incorrect, this proportion rises to 32 per cent. In the third situation, where his judgment is indicated to be accurate, this proportion falls again to only 4 per cent. Thus in the opinion of our respondents the toleration of personal initiative in the Egyptian civil service seems to depend a great deal upon how the situation turns out; the exercise of personal initiative is not so much defended on its own ground irrespective of its outcome. There are of course many Egyptian government officials who hold the other view; their position is exemplified in the comment of one respondent who, in replying to questions about the third situation, said the inspector ought not to be disciplined and gave the following reason:

"Regardless of the fact that this official's fears were realized and that his assessment was correct, he has performed his duty." (No. 404, 37 years old, agricultural technician, Ph.D. in the United States.)

The foregoing data have presented the views the respondents expressed or implied about other civil servants. This is a frequent questionnaire technique used to elicit opinions held by the respondents themselves. But we have more direct evidence that our respondents' own support of personal initiative is likewise dependent upon the result rather than the principle of its exercise. Consider the reasons given in each of the situations by those who seemed to defend the exercise of personal initiative, that is, by the respondents who say that the superior ought *not* to discipline the inspector. In the first situation (outcome unspecified), of the 243 who say the inspector ought to be disciplined for taking the initiative, 46 per cent give as their reason for adopting this position that the inspector did the right thing in closing the factory, 33 per cent say he did what he thought best, 20 per cent say he did his duty (the remaining 1 per cent—2 persons— say he should merely be warned). Thus 53 per cent take a stand in defense of the civil servant's right and duty to do as he sees fit within his authority; as for the 46 per cent who say he did the right thing, it is not clear whether they mean that the right thing was closing the factory or taking the initiative. Their probable meaning, however, becomes clearer in the next two situations. In the second situation (inspector's judgment turns out wrong) most of the 193 who say the inspector ought not to be disciplined have a clearer idea of the issue involved. That they oppose disciplining him even though his judgment was wrong is in itself an indication of greater awareness of the principle at work in this situation. This is revealed by the fact that of these 193 respondents 83 per cent give as their reason their belief that the inspector did what he thought best or did his duty. When we come to the last situation (inspector's judgment turns out to be right) it appears that the respondents lose sight of the principle of the exercise of initiative on its own grounds. For the 236 who now say the inspector ought not to be disciplined, only 25 per cent, a lower proportion than even in the first situation, give as their reason their belief that he did what he thought best or did his duty; 140 respondents, or 59 per cent, a sizable majority, give as their reason for believing he ought not to be disciplined the fact that his judgment turned out to be right. Thus the fidelity of the respondents as a group to the principle of the exercise of personal initiative on its own ground was not strong enough to maintain consistency through the three phases of this imaginary situation; and such clarity of viewpoint as emerged in the second phase was considerably dissipated in the third, where a majority of the respondents who thought the civil servant ought not to be disciplined for taking the initiative had in mind less his right or duty to act on his own than the fact that on this particular occasion his judgment turned out to be correct.

These findings confirm the impression of many observers that the Egyptian civil servant has been conditioned to "play it safe" by avoiding responsibility wherever possible, rather than to act independently within his authority. By summarizing the responses to the same question in each of the three situations we have been discussing, we can get further light on this tendency.

We may begin with the question as to whether or not the inspector acted properly in closing the factory. In the first situation (outcome unspecified), 90 per cent say he acted properly. In the second situation (judgment turns out to be wrong), the proportion willing to defend the inspector falls to 74 per cent. In the third situation (judgment turns out to be right) the proportion approving his action rises again to 88 per cent. Let us look at these data in a different way. In the first situation 221 respondents said the inspector acted properly. Of these 221, 44 changed opinions in the second situation, where the inspector is said to have exaggerated the danger, leaving only 177 who approved of his closing down the factory. The number who approved his conduct in the third situation rose to 197. Finally, consider the 63 respondents who, when the inspector's judgment turned out to be wrong, disapproved of his action in closing the factory; 40 of these 63 switched sides by approving his action when his judgment turned out to be right.

A comparison of these respondents who change sides so readily with all the others as to score on the Bureaucratic Scale is revealing. Consider the 40 respondents just mentioned, who disapprove of the inspector's action when his judgment is wrong but approve of it when his judgment is right, thus playing it safe and ignoring the principle of the exercise of personal initiative on its own ground. Their average (mean) score on the Bureaucratic Scale is only 0.68, compared with an average of 2.26 for the other 209 respondents. This difference (significant at the .01 level) indicates that these 40 "changers" have appreciably less Western bureaucratic tendencies than the other respondents. It is interesting, too, that there is no significant difference in degree of professionalism; the mean score of the 40 respondents on the Professionalism Index is 2.15, while the mean score of the other respondents is 1.81.

A similar comparison leads to a similar result. There are 44 respondents who say that the inspector should be disciplined when his judgment turns out to be wrong but that he should not be disciplined when his judgment is vindicated, thus ignoring the issue of personal initiative and "playing it safe." These 44 respondents have a mean Bureaucratic Scale score of only 1.52, compared with the 2.25 for the other 205 respondents. Hence this group is likewise far from the Western bureaucratic pattern that envisages, at least in formal terms, a relatively wide degree of personal initiative. Here again there is no significant difference in degree of professionalism; the mean Professionalism Index score of the 44 respondents is 2.36, while that of the other respondents is 2.04.[2]

Many of the findings based upon this imaginary situation of the inspector show that our respondents, by their replies, imply that the Egyptian civil service has not encouraged or rewarded the exercise of personal initiative. They show, furthermore, that a large proportion of the respondents themselves do not consistently or with full understanding defend the exercise of initiative, but seek to play it safe bureaucratically.

Another imaginary situation affecting personal initiative is the one (referred to earlier) involving the economist in the civil service. Question 28 asks the respondent to imagine the following situation: "A department head in the civil service asks one of his staff members, an economist, to prepare a memorandum in support of a certain policy that has been followed for some time. In studying the matter, the economist finds that he can defend this policy only if he presents arguments that differ with what is generally accepted among most economists in and outside of the government."

The purpose of this item was to learn how the respondents react to a conflict between a civil servant's responsibility to his

---

2 In both of these cases in which these averages are compared, one of the items of the questionnaire used in computing the average is also one of the items in the Bureaucratic Scale. This fact somewhat increases the likelihood that these groups of 40 and 44 respondents will have a lower scale score than the entire sample, but the comparison is nevertheless indicative because several other items entirely independent of one another are involved.

superiors in the bureaucracy and to his professional colleagues outside of it.

Asked whether the economist ought to prepare the memorandum or whether he should refuse to so so under these circumstances, a slight majority, 52 per cent, say he ought not to do so, and they give two reasons: the civil servant should not contradict his professional colleagues in economics, and he should not do something that violates his own opinions. Yet when asked whether or not the department head could expect the economist to prepare a memorandum under such circumstances, a very large majority, 79 per cent, agreed that he could. This discrepancy suggests that among the higher civil servants there is a greater desire to exercise personal initiative than is acceptable or customary in the Egyptian public bureaucracy. The administrative climate is again revealed to be hostile to the development of individual initiative even within the framework of normal bureaucratic loyalties.

This general subject is touched upon in another imaginary situation, described in question 46 as follows: "A civil servant is employed in a post in which it is his duty to devise ways to improve sanitation and cooperation in rural villages. After much study in the field, he prepares a memorandum presenting a full program toward this end. His superiors reject it. Instead, they adopt a program which, in his opinion, would not be in the interest of the villagers whose conditions he has studied in detail. His superiors, nevertheless, ask him to carry out this policy in the field."

The purpose of this item was to get the respondents' reaction to a conflict between a civil servant's loyalty to his superiors in the bureaucracy and his conception of his duty to that section of the public whose interests he is supposed to serve.

Asked whether his superiors can expect the civil servant to carry out their program despite his belief that it would not serve the villagers, 74 per cent of the respondents say they can. This proportion is about the same as the 79 per cent, in the case of the economist (in which the conflict was between loyalty to bureaucracy and professional group), who likewise say the civil servant can be expected to comply with his departmental superior's request. As in the case of the economist, although not to the same extent, here too there is a sizable discrepancy between the proportion who say the civil servant can be expected to carry out orders and the proportion who agree that he ought to, for 61 per cent take the latter position. This discrepancy thus points in the same direction: that our respondents seem to favor a degree of personal initiative that is neither customary nor expected in the Egyptian civil service. This viewpoint, however, does not exclude expression of the official's own opinion, as is indicated in the following comment of one respondent who said the civil servant in the story should carry out the policy set by his superiors:

"As a government official he is charged with carrying out the policy laid down by his superiors. He has performed his duty and has expressed his viewpoint, so he isn't responsible after that for not executing his own view, because he is only a government employee." (No. 413, 38 years old, technician in grade 4.)

The Background of Subservience

When Lord Cromer came to reflect upon his long experience in Egypt, he wrote that the Egyptian official shirks responsibility, fears blame, and so shrinks from the British administrative system, which allows a considerable degree of personal discretion. Instead, Cromer observed, the Egyptian official "flies for refuge to the French system" with its elaborate codes prescribing all procedures in their minutest details.[3] Just why the Egyptian civil service should follow the French rather than the British administrative tradition despite the fact that the British controlled Egyptian administration from 1882 until well after Cromer's departure in 1906, is a question of historical development and cultural influence that lies beyond the scope of this study.

Whatever the influence of British or French political organization, there are factors making for civil service timidity that may be found closer to home. Before briefly considering some of them, however, we ought to distinguish between administrative subservience and the customary politeness of the Near East which sometimes seems excessive to the Westerner.

Much that the Western observer sees as subservience in Egyptian administration is probably nothing more than the

[3] The Earl of Cromer (Evelyn Baring), *Modern Egypt*, 2 volumes, Macmillan, London, 1908, vol. 2, p. 240.

overt deference shown by younger officials to older or by subordinates to superiors, and a formal politeness between equals that is not familiar in the West (especially in the United States). The half-bows, the salutes, even the occasional hand-kissing that can be seen, are qualities of the entire culture. Personal relations in Egypt are conducted with this sort of social lubrication, which is reflected linguistically in the large number of terms of respect and deference that are not only available but also in constant use.

Apart from this behavior trait, however, real administrative subservience does exist, as many observers have reported and as our interview data have shown. One historical influence that helps account for it is the fact that Egypt was ruled by foreign powers for centuries until the last few years. Foreign rulers prefer centralized administrative systems, which do not encourage the development of initiative in the lower ranks of the hierarchy. When Egypt began to gain an increasing degree of self-government, the civil service, as we saw in the previous chapter, became the tool of the palace and the political parties. Uncertainty about his future in the service induced subservience by the government official to those who controlled his job. Precisely because the government post, no matter how minor, was an attractive occupation, relatively well-paid and conferring high status, its occupant dreaded losing it. Other employment commensurate with his education, his expectations, and his tastes was not easy to find. Even today this is true, as revealed in the answers to question 18, which asks whether the respondent has been offered opportunities for employment outside the government. Only 24 per cent report having received such offers, although their dissatisfaction with government emloyment (as reviewed in Chapters 4 and 5) would seem to make them at least alert to other possibilities.

Even if one agrees that subservience is more characteristic of Egyptian civil servants than of those in the West, and that the factors just briefly reviewed explain this difference, the larger question remains of how much personal initiative is compatible, in a public bureaucracy, with responsibility to the political leadership and the nation. Large doses of individualism in public administration can disrupt the orderly conduct of business anywhere and subvert the policies adopted by elected representatives

165

or leaders selected in other ways. The Egyptian civil servant, however, is far from this extreme; he is still suffering from too much subservience to the man on the next administrative rung. To use a high degree of personal initiative is not the ideal practice in a public bureaucracy, yet to abjure all discretion is not the desirable alternative. In Egypt responsibility to the hierarchy has developed at the expense of the growth of initiative and of responsibility to the post itself and to the public the government official is supposed to serve. This uneven development takes the form of subservience and timidity, of reluctance to exercise even that degree of discretionary power that is permitted by the formal distribution of functions in the bureaucracy.

Administrative and Technical Workers

An important facet of subservience emerges in the differences between the 38 respondents in administrative posts and the 211 in technical posts. First, the administrative workers seem more oriented toward the bureaucracy, the civil service hierarchy, while the technical workers are clearly more oriented toward their professions. Second, the technical workers are more concerned with narrow working conditions in the service than with larger questions of policy or the civil servant's broader responsibilities. The technical workers also tend to be more individualistic in their approach to the job and less oriented to groups of any kind. Third, since their view of the government service is a narrower one, the technical workers tend to be less critical of the service in general. Fourth, the technical workers' greater indifference to broad matters of policy and their greater concern with the immediate conditions of work induce a greater degree of subservience than is revealed among the administrative workers.[4]

The technical workers' greater orientation to professionalism is clearly shown in Table 44; among them 36 per cent score high on the Professionalism Index, compared to only 8 per cent among the administrative workers who score high. The opposite rela-

[4] Most of the relationships discussed in these four types of comparison between technical and administrative workers are not statistically significant. As in the earlier analyses, we take into account here the accumulation of many differences in the same direction, even though each difference may not be statistically significant.

TABLE 44

Score on Professionalism Index, by Function

	ADMINISTRATORS	TECHNICIANS
	Per Cent	*Per Cent*
High professionalism	7.9	35.5
Low professionalism	92.1	64.5
Total	*100.0*	*100.0*
(Cases)	(38)	(211)

Note: Significant at .001 level.

tionship holds, although not nearly so sharply, with respect to degree of Western bureaucratic attitudes as measured by the Bureaucratic Scale. As Table 45 shows, 47 per cent of the

TABLE 45

Score on Bureaucratic Scale, by Function

	ADMINISTRATORS	TECHNICIANS
	Per Cent	*Per Cent*
High bureaucracy	47.4	37.0
Low bureaucracy	52.6	63.0
Total	*100.0*	*100.0*
(Cases)	(38)	(211)

Note: Not statistically significant.

administrative but only 37 per cent of the technical workers score high on this scale. While this difference is not statistically significant, it is relevant because it is consistent with the highly significant relationship just indicated between occupation of technical posts and high degree of professionalism. As we might expect from the technicians' greater orientation toward professionalism and the administrators' greater tendency toward Western bureaucratic patterns, the former have a much higher proportion who are members of professional associations. As Table 46 shows, among the technicians, more than three quarters reported holding such memberships, compared with only 37 per cent of the administrators.

Finally, we may consider the view of each group regarding the relative importance of various determinants of job prestige (question 35). Since the technicians are more professionally oriented, we should expect that among them a higher proportion than among the administrators will attach the greatest im-

TABLE 46

Membership in Professional Associations, by Function

	ADMINISTRATORS Per Cent	TECHNICIANS Per Cent
Members	36.8	76.3
Non-members	63.2	23.7
Total	*100.0*	*100.0*
(Cases)	(38)	(211)

Note: Significant at .001 level.

portance to "skill required to do the work" and "opportunity to serve the public," for these two elements of occupational prestige stress skill and public service, which in turn are elements of professionalism. A higher proportion of technicians than of administrators places each of these two factors above all of the others: the proportions among technicians are 20 per cent and 14 per cent, and among administrators only 13 and 5 per cent. It would be expected, correspondingly, that technicians would *not* rate "opportunity to serve the state" so highly as would administrators, since this element of job prestige seems to be directly related to bureaucratic rather than professional loyalties. There is virtually no difference between the proportion of administrators who rank this element first, 36.8 per cent, and the proportion of technicians, 38.3 per cent, who do so. This item, therefore, neither confirms nor denies the general point that technicians tend to be oriented to professionalism and administrators to bureaucratic values.

Since they are less oriented toward the bureaucracy, technical workers tend to take a more individualistic approach to matters of policy but to be concerned less with these broad aspects of their civil service posts than with the narrower aspects, such as their immediate conditions of employment.

The imaginary situation involving the civil servant whose superiors ask him to carry out a policy that he feels will harm the villagers he is supposed to serve (question 46) calls for the reasons given by the 97 respondents who say the civil servant ought to refuse to carry out the policy. These reasons are twofold: (1) the civil servant should follow his own views, or (2) he should not do anything against the interests of the villagers. The first reason reflects a preoccupation with the government official's own attitude, and implies that his main obligation is to his own ideals and opinions, while the second reflects greater loyalty to a group, in this case the special section of the public whose interests are supposed to be protected and advanced. Among the administrators only 41 per cent offered the more individualistic reason, while 60 per cent of the technicians did so.

A similar distinction (although likewise itself not statistically significant) is revealed in the reasons given by administrators and technicians in the imaginary situation involving the government economist who is asked to prepare a memorandum that would contradict what is accepted among economists generally (question 28). Here again two reasons are given by the respondents who say the civil servant ought to refuse to prepare the document: (1) he should do what he thinks right, and (2) he should not contradict his professional colleagues among the economists. Again technicians have a higher proportion giving the more individualistic reply that the civil servant should refuse to violate his own views. Among the technicians 51 per cent give this kind of reply, compared with 44 per cent among the administrators.

Although they take a more individualistic approach to broader questions, the technical workers actually display less concern about such matters than they do about the more immediate aspects of their posts; their focus of interest is somewhat narrower. This difference in focus is sharply revealed in what the administrators and technicians say they dislike about the civil service (question 23). There is a statistically significant difference between the criticisms they freely mention. Among the administrators, all but one (97 per cent) mention some relatively broad aspect of the service such as that it involves too much routine, or kills individual initiative, or that there is too much favoritism and inefficient use of personnel; among the technicians, however, the proportion who mention these criticisms, 84 per cent, is significantly lower. Correspondingly, only 3 per cent of the administrators mention more immediate aspects of the job such as conditions of employment, whereas 16 per cent of the technicians offer such complaints.

In their replies to another question the technicians again display a proportionately greater interest in the narrow conditions of employment than in the broader implications of service in the government. As we have already seen in Chapter 5, on status and prestige, about half the respondents say the government ought to permit the civil servants without exception to hold other jobs at the same time (question 33). Consistently with the differences just reviewed, among the technicians a higher proportion take this position. Among them 52 per cent are willing, under present circumstances, to overlook the larger ethical questions involved in permitting civil servants to hold outside jobs, whereas among the administrators, generally more oriented to the bureaucracy in its broader relationships, only 45 per cent are so concerned with low salaries that they are willing to go this far.

Accompanying the relative indifference of technicians to these broader issues is a complementary reluctance to take a position critical of the civil service. The administrators, concerned with more and broader aspects of the service, tend to be more critical of it.

Asked what they like about the government service (question 22), the respondents give three types of answers: about a third mention the opportunity to perform some sort of public service, more than half mention a material advantage or personal benefit, and slightly more than a tenth say they like nothing about it. Proportionately fewer technicians than administrators, 11 per cent compared with 16 per cent, are so critical as to say they do not like anything at all about it. The technicians are likewise less critical when a higher proportion of them, 35 per cent as against 30 per cent for the administrators, are able to say they like the opportunity their jobs afford them to perform a public service.

They tend, also, to be less critical than administrators of the upper echelons of the public bureaucracy, as revealed in the answers to some of the questions following the imaginary situation about the inspector who acts on his own initiative in closing a factory he believes to be unsafe (question 36, discussed earlier in this chapter). For example, in the first situation, nearly a third of the administrators predict that the inspector's superior will discipline him for taking the initiative, but only a quarter of the technicians express so little confidence in the bureaucratic leadership. Even more revealing is the difference between the administrators and technicians in another aspect of this item.

170

There are 102 respondents who say the superior will discipline the inspector when the latter's judgment turns out to be wrong but not when his judgment turns out to be right. Among the administrators 45 per cent take this highly critical position, but only 40 per cent of the technicians do so.

One facet of this relative indifference of technicians may be their tendency, which we referred to above, to be more concerned with their own tasks and less with broader matters. A comparison between the ways in which they and the administrators rank "good salary and working conditions" as a determinant of occupational prestige throws some light on this tendency. We have already seen that the technicians attach more importance to "skill" and "public service." We can now see that this preference is complemented by less concern with the material aspects of government employment as elements of job prestige. Forty-five per cent of the administrators give first place to "good salary and working conditions" as a determinant of prestige, whereas only 29 per cent of the technicians think this material aspect of employment so important.

The relative indifference of technicians may, indeed, go far to explain another finding, that they show a higher degree of job-satisfaction than do the administrators. More concerned with the conditions of performance of their own tasks, less concerned with broader aspects of policy and with material advantages, less disposed to be critical of the hierarchy, the technicians are perhaps understandably more satisfied with their jobs than are the administrators. Among the technicians 22 per cent have a high degree of job-satisfaction, compared with only 13 per cent among the administrators.

Let us turn to the last of the four distinctions we are considering between the administrators and the technicians among our respondents, that is, that the technicians are not only less critical but also tend to be more subservient to authority than are the administrators. The evidence for this conclusion comes from their responses to questions following three imaginary situations already discussed in this chapter, the ones involving the factory inspector, the government economist, and the civil servant interested in village reform.[5]

[5] It warrants repetition here that most of the relationships on which this conclusion is based are not statistically significant but that we take

In the first phase of the situation involving the inspector (question 36), it will be recalled, he closes the factory on his own initiative but the respondents are not given any indication as to whether his judgment turned out to be right or wrong. Asked whether the inspector acted properly, a higher proportion of administrators (97 per cent) than of technicians (89 per cent) defended this civil servant's taking the initiative. In addition, among the technicians a higher proportion assert that the inspector *ought* to be disciplined for having taken this degree of initiative; among them 9 per cent, compared with only 3 per cent among the administrators, feel that initiative in this case calls for disciplinary action.

When we turn to the second phase of this imaginary situation, in which the respondents are told that the inspector's judgment turns out to be wrong, the differences are of the same kind; 84 per cent of the administrators but only 72 per cent of the technicians still defended the inspector's taking the initiative even when his judgment turned out to be mistaken. Consider, too, the decline in the number of the inspector's defenders from the first to the second phases; among the administrators his defenders fell from 34 to 32, or only 6 per cent, whereas among the technicians the information that the inspector turned out to be wrong produced a decline from 187 to 152, or 19 per cent, in the number who continued to defend his taking the initiative.

In the second phase, as in the first, the proportion of technicians saying the inspector *should* be disciplined is greater than the corresponding proportion among the administrators; the percentages are 16 and 23, respectively.

As in the case of their opinions as to the propriety of the inspector's action in the first and second phases, there is an interesting change in the respondents' attitude on the question whether or not the inspector should be disciplined for taking the initiative. In the first phase, 34 administrators defend the inspector by saying he ought not to be disciplined; in the second phase, in which the inspector's judgment turns out to be wrong, 31 administrators still say he ought not to be disciplined; the

---

into account the accumulation of many small differences in the same direction.

decline is thus 9 per cent from the first to second phase. Among the technicians, however, the corresponding decline in those who defend the inspector's taking the initiative is greater, from 190 to 162, or 15 per cent.

There is still another way of looking at the answers given by the administrators and technicians to the questions based on this situation involving the factory inspector. It will be recalled that a third phase supposes that his judgment turns out to be right. Now there are 40 respondents who switched sides from the second phase to the third, that is, who say that he acted improperly in taking the initiative when his judgment turns out to be wrong but that he acted properly when it turns out to be right. Who are these 40 respondents who are playing it safe? Among the administrators, only 11 per cent play it safe this way, whereas among the technicians 17 per cent do so.

Let us now consider, correspondingly, the 44 respondents who switch sides from the second to the third phases in replying to the question whether or not the inspector *should* be disciplined by his superior for taking the initiative. Here again the technicians show themselves to be less reliable defenders of personal initiative than the administrators. Among the latter, only 13 per cent play it safe in this particular way, whereas among the technicians 18 per cent do so.

In their answers to the imaginary situation (question 28) involving the government economist who is asked to prepare a memorandum that would run contrary to accepted economic doctrine, the administrators and technicians differ in the same way again. Asked whether the superior could nevertheless expect the economist to prepare the memo, 81 per cent of the technicians and only 68 per cent of the administrators said yes. One could argue that in any public bureaucracy a superior ought to be able to expect compliance with such a request; that, however, is not the issue here. Irrespective of whether or not it is appropriate (by any given standard) for the economist to comply with the request, those who say he ought not to do so are expressing the more independent attitude.

In another imaginary situation, it will be recalled, a civil servant is asked to carry out in the villages a policy which he believes will not benefit the people in them (question 46). The respondents are asked whether the civil servant's superiors can expect him to carry out such a policy and whether or not he himself should do so. To the first question a higher proportion of technicians say yes; only 66 per cent of the administrators but 75 per cent of the technicians take this position. On the second question, about what the respondents think the civil servant ought to do, 45 per cent of the administrators say he ought to refuse to comply with such a request but only 38 per cent of the technicians advocate this degree of personal initiative. These results conform with those just reviewed in the imaginary situation about the economist. One might likewise say that compliance is called for in such a case, but again that is not the issue. It is apparent that, rightly or wrongly, the administrators favor a larger degree of personal initiative.

The evidence reviewed in this section reveals that the technicians are more oriented toward professional than bureaucratic values, are more individualistic in their reasons for opposing the hierarchy whenever they do so, are concerned with narrow tasks rather than broad aspects of government employment, are less critical of the hierarchy in general and tend to be more subservient.

Summary and Conclusions

The findings of our questionnaire survey confirm the impression of many Egyptian and Western observers that the Egyptian civil servant is a rather timid official fearful of his superiors and unwilling to use even such personal initiative as is permitted (even if not encouraged). We have sought to find the historical roots of this quality in the fact of foreign domination and the nature and aims of those who dominated.

We have also sought to understand the differences between those civil servants who are more and those who are less timid and subservient. Our findings have pointed to the conclusion that greater initiative, as measured by our Bureaucratic Scale, is characteristic of the older respondents, those in the highest grade, those upwardly mobile in occupational status, and those more satisfied in their jobs—in short, those longer exposed to Western patterns of attitude and behavior and to Western bureaucracies, and most committed to the public bureaucracy in Egypt itself.

Much of our data indicate, furthermore, that the senior officials who responded to the questionnaire imply that the Egyptian civil service has not particularly rewarded the exercise of personal initiative. The respondents also display a fear of exercising such initiative and, perhaps because of the inherited atmosphere of sycophancy, a preference for playing it safe bureaucratically. Finally, as we have just seen, the officials in technical posts are less critical and more subservient than those in administrative jobs.

Chapter 8. Public Bureaucracy and the Task of Government in East and West

Like other Arab and Asian countries, Egypt has embarked on a process of industrialization and political change that seems sure to endow the civil service with greater importance than before. New governmental functions and a new attitude toward the rulers and the public bureaucracy are developing. The country's leadership is seeking to break sharply with almost every feature of the immediate past and with many older traditions as well. But, as the regime has been learning daily, the past is not easily changed or ignored. Prime Minister Gamal Abdel Nasser vividly describes his expectation of quick change and his shock of disillusionment at discovering the power of the dead hand of tradition. Before the army's seizure of power on July 23, 1952, he writes:[1] "I imagined that the whole nation was on tip-toes and prepared for action. . . . After July 23rd I was shocked by the reality. The vanguard performed its task; it stormed the walls of the fort of tyranny . . . and stood by expecting the mass formations to arrive. . . . It waited and waited. Endless crowds showed up, but how different is the reality from the vision! . . . We needed action but found nothing but surrender and idleness."

One of the regime's chief instruments of change is necessarily the higher civil service with all its inherited traditions, attitudes, and methods of work. Many changes have recently been introduced regarding personnel and procedure but the human legacy —the civil servant—is less easily changed. We have tried to relate our findings about the civil servant today to the historical pattern created by the combination of local cultural influences with foreign political domination.

The Problem of Further Change

Having come this far on the road to building a modern public bureaucracy, Egypt is not likely to reverse its path, irrespective

[1] Gamal Abdel Nasser, *The Philosophy of the Revolution*, Dar Al-Maaref, Cairo, 1954, pp. 19-20.

176

of the kind of regime in power. Further professionalization and rationalization can be expected. The vast expansion of the mission and functions of the civil service during the period of its modernization makes especially difficult both tasks—that of carrying out the new jobs and that of changing the character of the service itself. Charles Issawi points out that in the West civil service reform took place at a time when its functions were not so closely related to economic development. It is especially difficult, he contends, "to reform the civil service at a time when it plays such an important part in the life of the country, is surrounded by so many temptations and exerts so much power. . . ."[2] What effect will this double task have upon the fulfillment of each one? How will the status of the civil service be affected, in the long run, by the military regime under which it has been functioning? How long will its status continue to decline, under the impact of the influences analyzed in Chapter 5, before it begins to rise because of the service's augmented functions? Can the quality of the government workers' performance, indeed, be improved while their status declines? How will the service meet the new tasks, under full independence, of economic development and social reform? This is a particularly important question that is now occupying the attention of Indian students of public administration—how can the bureaucracy shift from concern mainly with the details of taxation and public order to the more complicated matters of land reform, industrial development, labor-management relations, and so on?[3]

Other questions arise out of our findings in this study. We have discussed the evidence pointing to a decline in the attractiveness of civil service posts, but this evidence is confined to the higher civil servants in our sample. It needs to be supplemented by study of the attitudes of those in the lower grades and of students now in the secondary schools and universities to determine just how they look at government and private employment. We have also discussed the evidence suggesting a decline in the socio-economic status and prestige of the civil servant. Here,

[2] Charles Issawi, *Egypt at Mid-Century*, Oxford University Press, London, 1954, p. 94.

[3] B. B. Majumdar, ed., *Problems of Public Administration in India*, Indian Political Science Association, Publication No. 1, Patna, 1954, pp. 7, 13, and *passim*.

too, we need further studies, this time of public attitudes toward government and its administrative arm.

Still other questions arise concerning the civil service itself. We have learned something of the socio-economic background of Egyptian senior officials but still know very little about this élite group compared with others. Are there differences in socio-economic background between the civil servants and the independent professionals or the executives in private industry or the middle and top leaders of political parties before their prohibition in 1952-1953? Government jobs were an important focus of nationalist struggle in Egypt. What was the role of the government job-holder himself in this struggle, and how has this role affected his attitude toward the ideal of political neutrality for the civil service of independent Egypt? Has the service acted as a political safety valve, draining off those who might become disaffected and alienated? What is the difference between the civil servant and political radical? Is it only a job? What is the place of the educated classes in a technologically underdeveloped society with limited opportunities and the competition of Westerners? The answers to such questions would tell us a great deal more about the social role of the public bureaucracy in Egypt.

The Study of Bureaucracy

Our findings raise even broader questions about public administration and government. We saw in the discussion of professionalism and varying loyalties that administrative efficiency and fidelity to function are possible in various kinds of society and can be attained by various means. What brings on real difficulty is a society in transition, in which loyalties are shifting. Such a situation developed in the United States, for example, in the second quarter of the nineteenth century and was given its sharpest expression during Andrew Jackson's presidency. As Leonard White has said, until Jackson took office in 1829 the civil service was a permanent, stable corps moving toward political neutrality.[4] It was, however, the administrative arm of an aristocratically-oriented governing class that was fast

---

[4] Leonard D. White, *Government Career Service*, University of Chicago Press, 1935, pp. 2-3, and *The Jacksonians*, Macmillan, N.Y., 1954, pp. 300-301.

being overcome by an urban and rural middle class with notions of equality. Jackson expressed the interests of these classes. In public administration this expression took the form of an expansion of the sources from which the government drew its officials. From one point of view such a policy was a spoils system designed only to aid Jackson's own political party; but from another point of view it was rotation-in-office, a means of removing a bureaucracy loyal to a very small social class. As Arthur M. Schlesinger, Jr., has put it, "The spoils system, whatever its faults, at least destroyed peaceably the monopoly of offices by a class which could not govern, and brought to power a fresh, and alert group which had the energy to meet the needs of the day."[5]

The Jacksonian policy brings us to the heart of an issue that has troubled democratic governments. On the one hand public administration ought to be efficient and reliable and offer a permanent career good enough to attract men and women of intelligence and understanding. On the other hand, the civil service ought to be responsive to elected heads of the government and not become so entrenched that it can establish policy itself. This balance between a career service and responsiveness has been the goal of the modern civil service system. Efficiency and technical competence are sought by means of recruitment on the basis of ability and by granting security of tenure. This type of open, competitive recruitment also prevents monopolization of posts by a party or a narrow social class. Responsiveness is sought by making the civil service as politically neutral as possible and by encouraging a professional spirit that stresses technical functions rather than policy formation. In this way democratic governments try to balance the advantages of permanence and change in public service. Yet not all democracies have the same system governing the civil service. The British civil service, for example, is tightly-knit and insulated from the public, while the American civil service is more fluid and certainly less insulated by tradition and regulation from the public or the legislature. What is the relationship, then, between the spirit and form of the bureaucracy and its attitude to the public? Is the closed, inbred bureaucratic corps also impervious to public

[5] Arthur M. Schlesinger, Jr., *The Age of Jackson*, Little, Brown, Boston, 1946, p. 47.

opinion? Is such a bureaucracy likely to want to affect policy and to be in a position to sabotage it? We have seen that the Egyptian higher civil service is considerably inbred and devoted to self-protection but displays little interest in high policy and even less capacity to affect it. To what extent is this true in other countries, technologically advanced as well as "underdeveloped"? What, indeed, are the differences in bureaucratic structure and behavior between these two types of state?

We have touched upon this last question in the discussion of the nature of the Bureaucratic Scale and the Professionalism Index (see Chapter 3 and Appendix 4).[6] To construct these measures we had to decide what are Western bureaucratic and professional characteristics. This process led us to distinguish three elements each in bureaucratic and professional behavior. For the former we mentioned rationality, hierarchy, and discretion, and for the latter skill, self-protection, and public service. It is generally assumed that a high degree of bureaucratic orientation or professionalism means a greater display of all three elements of each. Our study, however, suggests that these three qualities do not always vary together. Thus the civil servant highly exposed to Western influences may stress rationality and the use of personal initiative but not the prerogatives of status in the hierarchy; or, with respect to professionalism, a civil servant may stress the importance of skill and public service rather than self-protection.

Consider first what we have been calling Western bureaucratic orientation. May we say that one official is "more bureaucratic" than another because he is more dependent upon his superiors and is quicker to throw upon them the burden of a decision that is properly within his own competence? May we say, in other words, that the more willing an official is to use the full measure of discretionary power that his post permits, the less bureaucratic he is? What is involved in these questions is the degree to which personal initiative is related to bureaucratic behavior. The exercise of such initiative is not structurally excluded from bureaucracy, yet it is usually characterized as unbureaucratic behavior in scholarly studies as well as in popular

[6] For a fuller discussion of the points made in the following pages, see the author's article, "Bureaucracy East and West," *Administrative Science Quarterly*, Vol. 1, No. 4, March 1957.

discussion. Its opposite, extreme caution, playing it safe, covering one's self by getting a decision from the official on the next
level of the hierarchy, is likewise thought of as a typical behavioral concomitant of bureaucratic structure.

The uncertainty surrounding this aspect of bureaucratic behavior in the West is compounded when one looks to notions
derived from studies of such behavior for guidance in the analysis
of bureaucratic patterns in another culture. If, for example, one
wants to determine to what degree Egyptian bureaucratic behavior resembles its Western counterpart and the socio-economic
background of those Egyptian civil servants who are most like
Western civil servants, there must be a firm idea of what
actually constitutes Western bureaucratic patterns. Suppose,
then, we ask whether the Egyptian official who displays great
dependence upon his superiors is more or less bureaucratic than
one who is more willing to rely on his own judgment in affairs
within his competence. If our model of bureaucracy, so to speak,
implies that the tendency toward caution in this respect is
typically bureaucratic, then the more cautious official is the more
highly bureaucratic. If, however, the model implies that typically
bureaucratic behavior does not exclude the full exercise of such
personal initiative as is permitted by the rules, then the more
cautious official is not necessarily the more bureaucratic.

To add to our difficulties, suppose we find that we must consider not one but two models—one Western and one Egyptian.
Suppose, further, that the Western model implies that the more
bureaucratic official is the one who is more willing to exercise
the permitted degree of personal initiative, while the Egyptian
(or Eastern, or pre-industrial) model implies that the more
timid official is the more highly bureaucratic. We should then
have to say that the more timid Egyptian official is the more
bureaucratic if measured along the Egyptian scale but less
bureaucratic if measured along the scale of Western bureaucracy
we have just postulated. We now confront our problem in its
full extent; we are limited by the shortcomings of the theory of
bureaucracy.

By means of our questionnaire we had hoped to learn what are
the socio-economic characteristics of those Egyptian higher civil
servants whose attitudes toward the government, the service, and
the public most closely resembled what we could infer, from

such studies as have touched this matter, is the Western bureaucratic norm. We should expect that those Egyptian officials highly exposed to Western influences through travel, study in the West, and familiarity with Western mass media of communication, would come closest to the Western norms. We should expect, then, that the most highly exposed respondents would have the highest score on a scale of items touching bureaucratic behavior. But we find something different. The results show that the most highly exposed respondents are concentrated at the midpoint of the scale rather than at highest point. This outcome suggested a re-examination of the items that went into the scale purporting to measure bureaucratic attitudes. Upon analysis it appeared that these items did not all touch the same aspect of official behavior, that, indeed, what we had assumed was a unitary, irreducible predisposition could in fact be analyzed into several components. Significantly, too, these components, we learned, did not necessarily vary together. Rather, since they were different aspects of what we call the bureaucratic pattern they were differently related to a given characteristic.

Our re-examination of the items led to the consideration of the three aforementioned dimensions of bureaucratic behavior that accompany corresponding structural features of bureaucratic organization: rationality and impersonality, emphasis upon hierarchy and the prerogatives of position, and the attitude toward the use of personal initiative and discretion. These three components are, of course, intimately related to one another. The first, rationality and the emphasis upon efficiency, involves the second, the maintenance of a system of division of labor and authority. The second, hierarchy, permits varying degrees of the third, discretion. And discretion or personal initiative often is demanded if the first, rationality and efficiency, is to be realized. They may, however, be considered separately to see just how far a high degree of each of these aspects of bureaucratic behavior is associated with a high degree of any of the other two.

Although the questionnaire answered by our sample of Egyptian civil servants was not designed as such a test, the responses do throw some light upon this problem. As already mentioned, we had expected that high exposure to Western influences, for example, would place a respondent in the group high in predisposition to bureaucratic behavior. But the data concerning the three components of such behavior do not entirely fulfill this expectation. On the items of the questionnaire which touch upon the first component, rationality and efficiency, respondents highly exposed to the West indeed scored high, indicating a high predisposition to this particular quality of bureaucratic behavior. On those items touching the second component, hierarchy, the highly Western respondents scored low, indicating a low predisposition to this bureaucratic pattern of behavior. Finally, on the items concerning the use of discretionary power and personal initiative, the results are inconclusive. Thus high exposure to Western influence does not mean a uniformly high predisposition to all facets of bureaucratic behavior among our sample of Egyptian higher civil servants.

Let us consider the way in which another characteristic, age, affects the data. On rationality and efficiency, the older respondents score higher than the younger. On hierarchy the reverse obtains. On discretion and initiative, the evidence is again inconclusive. Still another characteristic we may try is the place of higher education, that is, the responses of civil servants who took their baccalaureate or higher degree in Europe or the United States, compared with the responses of those who studied in Egyptian institutions. On rationality and efficiency those educated in the West score higher. On hierarchy, those educated in Egypt score higher. On discretion and initiative, the Western-educated again score higher.

Thus none of these three variables, exposure to Western influences, age, and place of higher education, uniformly yields high or low scores on the three components of bureaucratic behavior we have postulated. What emerges is a picture of the older, Western-educated, and Western-exposed civil servant as more highly predisposed to emphasize rationality, efficiency, and universality, and less predisposed to emphasize the power of position, the authority of the superior official, and the propriety of obedience by the subordinate. That these three characteristics, incidentally, should affect the data in the same way is not surprising, for they are significantly related to one another in our sample of Egyptian civil servants.

The questionnaire data are relevant to professionalism, too. This concept, likewise, we found to be susceptible of analysis

183

into three component parts. We were led to this point for the same reason as in the case of attitudes on bureaucratic behavior. We had expected to find that respondents who scored high on an index of items touching professional loyalties would also be the ones most highly exposed to the West. They were, instead, concentrated among the group only moderately exposed to the West. Again we examined the items making up the index and concluded that they seemed to bear upon predispositions that did not necessarily respond uniformly to a given stimulus. We saw three components of what we had been taking to be the irreducible concept of professionalism: emphasis upon skill and self-regulation, emphasis upon self-protective devices, and emphasis upon public service.

As in the case of bureaucratic orientation, these component parts are of course related to one another. The first, emphasis upon skill, is promoted by the second, the power to exclude those not meeting the group's standard of competence. The goal of the second, by means of licensing and control of recruitment, is ostensibly the third, protection of the public. Again, however, they may be separated to enable us to see whether they uniformly accompany one another or whether they vary in the degree to which they are related to a given characteristic. Our data on these matters are less satisfactory than the data regarding bureaucratic orientation, but they do indicate that this line of analysis is worth pursuing. Exposure to Western influences, for example, affects two of the three components differently. The respondents who are highly exposed to the West tend to emphasize the skill component of professionalism but not the self-interest or self-protective component. On the service component, however, the results are not conclusive.

Bureaucratic and professional predispositions, then, are not unitary tendencies among our sample of Egyptian higher civil servants. Each has several components that do not accompany one another in the same degree when considered against certain characteristics. It may be that these differential effects would be found in studies of Western bureaucracies too, that they differ among themselves in the degree to which they stress one or another component of bureaucratic values and professionalism. Similarity in bureaucratic structure, in other words, does not preclude difference in the behavioral concomitants of structure.

This is especially so when we compare Western and non-Western bureaucracies. We may indeed find similarity of structure, usually the result of the sort of cultural diffusion that in part is shaping the changes now going on in the Egyptian civil service itself. But, as we have seen in preceding pages, similarity of organizational structure may be accompanied by wide differences in the behavioral patterns—the institutions—associated with these organizations. Thus the study of bureaucracy in a non-Western setting points to the limitations of current bureaucratic theory, developed mainly in the West. It has shortcomings for the analysis of bureaucratic and professional behavior in a non-Western culture as well as in our own.

A final implication of our findings for future research is their suggestion that the two aspects of Westernization or modernization—bureaucratic orientation and professionalism—exert different degrees of attraction for different occupational types. Technicians in Egypt (and perhaps other non-Western countries) seem to move most rapidly toward Western professional norms while administrators move most rapidly toward Western bureaucratic norms. It is not that either type takes on a new pattern more readily than the other but that each more readily adapts itself to that new pattern which is most closely related to the values and institutional characteristics of the local culture that it has already made its own.

As one of the most important sections of the middle class in Egypt, civil servants have been transmitters of cultural innovations and borrowings. In this respect, too, they may be declining in significance as other middle class groups become more numerous and as education spreads among the working class. A responsible, articulate, and organized middle and working class does not yet exist in Egypt, but may be now coming into being. It is often said that the present military regime seeks to "represent" the middle class. If it does, it is not the present middle class it seeks to represent—a middle class of the older kind of clerical government bureaucracy, the liberal professions and small trade. Rather, it seems to look toward a middle class with technological, managerial, and entrepreneurial functions, a class that is now only taking shape. The military regime, it might be more accurate to say, has really been seeking to create a class to represent.

Appendices

Appendix 1

The Questionnaire

Following is the original questionnaire in Arabic, with an English translation. It will be noted that items 19, 54, and 56 are lacking; these were questions originally included but not used. The numbering of the items is retained in order to facilitate references to them in the text, the coding, and the translations.

اسم السائل .... التاريـخ ....

١ الرقــم ....

٢ الـوزارة .... المصلحة ....

٣ الوظيفة ....

٤ الدرجـــة ....

٥ الاختصاصات ....

٦ سنة الميلاد ....

٧ محل الميلاد ....

٨ الدراسة ....

أ) الشهادة الثانوية أو المتوسطة   أتــم .... لم يتم ....

ب) موءهلات عالية وفنية

ج) دراسات أخرى

٩ ماهو هدف واختصاصات الوزارة التى تعمل بها ؟

١٠ ما هو دور وظيفتك التى تقوم بها لتحقيق أهداف الوزارة ؟

١١ ما هى الوظائف الحكومية التى شغلتها قبل وظيفتك الحالية ؟ (السائل : ابدأ بآخر وظيفة ومنها الى الأولى ٠)

١٢ كيف حصلت على أول وظيفة فى الحكومة ؟

دعنا الآن نعود لحظة الى ما قبل دخولك خدمة الحكومة ٠

١٣ كم كان عمرك عندما فكرت أول مرة فى أن تتخذ خدمة الحكومة مستقبلا لك ؟

١٤ لماذا فضلت خدمة الحكومة على الأعمال الحرة ؟ (السائل : حاول أن تتوصل الى الاجابة المفصلة ٠)

١٥ كيف وصل الى علمك خبر أول وظيفة حصلت عليها فى خدمة الحكومة ؟ (السائل : اذا لزم الحال ، أذكر أمثله : عن طريق صديق أو قريب أو أستاذ فى الجامعة ، الخ ٠)

١٦ ما هى الأعمال التى قمت بها قبل التحاقك بخدمة الحكومة ؟
تكرم بالبدء من آخر عمل ثـم ارجـع بالترتيب الى الأول •

١٧ أ) أتظن أنك قد تترك خدمة الحكومة نهائيا لسبب من الاسباب ؟
نعم .... لا ....

ب) (السائل : ان كان الجواب نعم ، إسأل •)   فى أى ظرف قد
تترك الخدمة ؟

١٨ أ) منذ أن أصبحت موظفا حكوميا ، هل اتيحت لك فرصة للعمل خارج
الحكومة ؟   نعم .... لا ....

ب) (السائل : ان كان الجواب نعم •) أذكر شيئا عن العرضين
الاخيرين من هذا النوع •

الوظيفة	طبيعة عمل المؤسسة	سنة العرض	الإجابة واسباب الرفض أو

القبول والآن أحب أن أسالك بعض الأسئلة عن خدمتك فى الحكومة •

٢٠ تراعى الحكومة عند التوظف ـ كما تعلم ـ الدرجات العلمية والخبرة
فهل تظن ان الحكومة يجب أن تراعى عوامل اخرى عند التعيين فى هذه
الوظائف ؟   فمثلا ....

أ) المكانة الاجتماعية ؟   نعم .... لا ....

ب) صلة النسب ؟   نعم .... لا ....

ج) الثروة ؟   نعم .... لا ....

ه) الدين ؟   نعم .... لا ....

د) المذهب السياسى ؟   نعم .... لا ....

٢١ كيف تصف الموظف الحكومى المثالى ؟   (السائل :   اذا لزم الأمر
اسأل : أى صفـات يجب أن يتمتع بها ؟   أى شخص يجب أن يكون ؟
ابحث عن صفات فردية معينة كالذكاء والاجتهاد والولاء والامانة الخ •)

٢٢ ما الذى يحبب اليك العمل بالحكومة ؟

٢٣ ما الذى لا ترتاح اليه فى خدمة الحكومة ؟

والآن أريد أن أسالك بعض الاسئلة عن أمور أخرى تتصل بعملك •

٢٤ أى لغة من اللغات الاجنبية المذكورة بعد تقرأها وتتكلمها بسهولة ؟

	تقرأ بسهولة	تتكلم بسهولة
الانجليزية	....	....
الفرنسية	....	....
الالمانية	....	....
الايطالية	....	....

(لغات أخـرى) ....
....

٢٥   أى بلد من البلاد الآتيـة قد زرت ولو لمد ة قصيرة ، أو اقمت بهااكثرمن
سنة ؟

أقمـت	زرت	
....	....	انجلـــــترا
....	....	الولايات المتحدة
....	....	فرنـسـا
....	....	المانيـــا
....	....	ايطاليـا
....	....	تركيـا
....	....	سـوريـا
....	....	لبنـان
....	....	(بلاد أخرى) ....

٢٦   أ)   أى الجرائد تقرأ فى مختلف اللغات ، وكم مرّة تقرأها ــ بمعنى ،
أتقرأ كل عدد ؟ أتقرأها غالبا ؟ أتقرأها أحيانا ؟
ب)   أى المجلات تقرأ فى مختلف اللغات ، وكم مرّة تقرأها ــ بمعنى ،
أتقرأ كل عدد ؟ أتقرأها غالبا ؟ أتقرأهـا أحيـانا ؟
(السائل :   اذكر بالترتيب اسم كلّ مجلـة وأسأل السؤال الاتي عن كل
مجلة فاذا كان المجيب لا يستطيع أن يتذكر مقالة من مجلة معينة أكتب
« لاشـيء » فى المكان المناسب فى آخر خانـة فى الجـدول أعـلاه ٠)
هل تتكرم بذكر مقال استمتعت بقراءتـه حديثا فى هذه المجلة ؟
٢٧   لأى هيئة مهنية أو اجتماعية أو غيرها تنتمـى ؟

والآن لنعود الى بعض الاسئلة التى تتصل بخدمة الحكومة ٠
٢٨   هنا ورقة تصف حالة تصويرية ٠   عندما تقرأها أريد أن أسألك بعض
أسئلة عنها ٠
(السائل : اعطى الورقة التالية الى المجيب وعندما يكون مستعدا للاجابة
عن الاسئلة ، إستمر ٠)

[حالـة الاقتصادى]

تصـور الحالة التاليـة :   يطلب رئيس احدى المصالح الحكومية من
أحد موظفيـه ــ وليكن رجـلا اقتصاديـا ــ أن يعد مذكرة لدعم سياسة
معينة اتبعت بعض الوقت ٠   ومن دراسـة الموضوع ، يرى الاقتصادى
أنـه يستطيع أن يدافـع عن هذه السياسة اذا هو قدم براهين تخالف ما

هو مقبول عامة عند أكثر الاقتصاديين فى الحكومة وخارجها •

أ)   هل لرئيس المصلحة أن ينتظر من الموظف الحكومى أن يعد مثل هذه المذكرة ؟

نعم ....   لا ....

ب)   ما الذى تعتقده واجبا على هذا الموظف أن يعمله بالنظر الى ارتباطه بواجبه الحكومى وارتباطه بمهنته كخبير اقتصادى ؟ هل يعد التقرير أم يرفض اعداده ؟

يجب أن يعده ....   يرفض اعداده ....

ج)   لماذا تظن هذا ؟

د)   اذا أعد هذا الموظف الحكومى مذكرة كهذه ، طبقا لرغبات رئيسه ، وعرف عنه أنـه هو الذى أعدها ، ماذا يظن فيه زملاوءه الاقتصاديون ؟   (السائل :   ابحث عن اجابـة دقيقـة •)

٢٩   فيما يلى جملة صفات عن موظفين حكوميين •   من فيهم ترى أنه أحسن موظف حكومى ؟ أذكر رقم الاجابة التى تختارها • (السائل : اعطى بطاقة للمجيب ، ثم ضع علامة أمام الاجابة التى يختارها •)

أ)   ....   الذى يتبع اللوائح حرفيا

ب)   ....   الذى يتصرف فى تفسير اللوائح

ج)   ....   الذى يتصرف فى الأمور دون أن يناقض اللوائح تناقضا كبيرا

٣٠   أ)   أتظن أنه يجب على موظفى الحكومة أن تكون لهم نقاباتهم المهنية كما للاطبـاء والمحامين والمهند سـين ؟

نعم ....   لا ....

ب)   لماذا تظن هذا ؟

٣١   كثيرا ما يقال أن المرتبات الحكومية ضئيلة ، فهل تستطيع أن تعيش على ماهيتك كموظـف حكومـى ؟

نعم ....   لا ....

٣٢   أ)   ألديك موارد أخرى كمبان أو أطيان أو استثمار من أى نوع ؟

نعم ....   لا ....

ب)   (السائل :   اذا كان الجواب نعم ، اسأل •)   هل تستعمل بعض هذا الد خل فى مصروفاتك المعيشية ؟

نعم ....   لا ....

٣٣   أ)   كما تعلم ، لا يسمح لموظفى الحكومة أن يقومـوا بأعمال أخرى غير وظائفهم الرسمية الا فى ظروف خاصة وبأذن خاص • فهل تعتقد انـه يجب على الحكومـة أن تسمح لجميع الموظفين

بأن يقومـوا بأعمـال أخـرى كهذه دون اعتراض منها ؟

نعـــم .... لا ....

ب) لماذا تظن هذا ؟

٣٤ والآن سأعطيك بطاقة عليها الجـزء الأول من جملة • أرجو
اتمامها بكلمـــات من عنــدك • (السائل : اعطى بطاقة
للمجيب • عنــدما تتســـلم البطاقـة مكمـلــــة
من المجيـب، اثبـت الــــرد عليهــــا أدنــاه •)
[السلطة تعطى صاحبها الحق فى ٠٠٠٠٠]

٣٥ كما تعلم، للناس أسباب مختلفة فى استحسان وظيفة أو مهنة معينة •
اليك بعض هـــذه الأسباب رتبها حسب اهميتها بالنسبة اليك ؟
(السائل : اعطى البطاقة الى المجيب•) اعطى أهم سبب رقم
١ وما يتلوه فى الأهمية رقم ٢ وهكذا •

أ) .... الماهية الحسنة وشـروط حسنة للخدمة

ب) .... اظهـار الكفاءة الشخصية لأداء العمل

ج) .... الفرصة لمقابلة العظمـــاء

د) .... الفرصة لخدمة الجمهـــور

ه) .... الفرصة لخدمة الدولــــة

٣٦ والآن سأقدم اليك حالة تصويرية اخرى، وبعد قراءتها سأسألك بعض
اسئلة عنها • (السائل : اعطى الورقة التالية الى المجيب وعند
مايكون مستعدا للاجابة عن الاسئلة ، استمر •)

[حالة المفتش]

تصـور الحالة التاليـة : يقوم موظف حكومى بالتفتيش على المصانع
وواجبه التحقق من أن تكـون المصانع مطا بقة لقوانين الامان وسلامة
العمال • وفى أحـد المصانع رأى المفتـش أن الارض قد تهبط تحت
ثقل ماكينة، وتبعا للاجراءات المعتادة يخاطـب رئيسه تليفونيا
ولكنه يجـد أن رئيسـه بمأمورية رسميـة خارج مكتبـه ولن يعـود
اليــه فى ذلك اليوم، فيفحص الأرض مرة ثانية ويظل غير واثق من
انها سوف تتحمـل أكثر من بضع ساعات، فيخبر صاحب المصنـع
بمخاوفـه ولكن صاحب المصنع يقـول انـه لا داعى لمثل هذه
المخاوف اذ أن كبير المفتشين قد صادق على سلامـة المصنع منذ
اسبوعين فقط وكان على حالته الراهنـة وبالتالى يطلعـه على شهادة
التصديـق ولكن المفتـش يظل متشككا ويبادر باصدار الأمر باغلاق
المصنـع •

٣٦ أ) أتظن أن تصرف هذا الموظف الحكومى لا غبار عليه باغلاقه
المصنع ؟

نعـــم ....   لا ....

لمـاذا تظـن هذا ؟

ب) أتظن أن رئيس هذا الموظف الحكومى سيؤ اخذه لاتخاذه مثل
هذه الخطوة ؟

نعـــم ....   لا ....

ج) أتعتقد أن رئيس هذا الموظف الحكومى يجب أن يواءخذه لاتخاذه
مثل هذه الخطوة ؟

نعـــم ....   لا ....

لماذا تظـن هذا ؟

د) والآن دعنا نفرض فى نفس الحالة ان فحصا ثانيا فى اليوم التالى
يظهر انه لم يكن هناك فى الحقيقة سبب للمخاوف ومن ثم فان صاحب
المصنع لم يطالـب بعمـل أيـة اصلاحات • أتظن أن تصرف
هذا الموظف الحكومى لاغبار عليه باغلاق المصنع ؟

نعـــم ....   لا ....

ه) اتظن ان رئيس هذا الموظف الحكومى سيواءخذه لاتخاذه مثل
هذه الخطوة ؟

نعـــم ....   لا ....

و) ان رئيس هذا الموظف الحكومى يجب أن يواءخذه ؟

نعـــم ....   لا ....

لماذا تظـن هذا ؟

ز) وأخيرا، فى هذه الحالة نفسها، لنفرض أنـه بعد ساعات قليلة من
اغلاق المصنع بناء على أمر المفتـش هبطت الارض ولم يصب احد
بضـرر لان الجميع كانوا قد ذهبـوا الى بيوتهم • أتظن أن
تصرف هذا الموظف الحكومى لاغبار عليه باغلاقه المصنع ؟

نعـــم ....   لا ....

ح) أتظن أن رئيس هذا الموظف الحكومى سيؤاخذه لاتخاذه مثل
هذه الخطوة ؟

نعـــم ....   لا ....

ط) أتعتقد أن رئيس هذا الموظف الحكومى يجـب أن يواخذه لاتخاذ
هذه الخطوة ؟

نعـــم ....   لا ....

لماذا تظـن هذا ؟

194

٣٧ أ) عندما تتولى الحكم حكومة جديدة ، هل يجب ان يكون لها الحق
فى فصل كل كبار موظفى الحكومة ، وتستبدلهم بأتباعها ؟

نعـــم .... لا ....

ب) لماذا تظن هذا ؟

٣٨ ها هى ذى بطاقة اخرى عليها الجزء الاول من جملة • أرجو اتمامها
بكلمات من عندك • (السائل : اعطى البطاقة للمجيب •
عندما تسلم البطاقة مكملة من المجيب ، اثبت الـرد عليها أدناه •)
[يجب على الاشخاص الذين يشغلون وظائف عامة ذات نفوذ ان • • •]

٣٩ أ) افرض انـه قد طلبـمنك انتنصح شابا ذكيا ـ وليكن ابن عم صغير
لك ـ عـــن مستقبله ، اى طريق فى الحياة تنصح له ان يسلك ؟

ب) لماذا تنصحه ان يسلك مثل هذا الطريق ؟

ج) (السائل : ان لميذكر خدمة الحكومة فاسأل •) ما رأيك
فى خدمة الحكومــــة كمستقبل لشاب ذكى ؟ (السائل :
ابحث عن آراء المجيب فى تحبيذه خدمة الحكومــة او عدم
تحبيذه لها •)

٤٠ اذا أراد شاب أن يصبح موظفا حكوميا فما هو خير طريق يسلكه ليحصل
على وظيفة ؟

٤١ أ) هل وظيفتك لها اتصال مباشر بالجمهور ؟

نعـــم .... لا ....

(السائل : اذا كان الجواب نعم فاستمر •)

ب) نريد أن نكون فكرة عن عملك اليومى • فدعنا نأخذ اخر
ثلاثة اشخاص ، وهم ليسوا من موظفى الحكومة ، أتوا ليروك فى
مصالح رسميـة • فلنبدأ بآخر شخص جاءليراك ـ ماذا كانت
مشكلته أو ما السبب الذى حدا به الى أن يستشيرك ؟ عن
اى طريق عرف انك انت الموظف المختص ؟ كيف تصرفتفى
مسألته ؟ (السائل : بعد آخر شخــــص اسأل المجيب ان
يرجـع الى من جاء قبل هذا وهكذا الى أن تنتهى الثلاث
حالات •)

ج) هل الحالات التى ذكرتها هى نموذ ج لعملك اليومى ؟

نعـــم .... لا ....

ب) (السائل : اذا كان الجواب بالنفى ، فـا سـأل •) لم لا ؟

٤٢ يقدر الناس الوظائف والمهن تقديرا متباينا ، وها هى ذى بطاقةمبين
عليها بعـض مهن • ضع نمرة ١ أمام المهنة التىيقدرها الجمهور

أعظم تقدير ، ثم نمرة ٢ أمام الـتى تليها وهكـذا •

أ .... عامل مصنـع   ب .... تاجـر صغـير

جـ .... طبيــب   د .... كاتـب بالحكومة

هـ .... صاحب أطيان   و .... مـديـر بنـك

ز .... محـامـى   ح .... صاحب مصنـع

ط .... فــلاح   ى .... رئيس قلم بالحكومة

٤٣ هاهى ذى بطاقة اخرى عليها الجزء الاول من جملة • أرجو اتمامها بكلمات من عندك • (السائل : اعطى البطاقة للمجيب • عند ما تسلم البطاقة مكملة من المجيب، اثبـت الرد عليها أدناه •) [أحسن ما فى الوظيفة الحكومية ... •]

٤٤ أ) اتظن أن الجمهور يهتم فى الوقت الحاضر اهتماما كافيا بخطط الحكومة ؟

نعـم ....   لا ....

ب) لماذا تظن هذا ؟

جـ) (السائل : اذا كان الجواب بالنفى، فاسأل •) ما الذى يجب على الجمهـور أن يعملـه حتى يظهر اهتماما كافيا بخطط الحكومة ؟

٤٥ أ) (السائل : ان لم يجب على السؤال السابق اسأل •) أتظن ان الخدمـة الحكومية تتحسن اذا ازداد اهتمام الجمهور بخطط الحكومة ؟ نعـم ....   لا ....

ب) لماذا تظن هذا ؟

٤٦ هذه حالة تصويرية أخرى، وبعد أن تقرأها أرجو أن اسألك بعض أسئلة عنهـا • (السائل : اعطى الورقة التالية للمجيب، وعندما يكون المجيب مستعدا لاجابة الاسئلة، استمر •)

[حالة موظف الأرياف]

تصـور الحـالـة التاليـة : عـين موظف حكومى فى وظيفة ، واجبه فيها ابتكار طـرق لتحسـين الصحـة ونشر التعاون فى الارياف، وبعد دراسات كثيرة فـى هذا الميـدان أعـد مذكرة يقدم فيها برنامجا كاملا لهذا الغرض فيرفضـه روءسـاوءه ، ويتخذون عوضا عنه برنامجا ـ لا يكون حسب رأيـه ـ فـى صالح القرويين الذين درس احوالهم بدقـة ، ومع ذلك يطلـب منه روءساوءه أن ينفذ هذه السياسـة فى الميدان •

٤٦ أ) هل لروءساء المصلحة أن ينتظروا من الموظف الحكومى ان
ينفذ هذه السياسة ؟

نعـــم .... لا ....

ب) ما الذى تعتقده واجبا على هذا الموظف أن يعملـه بالنظر الى
ارتباطه بواجبـه الحكومى وواجبه كمواطن يريد أن يصلح
جمهرة القرويين ؟ أيوافق أم يرفض أن ينفـذ هذه السياسة ؟

أ .... ينفذ السياسة

ب .... يرفض أن ينفذ السياسة

ج) لماذا تعتقد ذلك ؟

د) (السائل : اذا قال المجيب أنه يجب على الموظف الحكومى
أن يرفض، اسأل •) ماذا يجب أن يعمل عندئذ ؟

٤٧ أ) افرض أن موظفا حكوميا حضر الى مكتبه فى الصباح ووجد
بضعة أشخاص ينتظرونـه، وبينهم أحد معا رفه • أيليق أن
يترك هذا الرجل منتظرا مادام الآخرون قد أتوا قبله ؟

نعـــم .... لا ....

ب) لماذا تظـن هذا ؟

ج) ماذا تعتقد الموظف العادى فاعلا حقيقة فى مثل هذه الحالة ؟
أيقابـل هــذا الرجل قبل الآخرين ؟

نعـــم .... لا ....

٤٨ هاهى ذى بطاقة اخرى عليها الجزء الاول من جملة • أرجو اتمامها
بكلمات مـــن عندك • (السائل : اعطى البطاقة للمجيب •
عندما تتسلم البطاقة مكملة من المجيـب، اثبت عليها الرد أدناه •)
[كون الفرد موظفا حكوميا يعطيه الفرصة ل • • • •]

٤٩ والآن نود أن نعرف رأيك فى ما يظنه رجل الشارع عن موظف
الحكومة •

أ) أتظن أن رجل الشارع يقدر العمل الذى يقوم به الموظف الحكومى
تقديرا كافيا ؟

نعـــم .... لا ....

ب) هل يحترم رجل الشارع موظف الحكومة ؟

نعـــم .... لا ....

لماذا تظـن هذا ؟

ج) هل يخشى رجل الشارع الموظف الحكومى ؟

نعـــم .... لا ....

لماذا تظـن هذا ؟

د) هل يعتقد رجل الشارع انه من الصعب الوصول الى الموظف الحكومى أم يعتبره خادما للشعب يسهل الوصول اليه ؟

صعب .... سهــل ....

٥٠ أ) افرض أن مواطنا عاديا راى أن من الضرورى التوجه الى موظف حكومى بخصـــــوص اعمال رسمية عادية أى طريق من الطرق الآتية يحسن به ان يتخذ ليصل الى غرضـه ؟

أ) .... أيتوجــه هذا المواطن الى صديق له يعرف الموظف الحكومى

ب) .... أيتوجــه هذا المواطن الى قريب لـه من موظفـى الحكومة

ج) .... أيتوجــه هذا المواطن الى مكتب الموظف رأسا ويضع أمامه مشكلته

ب) لمـــاذا تظن هذا ؟

٥١ والآن سأعطيك آخر هذه البطاقات وعليها بضع كلمات ٠ اقرأها ثم أكمل الجملــــة مبتدء بهذه الكلمات ٠ (السائل : اعطى البطاقة للمجيب ، عندما تتسلم البطاقة مكملة من المجيب، اثبت الرد عليها أدناه ٠) [ان أسوأ ما فى كون الشخص موظفا حكوميا ٠٠٠]

٥٢ وها هى آخر حالة من الحالات التصويرية فعند ما تقرأ ها أود أن أسألك بعض اسئلــة عنها ٠ (السائل : اعطى الورقة التالية للمجيب وعندما يكون مستعدا للاجابة عـــن الاسئلة ، استمر ٠) [حالـة نقل الموظف]

تصـــور الحـالـة التاليـة : أحيـط موظف حكومى علما بأنـه سينقل من القا هرة الى وظيفة جديدة فى الاقاليم ٠ وليس لديه أى اعتراض على العمل فى الاقاليم، ولكنه يشعــــر أنـه يجب عليـه أن يقيم مع والديه المسنين اللذيـن لا يمكن نقلهمــا من القاهرة ، حيث يعالجان ٠ وعلى ذلك يتوجه الى المدير العام فـــى الوزارة ، وهو صديق حميم له، ويطلب منـه ان يبقيه فى القاهرة ٠

أ) هل لهذا الموظف الحكومى أن ينتظر من المدير العام ابقاءه فى القاهرة ؟

نعـــم .... لا ....

ب) ماذا تظن هد المدير العام فاعلا، بالنظر الى ارتباطه بواجبه الحكومــى وعلاقته بصديقه ؟ أيبقى صديقـه فى القاهرة أم لا ؟

يبقيــه .... لا يبقيــه ....

ج) والآن دعنا نفرض ، في نفس هذه الحالة ، أن الموظف الحكومى الذى يريـــد أن يبقى فى القاهرة هو ابن عم المدير العام • هل لهذا الموظف الحكومى ان ينتظر من المديــر العام ابقاءه فى القاهرة ؟

نعـــم .... لا ....

د) ماذا تظن هذا المدير العام فاعلا فى هذه الحالة ، بالنظر الى ارتباطـــه بواجبه الحكومى وارتباطه بعائلتـه ؟ أيبقى ابن عمه فى القاهرة أم لا ؟

أ .... يبقيــه ب .... لا يبقيــه

ه) فى هذه الحالة ، هل لأقرباء المدير أن ينتظروا منه أن يبقى ابن عمـه فـى وظيفتـه بالقاهرة ؟

نعـــم .... لا ....

لماذا تظن هذا ؟

و) ماذا يظن أقرباء هذا المدير العام فيه اذا لم يبق ابن عمـه فى وظيفته بالقاهرة ؟

والآن وقبل أن نصل الى النهاية أرجو أن لا يكون لديك مانع من اعطائى بعض البيانات الخاصة •

٥٣ ما هى حالتك الإجتماعية ؟

أ .... متزوج

ب .... أرمـل

جـ .... مطلق

د .... أعزب

٥٥ أ) (السائل : اذا كان الجواب انـه متزوج أو سبق له الزواج ، فاسأل •) ألك أولاد ؟

نعـــم .... لا ....

ب) (السائل : اذا كان الجواب نعم ، فاسأل •) أذكر عمر كل منهم والـــى أى مرحلة وصل كل منهم فى دراسته • (السائل : خذ الأولاد بالسن مبتدء بالأكبر •)

ذكر أو أنثى	السن	الدراســــة

٥٧ فى اى جهة أقمت معظم وقتك قبل سن العشرين ؟

٥٨ ماذا كان عمل والدك الرئيسى فى ذلك الوقت ؟

٥٩ الى أى مرحلة دراسية وصل والدك ؟

٦٠ الى أى مرحلة دراسية وصلت زوجتـك ؟

٦١ الى أى مرحلة دراسية وصلت والدتك ؟

٦٢ والآن وقد وصلنا الى نهاية هذه المقابلة ، أتريد أن تعلق على أى
ناحية من نواحيهـا أوعن أشياء عالجناها ، وكذلك الأشياء التى لم نعرها
التفاتا ؟

English Translation

Interviewer's name .... Date ....
1. Number   2. Ministry   Department
3. Title of post   4. Grade   5. Duties
6. Year of birth   7. Place of birth   8. Education
a. Secondary school: Completed .... Not completed ....
b. Higher and technical education:
c. Other education:
9. What is the mission and function of the ministry in which you are employed?
10. What part does your post play in realizing the aims of the ministry?
11. What civil service positions have you held prior to your present post? (*Interviewer*: begin with the most recent previous post and work back to the first one.)
12. How did you obtain your first civil service post?

Now let us go back for a moment to the time before you entered the civil service.
13. How old were you when you first thought of a career in the civil service?
14. Why did you prefer the civil service to a non-government job? (*Interviewer*: probe for a detailed answer.)
15. How did you first learn about the first civil service post that you obtained? (*Interviewer*: if necessary, give examples: through a friend or relative, university professor, etc.)
16. What jobs did you hold before entering the civil service? Please begin with the most recent one and go back in turn to the first.
17a. Do you think that you might leave the civil service entirely for some reason? Yes............ No............
b. (*Interviewer*: if yes, ask:) Under what circumstances would you leave?

200

18a. Since becoming a civil servant, have you been offered any opportunities for employment outside the civil service?
Yes............ No............

b.   (*Interviewer*: if the answer is yes, ask:) Would you tell me something about the two most recent offers of this kind?

Position	Nature of the work	Employer	Year Offer Was Made	Response and Reasons for Rejection or Acceptance

Now I'd like to ask you some questions about your service in the government.

20. As you know, the government, in employing people, considers their degree of education and experience. Do you think the government should consider other factors in making these appointments? For example
     a. social position?   Yes............ No............
     b. family connections? Yes............ No............
     c. wealth?   Yes............ No............
     d. religion?   Yes............ No............
     e. political belief?   Yes............ No............

21. How would you describe the ideal civil servant? (*Interviewer*: if necessary, ask: What qualities should he have? What sort of person should he be? Probe for specific qualities such as intelligence, diligence, loyalty, honesty, etc.)

22. What do you like about government work?

23. What do you dislike about the government service?

Now I'd like to ask you some questions about some other matters related to your work.

24. Which of the following foreign languages do you read and speak fluently?

	Read Fluently	Speak Fluently
English	....	....
French	....	....
German	....	....
Italian	....	....
(other languages)	....	....
....	....	....
....	....	....

25. Which of the following countries have you visited for any
period of time or resided in for more than a year?

	Visited	Resided in
England	....	....
United States	....	....
France	....	....
Germany	....	....
Italy	....	....
Turkey	....	....
Syria	....	....
Lebanon	....	....
(other countries)	....	....
....	....	....
....	....	....

26a. Which newspapers do you read, in various languages, and
how often do you read them?—that is, do you read every
issue, or frequently, or occasionally?

b. Which magazines do you read, in various languages, and
how often do you read them?—that is, do you read every
issue, or frequently, or occasionally? (*Interviewer*: mention in turn the name of *each magazine* and ask the
following question concerning each one. If the respondent
cannot recall an article for a particular magazine, write
"none" in the appropriate place in the last column of the
table above.) Would you mention an article that you enjoyed reading recently in this magazine?

27. Which professional, social, or other kinds of organization
do you belong to?

Now let's return to some questions relating to the civil service.

28. Here is a sheet of paper describing an imaginary situation.
When you have read it, I'd like to ask you some questions
about it.

(*Interviewer*: give the next sheet to the respondent. When
he is ready to answer questions, proceed.)

[Story of the Economist]

[Imagine the following situation: A department head in the
civil service asks one of his staff members, an economist, to
prepare a memorandum in support of a certain policy that
has been followed for some time. In studying the matter,

the economist finds that he can defend this policy only if he presents arguments that differ with what is generally accepted among most economists in and outside of the government.]

a. Can the department head expect this civil servant to prepare such a memorandum?

yes............   no............:

b. What do you think this civil servant ought to do in view of his obligation to the government and his obligation as a professional economist? Should he prepare the report, or should he refuse to prepare it?

should prepare............   refuse............

c. Why do you think so?

d. If this civil servant prepared such a memorandum, following his chief's wishes, and it became known that he did, what would his colleagues among the economists think of him? (*Interviewer*: probe for specific answer.)

29. Here are several descriptions of civil servants. Who among them do you think is the best civil servant? Please mention the number of the answer you select. (*Interviewer*: give card to respondent and indicate his answer.)

     a. .... one who follows the regulations literally

     b. .... one who uses his own initiative in interpreting the regulations

     c. .... one who uses his own initiative without seriously violating the regulations.

30a. Do you think civil servants should have their own protective society, such as doctors, lawyers, and engineers have?

yes............   no............

b. Why do you think so?

31. It is often said that salaries in the civil service are inadequate. Are you able to live on your salary as a civil servant?

yes............   no............

32a. Do you have other resources such as buildings or land or investments of any kind?

yes............   no............

b. (*Interviewer*: if yes, ask:) Do you use some of this income for your living expenses?

yes............   no............

33a. As you know, civil servants are not permitted to hold other jobs except under certain circumstances and with special permission. Do you think that the government should permit all civil servants to hold other jobs without exception?

       yes............   no............

b. Why do you think so?

34. Now I'm going to give you a card with the beginning of a sentence on it. Please complete the sentence with your own words. (*Interviewer*: give card to respondent. When you receive the completed card from the respondent, write his answer in the space below.)

[Authority gives one the right to . . .]

35. As you know, people have different reasons for thinking highly of a certain post or occupation. Here are some of these reasons. Please arrange them in what you think is the order of their importance.

(*Interviewer*: give card to respondent.) Call the most important reason number 1, the next in importance number 2, and so on.

      a. .... good salary and working conditions

      b. .... skill required to do the work

      c. .... opportunity to meet important people

      d. .... opportunity to serve the public

      e. .... opportunity to serve the state

36. Now I'm going to give you another imaginary situation. After you read it, I'll ask you some questions about it.

(*Interviewer*: give next sheet to respondent, and when he is ready to answer questions, proceed.)

[Story of the Inspector]

[Imagine the following situation: A civil servant is assigned to factory inspection; his duty is to insure that factories conform to safety laws. In one factory he sees a floor that looks as if it might give way under the weight of a machine. According to the usual procedure, he telephones his superior but finds that he is away on official business and will not return that day. The inspector examines the floor again and is not certain that it will hold up for more than a few hours. He tells the factory owner of his fear. But the owner tells him that there is no ground for such fear, since the chief inspector had approved the factory only two weeks ago in the same condition. The owner shows him the certificate of approval, but the inspector is still doubtful and, taking the initiative, he orders the factory to be closed.]

a. Do you think that the civil servant acted properly in closing the factory?

        yes............   no............

Why do you think so?

b. Do you think the civil servant's superior will discipline him for taking such a step?

        yes............   no............

c. Do you think the civil servant's superior *should* discipline him for taking such a step?

        yes............   no............

Why do you think so?

d. Now let us suppose, in the same situation, that the next day further inspection shows there was really no ground for fear. In fact, the factory owner is not required to make any repairs. Do you think that the civil servant acted properly in closing the factory?

        yes............   no............

e. Do you think the civil servant's superior will discipline him for taking such a step?

        yes............   no............

f. Do you think the civil servant's superior *should* discipline him for taking such a step?

        yes............   no............

Why do you think so?

g. Now, finally, in the same situation, let us suppose that a few hours after the factory has been closed on the inspector's order, the floor actually gives way, but no one is hurt because everyone had gone home. Do you think that the civil servant acted properly in closing the factory?

        yes............   no............

h. Do you think the civil servant's superior will discipline him for taking such a step?

        yes............   no............

i. Do you think the civil servant's superior *should* discipline him for taking such a step?

        yes............   no............

Why do you think so?

37a. When a new government takes office should it have the right to dismiss all higher civil servants and to replace them with its own followers?

yes............   no............

b. Why do you think so?

38. Here is another card with the beginning of a sentence on it. Please complete the sentence with your own words. (*Interviewer*: give card to respondent. When you receive the completed card from the respondent, write his answer in the space below.)

[Persons occupying public posts of authority should . . .]

39a. Suppose you were asked to advise an intelligent young man—say, a young cousin of yours—on his career. What sort of career would you advise him to follow?

b. Why would you advise him to follow such a career?

c. (*Interviewer*: if civil service is not mentioned, ask:) What do you think of the civil service as a career for an intelligent young man? (*Interviewer*: probe for respondent's views for or against civil service career.)

40. If a young man wants to become a civil servant, what would be the best way for him to do so?

41a. Does your post place you in personal contact with the public?

yes............   no............

(*Interviewer*: if answer is yes, proceed.)

b. We should like to get an idea of your daily routine. Let's consider the last three persons, not in the civil service, who came to see you on official business. Let's begin with the person who came most recently—what was his problem, or what was the reason he had to consult you? How did he learn that you were the official he should see? How did you dispose of his case? (*Interviewer*: after the most recent person, ask respondent to go back to the one before that, and so on until three cases are completed.)

c. Would you say that these cases are typical of your daily work?

yes............   no............

d. (*Interviewer*: if answer is no, ask:) Why not?

42. People rate various posts and occupations differently. Here is a card listing several occupations. Just place number 1

alongside the occupation the general public thinks most highly of, number 2 for the next, and so on.

a. ...... factory worker   b. ...... small merchant
c. ...... doctor   d. ...... government clerk
e. ...... landowner   f. ...... bank director
g. ...... lawyer   h. ...... factory owner
i. ...... peasant   j. ...... government
                                 bureau chief

43. Here is another card with the beginning of a sentence on it. Please complete the sentence with your own words. (*Interviewer*: give card to respondent. When you receive the completed card from the respondent, write his answer in the space below.)

[The best thing about a government post is . . .]

44a. Do you think that the general public at present takes sufficient interest in the activities of the government?

    yes............   no............

b. Why do you think so?

c. (*Interviewer*: if answer is no, ask:) What should the general public do to show a proper interest in the activities of the government?

45a. (*Interviewer*: if not answered in the previous question, ask:) Do you think that the civil service would be improved if the general public took more interest in the activities of the government?

    yes............   no............

b. Why do you think so?

46. Here is another imaginary situation. When you have read it, I'd like to ask you some questions about it. (*Interviewer*: give next sheet to respondent. When he is ready to answer questions, proceed.)

[Story of Rural Civil Servant]

[Imagine the following situation: A civil servant is employed in a post in which it is his duty to devise ways to improve sanitation and cooperation in rural villages. After much study in the field, he prepares a memorandum presenting a full program toward this end. His superiors reject it. Instead, they adopt a program which, in his opinion, would not be in the interest of the villagers whose conditions he has studied in detail. His superiors, nevertheless, ask him to carry out this policy in the field.]

a. Can his superiors expect this civil servant to carry out this policy?

yes........... no...........

b. What do you think this civil servant ought to do, in view of his obligation to the government and his obligation as a citizen who wants to improve the lot of the villagers? Should he agree or refuse to carry out this policy?

...........should carry out policy

...........should refuse to carry out policy

c. Why do you believe that?

d. (*Interviewer*: if respondent says civil servant should refuse, ask:) Well, just what should he do?

47a. Suppose a civil servant arrives at his office one morning and finds several persons waiting to see him. Among them is an acquaintance of his. Is it proper to keep this man waiting because others came before him?

yes.. .... no...........

b. Why do you think so?

c. What do you believe the average civil servant would actually do in such a case? Would he receive this man before the others?

yes........... no...........

48. Here is another card with the beginning of a sentence on it. Please complete the sentence with your own words. (*Interviewer*: give card to respondent. When you receive the completed card from the respondent, write his answer in the space below.)

[Being a government official gives one the opportunity to . . .]

49. We would like to know, now, what the man in the street thinks of civil servants.

a. Do you think that the man in the street has enough appreciation of the job that the civil servant does?

yes........... no...........

b. Does the man in the street respect the civil servant?

yes........... no...........

Why do you think so?

c.   Does the man in the street fear the civil servant?

        yes............   no............

Why do you think so?

d.   Does the man in the street consider the civil servant difficult to approach, or does he consider the civil servant as a servant of the people and therefore easy to approach?

        difficult............   easy............

50a. Suppose that an ordinary citizen finds it necessary to go to a government official concerning ordinary official business. Which of the following ways would it be best for him to use in order to accomplish his purpose?

        a. .... He should see a friend who knows the government official.

        b. .... He should see a relative of his who is also a civil servant.

        c. .... He should go directly to the official's office and state his problem.

b.   Why do you think so?

51.   Now I'm going to give you the last of these cards with some words on it. Please read them, and then complete the sentence using these words as the beginning. (*Interviewer*: give card to respondent. When you receive the completed card from the respondent, write his answer in the space below.)

    [The worst thing about being a government official is . . .]

52.   Here is the last of these imaginary situations. When you have read it, I'd like to ask you some questions about it. (*Interviewer*: give next sheet to respondent. When he is ready to answer questions, proceed.)

[Transfer of Civil Servant]

[Imagine the following situation: A civil servant is officially informed that he is to be transferred from Cairo to a new post in the provinces. He has no objection to service in the provinces but he feels that he must be near his aged parents, who cannot be moved away from Cairo, where they receive medical treatment. He therefore goes to the director general in the ministry, who is a close friend of his, and asks the director general to keep him in Cairo.]

209

a. Can this civil servant expect the director general to keep him in Cairo?

yes............   no............

b. What do you think the director general would do, in view of his obligation to the government and his obligation to his friend? Would he keep his friend in Cairo, or not?

keep him............   not keep him............

c. Now, let us suppose in the same situation, that the civil servant who wants to remain in Cairo is a *cousin* of the director general. Can this civil servant expect the director general to keep him in Cairo?

yes............   no............

d. What do you think the director general would do in this situation, in view of his obligation to the government and his obligation to his family? Would he keep his cousin in Cairo, or not?

keep him............   not keep him............

e. In this situation, can the director general's relatives expect him to keep his cousin in the Cairo post?

yes............   no............

Why do you think so?

f. What would the director general's relatives think of him if he did *not* keep his cousin in the Cairo post?

And now, before we conclude, I hope you won't mind giving me some facts about yourself.

53. What is your marital status?   a. .... married
b. .... widowed   c. .... divorced   d. .... single

55a. (*Interviewer*: if married, or has been married, ask:) Do you have any children?

yes............   no............

b. (*Interviewer*: if yes, ask:) Please tell me the age of each one, and how far he has gone in school. (*Interviewer*: take children in order of age—oldest first.)

Sex   *Age*   *Education*

57. Where did you live most of the time before you were 20 years old?

58. What was your father's main occupation during this time?

59. How much formal education did your father complete?

60. How much formal education did your wife complete?

61. How much formal education did your mother complete?
62. Now that we have completed the interview, would you like to comment on any aspect of it—the things we have covered as well as some things we may not have covered?

Appendix 2

Letter inviting civil servants to be interviewed

Following is the letter, in the original Arabic and in an English translation, sent to a sample of higher civil servants asking them to participate in the study. It was signed by the following officials for their respective ministries: William Selim Hanna, Minister of Municipal and Rural Affairs; Abdel Razaq Sidqy, Minister of Agriculture; Ali A. I. El Gritly, Vice Minister of Finance and Economy; Ahmad Shafiq Zaher, Acting Under-Secretary of Education.

يقوم الدكتور مورو برجر ـ استاذ العلوم الاجتماعية بجامعة برنستون بالولايات المتحدة الامريكية ـ بدراسة لبضع نواح فى ميدان العمل الحكومى فى مصر • ولذلك أبعث اليكم بهذه المذكرة راجيا انتساهموا ـ قدر المستطاع ـ فى معاونته لاتمامها •

وقد أرسلت جامعة برنستون هذا العام ـ وهى احدى الجامعات الامريكية الهامة ـ الدكتور مورو برجر الى الشرق الاوسط ـ وهو بمصر الآن ـ ليجمع المواد العلمية لسلسلة من المحاضرات التى ينوى القاءها فى العام القادم عن الحياة الاجتماعية والاقتصادية فى الشرق الاوسط •

وسيكون اهتمام جنابه مركزا فى نواحى العمل الحكومى المختلفة بين كبار موظفى الحكومة ، اذ يهتم بدراسة مقومات واختصاصات ووضع العمل الحكومى بين كبار الموظفين حتى يتمكن من استيعاب طبيعة الحياة الاجتماعية هنا •

وقد أعد الدكتور برجر ـ كجزء من دراسته ـ مجموعة من الاسئلة لكى يجيب عليها حوالى خمسمائة من كبار موظفى الحكومة فى وزارات عدة • هذا وقد سمحت للدكتور برجر بمزاولة أبحاثه ودراسته فى هذه الوزارة •

والدكتور مورو برجر يتبع فى دراسته وأبحاثه طريقة علمية نموذجية حتى يحصل بواسطتها على نموذج أو مثال صادق يمثل الموظف الحكومى فى الدرجات الثانية والثالثة والرابعة فى مختلف ادارات ومصالح هذه الوزارة • وتبعا لهذه الطريقة ـ وهى تشبه فى مضمونها ما يقوم به معهد جالوب وغيره للأبحاث ـ فقد اختير اسم سيادتكم كأحد الذين سيتكرمون بالاجابة على اسئلة الدكتور برجر فى مقابلة خاصة •

وستكون المقابلة فى الصباح ولن تستغرق اكثر من ساعة ونصف ،

212

وسيقوم بتوجيه الاسئلة الى سيادتكم باللغة العربية احد الاشخاص المدربين على هذا النوع من البحث • ويود الدكتور برجر ان يؤءكد لجميع اولئك الذين سيتكرمون بالمساهمة فى هذا المشروع أن كل ماسيقال فى هذه المقابلة لن يعرض على احد ، بل ان اسم المجيب لن يثبت على نمـوذج الاسئلة •

وليكن معلوما ان هذه الدراسة وهذا البحث لم يعملا لتحرى وجهات نظر موظف الحكومة كفرد بل لجمع بعض حقائق عن موظفى الحكومة كمجموعة ولذلك أعتقد ان هذه الدراسة ستكون موضع اهتمامكم •

ورغبة فى حصر اسماء الذ ين سيشتركون فى هذا البحث ، أرجو أن تملأ البطاقة المرفقة ثم تعيدها فى خلال أربعة أيام الى ....

...........•* وبعدئذ سيتصل بك تليفونيا او يحضر لمقابلتك الشخص الذى سيقوم بتوجيه الاسئلة اليك ليحدد ميعاد ومكان المقابلة •

واخيرا أتقدم اليكم ـ وكذلك الدكتود برجر ـ بوافر الشكر لمساهمتكم فى هـذه الدراسـة •

———

* وكيل مدير المستخدمين بالوزارة

Dr. Morroe Berger, professor of sociology at Princeton University, in the United States, is conducting a study of some aspects of government operations in Egypt. Accordingly, I am sending you this memorandum in the hope that you will, to the extent that you can, help him to complete it.

Princeton University, one of the important universities in America, this year has sent Dr. Berger to the Middle East—he is now in Egypt—to collect scientific data for lectures which he plans to give next year on social and economic life in the Middle East.

His interest is centered on various aspects of the work of the higher civil servants, their background, functions and status, to help him understand the nature of social life here.

Dr. Berger has prepared, as part of his research, a series of questions to be answered by about five hundred of the higher civil servants in several ministries.

I have permitted Dr. Berger to carry out his study in this Ministry.

In his study Dr. Berger follows a scientific sampling method to obtain a representative sample of civil servants in the second, third and fourth grades in the various departments and bureaus of this Ministry. According to this method, which in general resembles the work of the Gallup poll and similar agencies, your name was selected as one of those who might be willing to answer the questions in a private interview.

This interview will take place in the morning and will not take more than an hour and a half. The person who will ask these questions, in Arabic, will be someone trained in this kind of research. Dr. Berger would like to assure all those who participate in this project that anything said in this interview will be kept confidential; in fact, the name of the respondent will not appear on the questionnaire.

It should be understood that this study is being undertaken not to find out the views of the civil servant as an individual but to obtain some information about the civil servants as a group. Accordingly, I believe that this study merits your serious attention.

For the purpose of ascertaining the names of those who will participate in this study you will, I trust, fill out the accompanying card and will return it within four days to ....
...........................* Later on, an interviewer will get in touch with you by telephone or will come to see you personally to arrange a time and place for the interview.

Finally, I—and Dr. Berger as well—want to thank you for your participation in this study.

Letter from the Director of the Study to the Respondents

Following is the letter, in the original Arabic and in an English translation, from the director of the study given to each respondent by the interviewer at the start of the interview.

من الدكتور مورو برجر الى حضرة السيد المجيب
كم كنت أود أن أقابلكم شخصيا لأخبركم بنفسي عن هذا البحث وأقدم
لكم جزيل شكرى على مساهمتكم فيه • ولكنكم ترون أنه من الصعب
جدا أن أقابل جميع حضرات اولئك الذين سيساهمون فيه فردا فردا
ويبلغ عددهم بضع مئات • ولقد وقع الاختيار عليكم لأن اسم
سيادتكم قد جاء فى الترتيب المسلسل لهذه الطريقة العلمية التى
اتبعها فى أبحاثى لكى أحصل بواسطتها على نموذج أو مثال صادق لرأى
كبار موظفى الحكومة فى مصر •

* Personnel officer in the ministry.

ودعــنى أؤكــد لك أن كل ما سيــقال او يذكــر فى هـــذه المقابلــة لن يعــرض على أحــد كائنا من كان وحـتى اسم سيادتكـــم لن يثبــت على نمـــوذج الاسـئلة • وذلك لانى لسـت مهتما بتحـــرى وجهــات نظر موظف الحكومــة كفــرد ولكنى مهتم بجمع بضــع حقائـق عن رأى كبــار موظفـى الحكومة كمجموعة ، اذ أن الهـــدف الـــذى يرمـى اليــه هذا البحـث هو هـدف علمـى خالـص •

ومــرة اخرى تقبــل فائق شكرى لمعاونتك الصـادقة •

دكتور مورو برجر

أستاذ العلـــوم الاجتماعيــة

بجا معة برنستون

بأمريكا

I would have liked to meet you personally to tell you about this research and to thank you for participating in it, but you will understand that it would be very difficult for me to meet individually with several hundred of you. All of you were selected because your names came up in the regular order according to a scientific procedure which is followed to obtain a representative sample of the opinions of higher civil servants in the government of Egypt.

Let me assure you that everything you say in this interview will be kept confidential. Your name will not even appear on the questionnaire. This is so because I am not concerned with finding out the views of the civil servant as an individual but with obtaining some information about the views of the higher civil servants as a group, since the objective of this research is purely scientific.

Once again, thank you for your cooperation.

Appendix 3

Details of the selection of the Egyptian higher civil servants who responded to the questionnaire

Ministry	2d	Grade 3d	4th	Total
AGRICULTURE				
total civil servants in Cairo	9	26	94	129
invited to participate	6	16	56	78
agreed to participate	3	9	30	42
interviewed	2	9	28	39
EDUCATION				
total civil servants in Cairo	140	309	238	687
invited to participate	69	49	36	154
agreed to participate	31	29	11	71
interviewed	27	27	10	64
FINANCE AND ECONOMY				
total civil servants in Cairo	57	147	398	602
invited to participate	38	94	198	330
agreed to participate	13	46	62	121
interviewed	21[a]	39	47	107
MUNICIPAL AND RURAL AFFAIRS				
total civil servants in Cairo	21	33	84	138
invited to participate	9	17	28	54
agreed to participate	11[b]	8	21	40
interviewed	11[a]	9[a]	19	39
ALL FOUR MINISTRIES				
total civil servants in Cairo	227	515	818	1,556
invited to participate	122	176	318	616
agreed to participate	58	92	124	274
interviewed	61[a]	84	104	249

[a] The number of persons interviewed exceeds the number who had been invited or agreed to participate. This resulted from promotions that occurred between the time the civil servant was invited or agreed to be interviewed and the time the interview took place.

[b] The number of persons who agreed to participate exceeds the number who had been invited. This was the result of promotion between the time the civil servants' names were obtained from the ministries' records and the time they received the written invitation to participate.

Appendix 4

Construction of the scales and indexes

This study uses four scales and indexes in order to measure the respondents' degree of bureaucratic orientation, professionalism, exposure to Western influences, and job-satisfaction. They were constructed in the manner described below.

Bureaucratic scale. To measure the respondents' degree of approximation of Western bureaucratic norms a Guttman scale of three items was constructed. These items are questions 23, 36d, and 36f in the questionnaire.

Question 23 asks: "What do you dislike about civil service employment?" The civil servant was thus permitted to say anything he wanted to, rather than to select his answer from a suggested list. The respondents mentioned many things they disliked, and these have been grouped as follows: routine and monotony, favoritism, inefficient use of personnel, low salaries, absence or killing of initiative, instability, and nothing at all. Among these replies, those complaining about favoritism, inefficient use of personnel, and the absence or killing of initiative seem to come nearest to such Western bureaucratic norms as impartiality, efficiency, and initiative. This type of response is therefore considered Western, and any other is not considered Western.

Question 36 was less simple. The respondents were asked to consider the following imaginary situation: "A civil servant is assigned to factory inspection; his duty is to insure that factories conform to safety laws. In one factory he sees a floor that looks as if it might give way under the weight of a machine. According to the usual procedure, he telephones his superior but finds that he is away on official business and will not return that day. The inspector examines the floor again and is not certain that it will hold up for more than a few hours. He tells the factory owner of his fear. But the owner tells him that there is no ground for such fear, since the chief inspector had approved the factory only two weeks ago in the same condition. The owner shows him the certificate of approval, but the inspector is still doubtful and, taking the initiative, he orders the factory to be closed."

With this situation before him, the respondent was asked

whether he thought (a) the civil servant acted properly in closing the factory, (b) the civil servant's superior *would* discipline
him, and (c) the civil servant's superior *should* discipline him.
The situation was then altered twice, and the same questions
asked.

The first change was: "Now let us suppose, in the same situation, that the next day further inspection shows there was really
no ground for fear. In fact, the factory owner is not required to
make any repairs."

The second change was: "Now, finally, in the same situation,
let us suppose that a few hours after the factory has been closed
on the inspector's order, the floor actually gives way, but no
one is hurt because everyone had gone home."

This multiple question was designed to test the degree to
which the respondent felt it proper and safe for a civil servant
to use his initiative. For the Bureaucratic Scale we used the
second of these three situations (the first change quoted above)
—that is, the one in which the inspector's judgment turns out to
have been wrong, since there was really nothing at fault in the
factory. Two questions about this situation are included in the
scale: (36d) "Do you think that the civil servant acted properly
in closing the factory?" (36f) "Do you think the civil servant's
superior *should* discipline him for taking such a step?" The
"Western" answer to the first of these questions is in the affirmative, that is, insistence upon the propriety of the civil servant's
acting on his own *initiative*, as he saw fit, despite the fact that
his *judgment* later turned out to be wrong. The "Western"
response to the second question is in the negative, that is, that
the superior should *not* discipline the civil servant for having
acted on his own initiative even when his judgment is later seen
to be wrong.

These three items yield four positions along the Bureaucratic
Scale—no Western answers, 1 Western answer, 2 Western
answers, and 3 Western answers. Table A-1 shows that 96
respondents answered all three questions in what we take to be
the ideal Western manner. These 96 higher civil servants, we
say, are high on the Bureaucratic Scale; the 153 others are low.
The value of this scale is not that it permits us to say that 96
out of 249 Egyptian higher civil servants show a high degree
of Western bureaucratic predisposition; such a statement does

TABLE A-1

Distribution of Respondents along Bureaucratic Scale

Scale Position		No. of Respondents
Low	0	37
	1	20
	2	96
High	3	96
	Total	249

not carry us very far in present circumstances because we have no precise comparable data for the higher civil servants of other countries. We cannot, therefore, say that the proportion of Egyptian officials high on bureaucracy is greater or smaller than that of any other national group of senior government employees; we *assume*, however, that Western civil service groups would, on the same questions, emerge with a larger proportion in the high group. The real value of the scale here, however, is that it enables us to compare the Egyptian civil servants who are high on the scale with those who are low. For example: are the highs younger or older than the lows? Are they more or less educated?

Professionalism index. Unlike the questionnaire items on bureaucracy, the four items on professionalism were not so related to one another that they could yield a Guttman scale. We therefore use them as an *index* of professionalism in much the same way as we use the scale of bureaucracy. The Professionalism Index is made up of questionnaire items 27, 28c, and 35 (2 parts).

Question 27 asks: "Which professional, social, or other kinds of organizations do you belong to?" Membership in a professional association was, of course, taken to be indicative of a more highly developed sense of professionalism than non-membership.

Question 28, like question 36 in the Bureaucratic Scale, asks the respondent to consider an imaginary situation: "A department head in the civil service asks one of his staff members, an economist, to prepare a memorandum in support of a certain policy that has been followed for some time. In studying the matter, the economist finds that he can defend this policy only if he presents arguments that differ with what is generally accepted among most economists in and outside of the government."

One of the questions based upon this imaginary situation asked: "What do you think this civil servant ought to do in view of his obligation to the government and his obligation as a professional economist? Should he prepare the report, or should he refuse to prepare it?" This item was intended to test the degree of the respondent's identification with a profession by setting the imaginary civil servant's profession against his governmental superiors. Those who said the economist in the story should refuse to prepare the memorandum that would contradict the economists were taken to have the more highly developed sense of professionalism. All the respondents who gave this answer offered one of two reasons for it: that the economist ought not to do something he did not believe right, or that he should not contradict his fellow-economists.

Question 35 sought to get at the respondent's notion of what gives one post more prestige than another. It reads as follows: "As you know, people have different reasons for thinking highly of a certain post or occupation. Here are some of these reasons. Please arrange them in what you think is the order of their importance. Call the most important reason number 1, the next in importance number 2, and so on. (a) good salary and working conditions (b) skill required to do the work (c) opportunity to meet important people (d) opportunity to serve the public (e) opportunity to serve the state."

Two of these five elements of occupational prestige relate to professionalism: (b) skill required and (d) opportunity to serve the public. Rating each of these elements first or second in importance was taken to be indicative of a higher degree of professionalism.

These four items yield five positions along the index in degree of professionalism: no "professional" answers, 1 "professional" answer, 2 such answers, 3, and 4. Table A-2 shows that 78 of the 249 respondents answered three or all four of these questions in the "professional," or "Western," manner. These 78, we shall say, are high on the Professionalism Index, the other 171 low.

As in the case of the Bureaucratic Scale, the value of the Professionalism Index is not that it permits us to compare the degree of professionalism among Egyptian and Western higher civil servants, but that it enables us to identify the socio-economic

TABLE A-2

Distribution of Respondents on Professionalism Index

Index Position		No. of Respondents
Low	0	8
	1	45
	2	118
High	3	71
	4	7
	Total	*249*

characteristics of those Egyptian senior officials who display a high degree of professionalism and of those who do not.

Exposure scale. It is not a simple matter to measure and establish an index of exposure to Western influences. If we mean merely a person's presence in the West or his use of certain Western products, it is relatively easy to construct an index. If, however, we are interested in *effective* exposure to the West, we are concerned not only with the presence of Western influences but also with the person's predisposition to be influenced by them. To embrace both the sheer exposure and this personal predisposition is indeed difficult. Two methods of measuring exposure may be considered.

One is the respondent's place of higher education. Those who attended universities in the West, that is, in England, the U.S., and Europe, would certainly have been physically exposed to Western attitudes, ideas, and behavior. Those who attended universities in Egypt, while also highly exposed to Western modes in comparison with those who did not go to college, would probably not have come into such intense and sustained contact with the West as those who went abroad for their higher education. But how can we measure a man's predisposition toward what he sees in the West? One Egyptian educated in Europe may return imbued with admiration for everything Western; another man may go home fearing and rejecting what he has seen. Both will have been influenced in some way, but the important question is, in what way, and why? The things we can measure in this study cannot provide the answer.

Place of higher education has two further drawbacks as an index of exposure to the West. First, 30 respondents, as we saw earlier in Table 5, have not attended a university anywhere.

A second and statistically more serious weakness is that only 35 of 217 college graduates have been educated in Western universities. To classify all others as not having been highly exposed to the West would be to limit this group so severely as to reduce the probability of obtaining statistically significant results from comparisons between those educated in the West and in Egypt.

To broaden the measure of exposure we have constructed a Guttman scale of four items, questions 25, 26a, 59, and 61.

Question 25 concerns travel abroad. A visit to or residence in any Western country was taken as exposure to Western influence.

Question 26a asks which newspapers the respondents read. Reading a newspaper in a Western language, with any degree of frequency, was taken as exposure to the West.

Questions 59 and 61 ask the extent of the formal education completed by the respondent's mother and father. For the father, relatively high exposure to the West was assumed if he had completed at least secondary school, for the mother if she had completed at least primary school.

These four items in the Guttman scale yield five positions along a continuum of exposure to the West—those with no Western responses, and with 1, 2, 3, or 4 Western responses. The distribution of the 249 respondents along this scale is shown in Table A-3. Those in positions 2, 3, and 4, a total of

TABLE A-3

Distribution of Respondents along Scale of Exposure to the West

Scale Position		No. of Respondents
Low	0	86
	1	57
High	2	62
	3	30
	4	14
	Total	249

106 civil servants, may be called more exposed to the West, the remainder less exposed.

As might be expected, these two measures of exposure, place of higher education and the group of items in the Exposure Scale, are related. Table A-4 shows that among the 35 higher civil

TABLE A-4

Exposure Scale and Place of Higher Education

SCALE POSITION		EGYPTIAN UNIVERSITIES *Per Cent*	WESTERN UNIVERSITIES *Per Cent*
Low	$\left\{\begin{array}{l} 0 \\ 1 \end{array}\right.$	39.6 26.4	2.9 2.8
High	$\left\{\begin{array}{l} 2 \\ 3, 4^a \end{array}\right.$	15.9 18.1	80.0 14.3
	Total	*100.0*	*100.0*
	(cases)	(182)	(35)

a Combined because of small number of cases in position 4.
Note: Significant at .001 level.

servants who attended Western universities, 94 per cent are high in exposure as measured by the Exposure Scale (that is, are in scale positions 2, 3, and 4), compared with only 34 per cent of the 182 educated in Egyptian universities.

The Exposure Scale, however, has its limitations. The main drawback is that it is only a static measure of externals. It does not take sufficient account of the *duration* of any kind of exposure. A month's visit to a Western country counts equally with four years spent in a Western university. A civil servant aged 35, who, let us say, has been reading a newspaper in English for five or ten years, is considered, in the scale, to be equally exposed in this respect to one aged 50, for example, who has perhaps been reading a newspaper in English for 20 or 25 years. Age itself is a quality that includes exposure.

The Exposure Scale suffers from still another limitation of this nature, for it discriminates in favor of the younger respondents. Any static measure of exposure is likely to do the same, because in externals the whole of Egyptian society has had more contact with the West as time has passed. Our four-item scale is biased by the inclusion of the two items on the educational level of the respondents' parents. Owing to the vast growth of education in Egypt in the last half-century, the parents of younger respondents are very likely to have had more schooling than those of the older respondents. These very changes, however, have been accompanied by others that have actually increased the exposure of the older civil servants over a longer period of time than the younger.

Finally, the Exposure Scale does not take into account one sort of exposure to Western influence that is important in itself and especially so in this study. It does not give weight to the fact that the older respondents, those with about 25 years of service or more, very likely had some contact with British officials in the Egyptian civil service, a kind of "exposure" that is of greatest relevance to the subject of this study, the development of Western bureaucratic and professional norms in Egypt.

The special difficulties involved in measuring exposure by this scale emerge when we consider (as we do in Chapter 3) what factors make for a high or low degree of bureaucratic orientation and professionalism. How is exposure, as one of these factors, related to degree of Western bureaucratic norms as measured by the Bureaucratic Scale? There is no relationship between them. One would have expected that the more highly exposed civil servants would be the ones higher in Western bureaucratic tendencies. How can we account for the fact that they are not? The question is the more interesting because of two other relationships: between age and bureaucracy, and between age and exposure. Table A-5 shows that age and bureaucratic

TABLE A-5

Bureaucratic Scale and Age (1)

BUREAUCRATIC SCALE POSITION		AGE 31-45 *Per Cent*	AGE 46-60 *Per Cent*
High		24.0	53.2
Low		76.0	46.8
	Total	*100.0*	*100.0*
	(Cases)	(125)	(124)

Note: Significant at .001 level.

orientation are indeed closely related. Among those aged 46 to 60, 53 per cent are high on bureaucracy, while among those aged 31 to 45 the proportion is only 24 per cent.

Table A-6 shows that there is a significant relationship between age and exposure if we divide the respondents into *three* age groups instead of *two* (as we have done in the text). Although age is significantly related both to exposure and bureaucratic orientation, the latter two scales are not significantly related to each other. The reason lies in the nature of the relation-

TABLE A-6

Exposure Scale and Age

EXPOSURE SCALE POSITION	AGE 31-40 Per Cent	AGE 41-50 Per Cent	AGE 51-60 Per Cent
0	34.9	31.0	39.7
1	25.4	23.9	19.2
2	17.5	23.0	34.2
3-4[a]	22.2	22.1	6.9
Total	*100.0*	*100.0*	*100.0*
(Cases)	(63)	(113)	(73)

[a] Combined because of small number of cases in position 4.
Note: Significant at .05 level.

ship between age and exposure as shown in Table A-6. The oldest group, 51-60, has by far the lowest proportion, only 6.9 per cent, with the highest exposure; they are the least exposed. But a breakdown by these three age groups, in Table A-7, shows

TABLE A-7

Bureaucratic Scale and Age (2)

BUREAUCRATIC SCALE POSITION	AGE 31-40 Per Cent	AGE 41-50 Per Cent	AGE 51-60 Per Cent
0,1[a]	23.8	23.9	20.5
2	47.6	42.5	24.7
3	28.6	33.6	54.8
Total	*100.0*	*100.0*	*100.0*
(Cases)	(63)	(113)	(73)

[a] Combined because of small number in position 1.
Note: Significant at .02 level.

that the oldest, 51 to 60, has the highest proportion on the Bureaucratic Scale, 54.8 per cent; they are the most bureaucratic. Thus the oldest are the *least exposed* and the *most bureaucratic*. This fact tends to bring down the significance of exposure in relation to bureaucratic orientation so that we do not indeed find what we might have expected: high exposure is *not* accompanied by high bureaucratic predisposition. The relation between age and exposure is such that the middle group, those aged 41 to 50, are the most highly exposed, as Table A-6 shows. We see now the effect of the type of items we have had to use to measure exposure to the West: they tend to reduce the number of older persons with high exposure. Thus the most bureaucratic group brings down the exposure level of those high on the Bureaucratic Scale, with the result there is no significant and direct relationship between the exposure of the civil servant to Western influences and the degree to which he accepts Western bureaucratic norms.

We return to the point we made earlier, that a valid measure of exposure must be a dynamic one that will include the influence of age. Our questionnaire does not permit us to devise such a measure. We must, therefore, consider exposure and age together, for age, as we have already pointed out, means exposure of our respondents to the West in two senses. First, as a group they are highly exposed in comparison to the rest of the Egyptian nation. All the respondents wear Western clothing. Three quarters of them were born in urban areas in a country still largely rural. Almost nine out of ten among them have been graduated from college in a country in which the vast majority is still illiterate. Forty per cent are the sons of civil servants. Sixty per cent can read at least English and one other foreign language. Virtually all of them are thus in considerable contact with Western influences. Differences in degree of exposure may perhaps be minor when measured by the externals in our scale. What may be really significant is the duration of this exposure, the degree to which it has been sustained. And this means the older are exposed over a longer time. The relative influence of age and exposure, considered *separately*, upon bureaucratic tendencies may be seen in Table A-8, which shows how age and such tendencies are related among respondents with high exposure and among those with low exposure. It consists of Table A-5 taken separately for those high and those low on the Exposure

TABLE A-8

Bureaucratic Scale by Age and Exposure Scale

	HIGH EXPOSURE		LOW EXPOSURE	
	31-45	46-60	31-45	46-60
	Per Cent		Per Cent	
High bureaucracy	20.8	41.4	26.0	63.6
Low bureaucracy	79.2	58.6	74.0	36.4
Total	100.0	100.0	100.0	100.0
(Cases)	(48)	(58)	(77)	(66)

Note: High exposure section significant at .05 level; Low exposure at .001 level.

Scale. As Table A-8 shows, the significant relationship between age and bureaucratic orientation holds despite the introduction of the factor of exposure. Our opinion that high bureaucratic orientation is related to age is thus strengthened. Each way we look at our respondents, the difference in age seems to be a very important one. We therefore refer to age differences frequently in the presentation of the data. We do not exclude the Exposure Scale or place of higher education entirely but use them where they are meaningful, that is, in connection with age differences.

Job-satisfaction Index. We measure job-satisfaction by means of an index of four items in the questionnaire: 17, 31, 42, and 49a.

Question 17 asks: "Do you think that you might leave the civil service entirely for some reason?" A negative answer was taken as an expression of high job-satisfaction.

Question 31 asks: "It is often said that salaries in the civil service are inadequate. Are you able to live on your salary as a civil servant?" A positive answer was taken to indicate high job-satisfaction.

Question 42 asks for the respondent's impression of how the general public rates various occupations:

"People rate various posts and occupations differently. Here is a card listing several occupations. Just place number 1 alongside the occupation the general public thinks most highly of, number 2 for the next, and so on.

a. .... factory worker		b. .... small merchant
c. .... doctor		d. .... government clerk
e. .... landowner		f. .... bank director
g. .... lawyer		h. .... factory owner
i. .... peasant		j. .... government bureau chief."

A rank of first through seventh for the occupation of government clerk was taken as an indication of high job-satisfaction, since it was assumed the respondents would, in answering this question, be reflecting their own assessments. Nearly three fifths of those who rated the government clerk placed him somewhere between first and seventh.

Question 49a asks: "Do you think that the man in the street

has enough appreciation of the job that the civil servant does?"
An affirmative answer was taken as an expression of high job-satisfaction.

These four items yielded five positions on the Job-Satisfaction Index: no answers indicating high satisfaction, one answer indicating high satisfaction, 2, 3, and 4 such answers. As Table A-9 shows, 198 out of 249 respondents are in positions 0, 1, and

TABLE A-9

Distribution of Respondents on Job-Satisfaction Index

Index Position		No. of Respondents
Low	0	33
	1	90
	2	75
High	3	43
	4	8
	Total	249

2; these we say are low on the Job-Satisfaction Index. The remaining 51 respondents are in positions 3 and 4, indicating high job-satisfaction.

Index

Date Due